Project Apostasy

The Development and Propagation of the Trinitarian Doctrine

by
Jesse Acuff

AuthorHouse™
1663 Liberty Drive, Suite 200
Bloomington, IN 47403
www.authorhouse.com
Phone: 1-800-839-8640

This book is a work of non-fiction. Unless otherwise noted, the author and the publisher make no explicit guarantees as to the accuracy of the information contained in this book and in some cases, names of people and places have been altered to protect their privacy.

© 2008 Jesse Acuff. All rights reserved.

No part of this book may be reproduced, stored in a retrieval system, or transmitted by any means without the written permission of the author.

First published by AuthorHouse   8/20/2008

ISBN: 978-1-4343-5168-5 (sc)

Printed in the United States of America
Bloomington, Indiana

This book is printed on acid-free paper.

Introduction

I am what some call a count-down Christian. This simply means that I progressed from a belief that viewed the Godhead as consisting of three co-equal, co-eternal beings (Trinitarian), to a belief in only two co-equal, co-eternal beings (The Binitarian view of the Worldwide Church of God under Herbert W. Armstrong), to a belief that there is only One God in the Godhead (The Biblical Unitarian view of The Church of God, Abrahamic Faith). I wrote most of the material included in this book some years ago while I was still a Binitarian. However, I have tried to adapt it to the biblical Unitarian view that I have now embraced as true.

During my years of study and research, it has been my habit to keep an open mind to other people's concepts and ideas. Although I have rejected most of them, there have been those that, once I was exposed to them, seemed very sensible. This was the case when I encountered the "One God" doctrine. I have learned that, in the words of Anthony Buzzard and Charles Hunting,

> "Biblical doctrine must be established by the plain, straightforward texts which bear directly on the subject in question. When the Bible's creedal declarations are taken at face value, according to the ordinary rules of language, they present a doctrine about God which cannot be reconciled with traditional belief systems."[1]

One of the most difficult things in one's life, after having inured oneself to a particular theological viewpoint, is to change that viewpoint.

When challenged about a particular belief, rejection is usually automatic. This makes it very difficult to "evangelize," if you will, those who have accepted error. Cherished beliefs are sacred cows that simply will not be easily dislodged from the pantheon of religious dogmatism that characterizes Christian orthodoxy, ancient and modern. The bias associated with such rigidity is staggering. The legalistic mindset that accompanies it stifles spiritual growth and understanding to a degree that makes it almost impossible for the glorious light of the Gospel of grace to penetrate that legalistic mind.

The great mistake that Bible students make today is that they exegete from a 21st Century point of view. I agree heartily with Buzzard and Hunting, when they observe,"True Christianity must be shaped by the ideas and concepts which circulated in their first-century apostolic environment, now viewed by us at a distance of 1900 years."[2] This, in fact, is one of the first principles of Hermeneutics. We cannot apply 21st century thinking to Scripture and expect to interpret it accurately. If we do, mistakes will surface that do not conform to the biblical view.

The Trinitarian Doctrine is one of the greatest of them. The Trinity was not always the majority belief among Christians. In fact, according to Buzzard and Hunting, "It may be surprising to some, but church historians record that believers in God as single person—unitarian Christians—were 'at the beginning of the third century still forming the large majority."[3] What happened? Orthodox theologians from the fourth and fifth centuries onward began to introduce Gnostic doctrine into the writings of the original apostles and wresting Scripture to conform to their own agenda. Unfortunately, when the unitarians challenged them, orthodoxy won and such doctrines as the Trinity became the norm instead of the exception in western Christian thought.

Largely, we have not asked the right questions when encountering a doctrine that does not make much sense, e.g. the Trinitarian Doctrine. What is the Trinity? If it is not characteristic of the true Godhead, why do we, as "Christians," worship God as if He were in fact, a trinity in unity, whatever that means? Where does Scripture ever disclose a doctrine of the Trinity? Were we to examine these sacred documents carefully and open-mindedly with the aid of the Holy Spirit to guide us, we would establish that, as Buzzard and Hunting declare, "There is no passage of Scripture which asserts that God is three. No authentic verse claims that the One God is three persons, three spirits, three divine, infinite minds, or three anything. No verse or word of the Bible can be shown to carry the meaning "God in three Persons." Any claim that there are three who compose the Deity must be based on inference, rather than plain statements. The Trinitarian concept relies upon sophisticated and often tortured logic which lacks solid support in the earliest Christian writings."[4]

A.W. Tozer, who writes as a Trinitarian, says that we must think rightly about God. If our thoughts about God are erroneous or inadequate, "It is impossible to keep our moral practices sound and our inward attitudes right. . ."[5] It is not enough that we *think* that our ideas of God are right; we must *know* that our thoughts about Him are right. How can we know? The Trinitarians are adamant that they are right because tradition tells them so. The biblical unitarians, on the other hand, know they are right because they adhere strictly to Scripture. A right conception of God must be basic, not only to systematic theology, but also to Christian's practical living."[6] In fact, Tozer states further,

> "That our idea of God correspond(s) as nearly as possible to the true being of God is of immense importance to us. Compared with our actual thoughts about Him, our creedal statements are of little consequence. Our real idea of God may lie buried under the rubbish of the conventional religious notions and may require an intelligent and vigorous search before it is finally unearthed and exposed for what it is. Only after and ordeal of painful self-probing are we likely to discover what we actually believe about God."[7]

Regardless of his position, I find Tozer's statements amazing and stimulating. For instance, when it comes to erroneous doctrine he declares, "I believe there is scarcely an error in doctrine or a failure in applying Christian ethics that cannot be traced finally to imperfect and ignoble thoughts about God."[8] I believe that these "ignoble" and "imperfect" thoughts about God, especially in the area of the Trinitarian Doctrine, are the root cause of much of what can be classified as idolatry in the Christian church so-called today.

Although he is working toward a Catholic view of the Holy Trinity, his thoughts nevertheless apply to all peoples in all walks of life who seek a true conception of God. Moreover, they apply as well to Catholic and Protestant alike.

> "It is my opinion," he continues, "that the Christian conception of God current in these middle years of the twentieth century is so decadent as to be utterly beneath the dignity of the Most High God and actually to constitute for professed believers something amounting to a moral calamity."[9]

Although Tozer is probably not aware of it, the moral calamity is Trinitarianism, Christianity's self-inflicted wound, a wound from which she has never recovered. It looms as large today as it ever did. It is a calamity which leads to the most abominable sin in God's sight—idolatry! In fact, Tozer says,

> "Among the sins to which the human heart is prone, hardly any other is more hateful to God than idolatry, for idolatry is at bottom a libel on His character. The idolatrous heart assumes that God is other than He is—in itself a monstrous sin—and substitutes for the true God one made after his own likeness."[10]

Well spoken! America today and Christianity in general are guilty of the most libelous actions when it comes to worship of the True God. America today is not a Christian nation but one, which, largely, adheres to rank, pagan idolatry.

The essence of this book is to show where and how it all started, and how it progressed from the beginning. Paul writes in Romans 1:21, "When they knew God they glorified Him not as God, neither were thankful; but became vain in their imaginations, and their foolish heart was darkened." Once their minds were darkened, they began to build idols fashioned after the likeness of men, birds, animals, reptiles, and creeping things. They began to bow down and worship these things becoming guilty of idolatry. All these concepts came from their minds and, as Tozer succinctly puts it, "Wrong ideas about god are not only the fountain from which the polluted waters of idolatry flow; they are themselves idolatrous. The idolater simply imagines things about God and acts as if they were true."[11]

Project Apostasy

This book is not intended to be a pogram against the Roman Catholic Church, the Protestants, Billy Graham, or any others who cling to the Trinitarian Doctrine. It is simply this author's opinion that it needs to be pointed out that they are mistaken in their theology because they do not believe the plain statements of Scripture concerning the makeup of the Godhead. Biblical monotheism claims thousands of times within the pages of the Bible that God is One and only One. When I see scholar's efforts to reinterpret the meaning of the Hebrew word *Echad* to mean a compound "one," I am saddened by their attempts to force the Doctrine of the Trinity into the biblical concept of God when it will not fit. I am reminded of the old song that says, "One is one and all alone and ever more shall be it so." It is a perfect description of the true makeup of the Godhead according to the monotheistic teachings of the Hebrew Bible and the New Covenant teachings of Jesus and the Apostles. In the end, as Tozer says, "The essence of idolatry is the entertainment of thoughts about God that are unworthy of Him."[12] Thoughts of God as being a Trinity are certainly not worthy of Him, and undeniably constitute idolatry on our part. Christianity needs to move off of the Trinitarian position if it ever hopes to worship God "in spirit and truth."

> *From the cowardice that shrinks from new truth,*
> *From the laziness that is content with half-truths,*
> *From the arrogance that thinks it knows all truth,*
> *Oh, God of truth, save Us!*

Chapter 1
The "Force"

The brainchild of George Lucas, Star Wars is the ultimate cowboys and Indians adventure acted out in a futuristic space-time continuum. "May the Force be with you," a single, innocuous sounding phrase from the movie, literally captured the hearts and minds of millions the world over. Ben (Obi-Wan) Kenobi, a once great warrior and Jedi Knight of the Old Republic spoke these passionate words. They were pronounced as a blessing upon the young, impetuous Luke Skywalker as he set about to do battle with the sinister leaders of the treacherous Galactic Empire. The Empire had broken the proud power of the Old Republic, and sought through force of arms to enslave its inhabitants by means of a harsh, dictatorial, military regime.

The "Force," whether used for good or evil, is a mysterious, invisible, magical power that pervades the universe. It can be used at will to perform miraculous, superhuman feats of strength and daring by those trained to tap its awesome power.

Luke Skywalker, the story's effervescent and courageous protagonist, championed the good side of the Force. The consummately evil, black-hooded and black-caped Darth Vader, a former Jedi Knight turned adversary, champions the dark side of the "Force."

While the good side of the "Force" stands for right and justice, the dark side is a malevolent destroyer. With it, Darth Vader determined to smash utterly the remaining strongholds of the rebel forces that remained loyal to the Old Republic. With it, he sought to suppress forever the good side of the "Force." Ultimately, however, the good side of the "Force" emerges victorious, even converting the evil Darth Vader to its cause.

Project Apostasy is about a "force" that seeks to destroy in this age, as in ages past, the remaining strongholds, not of rebels so-called, but of God's Church. Not unlike the dark side of the "Force" in Star Wars, it permeates the solar system and galaxy in which we live, if not the whole universe.

Did this evil "Force," embodied as Satan, exist from the beginning? Did the One claiming to be God and Creator of the universe create the Devil and the evil associated with him? Did God the Father create Satan in the beginning? Indications are that He did not. The One God is not the Author of sin and evil. Satan is! He was a liar and a murderer from the very beginning (possibly meaning – "of *his*, i.e. Satan's beginning").

". . . He (Satan) was a murderer from the beginning, and abode not in the truth, because there is no truth in him. When he speaks a lie, he speaks of his own: for he is a liar and the father of it" (John 8:44).

Satan has perpetuated the dark side of the force throughout the ages. Within prescribed limits, God has allowed this evil to continue for a very specific purpose; a purpose that is lost to the many. In His infinite love and compassion, God has blinded the minds of the vast majority—withheld His Holy Spirit from most—in unbelief (disobedience) because He intends to show them great mercy (Rom. 11:32). In His infinite wisdom, God knows that if He allowes man to go his own way, that if he leaves him to his own devices, he will be more receptive to the truth when Jesus Christ returns in power and glory to establish God's Kingdom upon this earth.

Our great and wonderful God is dealing with only a comparative few now, not the many as Evangelical Christianity supposes. Satan holds sway over the many. Satan has deceived the world into believing the exact opposite of what God's word really says.

"So the great dragon was cast out (of Heaven), that serpent of old, called the Devil, and Satan, **who deceives the whole world**. . ." (Rev. 12:9).

God cast him out because he tried to usurp His authority and set himself up as the ruler of the universe!

Out of the shadowy remoteness of antiquity, there arose a powerful, foreboding, super- intelligent force obsessed by delusions of grandeur and relentlessly driven by unrequited dreams of universal conquest.

Surreptitiously, this "Force" slithers serpent-like through the halls of recorded history, hissing out his utter contempt for God and maker. He bitterly proclaims his cancerous hatred for his Creator, who, knowing full well his potential for evil, formed him flawless and perfect in the day that he created him (Ezek. 28:15).

This manifestly evil "Force", personified as the great dragon, and serpent of old called the Devil and Satan, pauses occasionally to look furtively about with keen, unblinking eyes for inherent flaws and latent weaknesses with which to exploit his primary target—mankind. Satan's super intelligent, malicious mind constantly probes the ambiance of the times. With steely mental fingers, he locks tightly onto the social, economic, political, and religious mores of the masses. As quickly as he garners new information, he assimilates and analyzes it so that, at the appropriate moment, it can be unleashed on unsuspecting populations for purposes of evil. Satan's greatest pleasure is derived from giving the masses what they want, but only if it serves to further degrade their moral values and behavior. In this way, he sustains the apparent downward spiral of the human race into oblivion.

Lucifer

If God did not create this consummately evil "Force," this Devil, in the beginning, when did he originate? We do not know. All we know is that sometime between the creation of the hard universe God created a fantastically beautiful, immensely powerful, super intelligent spirit being whom He called Lucifer. Lucifer was *the* angel's angel, as it were. He was *the* paragon of the angelic realm, but he did not long maintain his first estate (Ezek. 28:17). He became a power grabbing, treasonous malcontent, contending murderously with his Maker for control, authority, and worship that were not rightfully his. The result was a great space war, the real **Star Wars**, if you will, for control of the universe. "And a war broke out in heaven: Michael and his angels fought against the dragon; and the dragon and his angels fought, but they did not prevail; nor was a place found for them in heaven any longer. So the great dragon was cast out, that serpent of old called the Devil, and Satan, who deceives the whole world: he was cast to the earth, and his angels were cast out with him" (Rev. 12:7-9).

God categorically defeated Lucifer and his angels and cast them headlong back to the earth, their original abode. Ultimately, Lucifer became Satan, the Adversary of God and man, the Darth Vader of the Angelic world.

In the final analysis, just as the dark side of the "Force" was destined for failure, so also is the great deception foisted upon the world by the god of this world (2 Cor. 4:4). The downward spiral into oblivion and the imminent, Satan planned destruction of mankind will be cut short (Mt. 24:22). God and those who follow Him (the saints, also called the Elect), will be for all time, victorious!

From the beginning to the soon coming end of the age spoken of in Matthew 24, Satan has worked diligently to annihilate mankind through a multitude of subtle, covert operations designed to destroy with "all deceivableness and lying wonders." Yet, with all he has accomplished over the past 6,000 years, his greatest deception still lies ahead.

Keenly aware of the ultimate consequences of Satan's end-time deception, the Apostle Paul warned the church at Thessalonica that there is coming a time when Satan will vent the full force of his wrath against the world and mankind. It is to be a time of unheard of tribulation engendered by a demonically possessed man. The book of Revelation, calls him the Beast and Antichrist.

> "Now brethren, concerning the coming of our Lord Jesus Christ and by our gathering together to Him, we ask you not to be soon shaken in mind, or be troubled, either by (an evil) spirit, or by word, or by letter, as if from us, as though the day of Christ had come. Let no one deceive you by any means: for that Day *will* not come, unless the falling away comes first, and the man of sin is revealed, the son of perdition; who opposes and exalts himself above all that is called God, showing himself that *he* is God. Do you not remember that when I was yet with you I told you these things? And now ye know what is restraining, that he may be revealed in his own time. For the mystery of lawlessness is already at work: only he who now restrains *will do so*, until he is taken out of the way. And then the lawless (one) will be revealed whom the Lord will consume with the spirit of His mouth, and shall destroy with the brightness of His coming.

> The coming of the lawless *one*, is according to the working of Satan with all power, signs and lying wonders, and with all unrighteous deception among those who perish (are perishing), because they do not receive the love of the truth, that they might be saved. And for this reason God shall send them strong delusion that they should believe (the) lie, that they all may be condemned who did not believe the truth, but had pleasure in unrighteousness (2 Thess. 2:1-12).

This end-time deception through Satan's man the Beast will be the greatest of all time! "For then there will be great tribulation, such as has not been since the beginning of the world until this time, no, nor ever shall be. And unless those days were shortened, no flesh would be saved (alive): but for the elect's sake, those days will be shortened (i.e. cut short). Then if anyone shall say unto you, 'Look, here is Christ!' or 'There!' do not believe *it*. For false Christ's and false prophets will arise and show great signs and wonders; so as to deceive, if possible, even the elect" (Mt. 24:21-24).

Satan and his servants will be so clever in their deception that the very elect, true Christians who have God's Holy Spirit will come very close to being deceived! If , then, the very elect come so close to being deceived, how will those without God's Holy Spirit escape?

Paul wrote the letter to the Thessalonians around 50-55 A.D. The wholesale departure of true Christians from God's truth in the New Testament era began about 70 A.D. It was the first event prophesied to develop within God's church. Paul explained how this apostatizing movement would occur in Acts 20:29-30. "For I know this, that after my departure savage wolves will come in among you, not sparing the flock. Also from among yourselves men will rise up, speaking perverse things, to draw away the disciples after themselves."

Self-appointed church leaders who accepted the vile and erroneous doctrines of the Babylonian Mystery Religion began, by about 70 A.D., to withhold the keys to God's truth and lock the doors to spiritual enlightenment against true believers. To insure that the doors remained locked to all but those whom they apostatized, they cast the keys of truth aside hoping forever to keep their disciples bound in iniquity and the spiritual darkness of Satan's apostate religion that became the great Mother Church of Rome. God's truth, however, is immutable and ineradicable. He has had His faithful witnesses in every age who have boldly proclaimed the Gospel of His soon coming, world ruling kingdom, despite Satan's attempts to suppress and destroy it.

Project Apostasy is Satan's story. We shall see in the following chapters how Satan immersed the world in the depths of apostasy and paganism.

Chapter 2
ORIGINS

How Did It All Begin?

Whether scientific, Scientific Creationist, or simply Creationist, origins can be very mysterious things. There are almost as many theories of the beginning of the universe as there are scientists, theologians, and religionists to concoct them. Astronomers say it all started with a "Big Bang." Most Christian theologians subscribe to the Divine Fiat (fy-aht) theory. Both remain resolute in their views on the eternity of matter. The Creationists maintain that there is no past eternity of matter. The evolutionists espouse a godless evolution of the universe via a mindless cosmic accident.

Who is right? Where did it all begin? Was there, as the Bible unequivocally states, a great First Cause who simply spoke to create it? Did all that we see about us from the tiniest microbe to giant, star-filled galaxies speeding through the vastness of space at millions of miles per hour, come about as the result of a mindless cosmic accident?

These are good questions that are sometimes hard to answer!

The Bible says, "In the beginning God created. . ." Science says, "In the beginning there was the Big Bang." The one claims that God brought matter into existence *ex nihilo*. The other claims that matter is eternal and autonomous!

The very foundation upon which evolutionary science bases its beliefs is laid down unerringly, dogmatically, and religiously in support of an autonomous universe, which does not require a Supreme Creator God to explain its existence. Whom do you believe—the One in the Bible claiming to be the All-powerful, Creator-God, or humanistic, evolutionary science, which dogmatically and religiously espouses a godless creation? Most importantly, is any of this relevant?

A young Christian man once told me quite emphatically that where we came from is not important. "What is important," he stated without reservation, "is where we are going." I cannot argue with the latter statement, but I heartily disagree with the former.

Hosea 4:6 says, "My people are destroyed for lack of knowledge..." This certainly applies to who we are! Where we came from is extremely important to our understanding of who and what we are, of where we are going, and why! If we are to set off in the right direction, we must be able to get a clear picture of where we have been historically, *and* religiously. Let us consider, then, two different historical viewpoints of the origin, or "the beginning," if you will, of the universe. Before we consider these two "beginnings," however, let me assure you, no part of this chapter is intended to either prove or disprove creation or evolution. Moreover, the material presented here is not an argument for or against creation or evolution. Rather, this author intends it to be nothing more than an historical perspective.

The Big Bang

Astronomers base this theory of beginnings upon the occurrence of a gigantic, fiery explosion of a cosmic hydrogen bomb so-called. Hence, the observation of Robert Jastrow that

> "The general scientific picture that leads to the Big Bang theory is well known. We have been aware for fifty years that we live in an expanding universe, in which all the galaxies around us are moving apart from us, and each other, at enormous speeds. The Universe is blowing up before our eyes, as if we are witnessing the aftermath of a gigantic explosion. If we retrace the motions of the outward moving galaxies backward in time, we find that they all come together, so to speak, fifteen or twenty billion years ago. All that time all the matter in the universe was packed into a dense mass (the eternal, autonomous existence of matter), at temperatures of many trillions of degrees. The dazzling brilliance of the radiation in this dense, hot universe must have been beyond description. The picture suggests the

explosion of a cosmic hydrogen bomb. The instant in which the cosmic bomb exploded marked the birth of the universe" (parenthesis added).[13]

What prompted this exotic sounding theory? Jastrow gives us the clues—"expanding universe," "gigantic explosion," "outward-moving galaxies," "cosmic hydrogen bomb,"—etc. Like many other important scientific discoveries, astronomers formulated the Big Bang theory because of experimental serendipity. It began with Vesto Melvin Slipher in 1926. Slipher was busy cataloguing light from about a dozen distant galaxies. To his utter amazement, he discovered that the light from these galaxies had shifted considerably to the red end of the spectrum. When Slipher measured this red shift, he discovered that the galaxies were moving away from the earth, and each other, at speeds of thousands of kilometers per second. It was a stunning revelation! The problem was that nobody in the scientific community understood exactly what it meant. Despite the immediate lack of understanding, the scientific community enthusiastically received Slipher's discovery. Some years later, Milton Humason and Edwin Hubble confirmed his work. However, Slipher's discovery was the first indication of an expanding universe. Thus, Slipher planted the seed and the fertile soil of the scientific minds of the era nurtured and watered the seed until it germinated and grew to maturity. It became the most salient theory of beginnings in the whole of the scientific community. At last, here was a plausible, albeit godless explanation of the origin of the universe. Nevertheless, there was no concrete "proof" of a cosmic hydrogen explosion until 1945.

Plagued by an irritating background noise in a radio-frequency detection device on which they were working, two Bell Telephone physicists, Arno Penzias and Robert Wilson, decided to investigate the interior of the giant horn-shaped antenna, and discovered pigeons roosting in it. They promptly removed the pigeons and the droppings that had accumulated, but the noise persisted. No matter where they pointed their radio telescope, the noise remained constant and persistent. It was as if the whole universe was "broadcasting" an immutable hiss. It puzzled them.

Meanwhile, Robert Dicke and his group at Princeton University were doing some calculations involving the theoretical residual temperature of the proposed Big Bang. They concluded that if the Big Bang occurred

15 billion years ago (the figure based upon Slipher's, Humason's, and Wilson's data), the cooling effect should have brought the temperature down from 10 billion degrees Kelvin to about 10 degrees Kelvin.

In 1949, two former students of George Gamow calculated a present day residual temperature of 5 degrees Kelvin, a temperature corresponding to minus 268 degrees Centigrade. Eventually, Penzias and Dicke got together at the Bell laboratories. After Dicke and his group saw Penzias' and Wilson's equipment and data, they felt very strongly that the Bell physicists had measured residual fireball radiation from the original Big Bang. Subsequent testing and measurements at different wavelengths confirmed Dicke's suspicions. For the first time, the Big Bang, proposed as the origin of the universe, gained a solid footing.

Divine Fiat

If you were a theologian of, say, the fundamentalist persuasion, you would probably turn to Genesis 1:1 or John 1:1-3 and present the Creationist's viewpoint of Divine Fiat (long Y, fy-aht), or creation *ex nihilo*. You would also probably assert dogmatically that God simply spoke and it came to be. No one, however, (not even the scientist, Scientific Creationist, or the creationist) will argue the point that some sort of creation event occurred at some moment in the remote past and the fact that the universe exists, and that we exist in it, is proof positive that a creation process took place, regardless of the method. The question here is not whether creation occurred, but when and how. It is not a scientific versus religious argument but a difference of philosophies based upon one's background.

One can think one's way into a pattern of living, or live one's way into a pattern of thinking. The scientist who lives his way into a pattern of thinking that is evolutionary in nature rejects God and devises physical experiments in an attempt to prove that everything came about because of natural laws working upon the material universe. His viewpoint is therefore naturalistic and humanistic. He looks at the material universe, extrapolates backwards in time, and tries to imagine the primordial conditions that existed at "the beginning." After thinking about all this very carefully, he concludes that there was some sort of "Big Bang." However, he has not devised an experiment from which he has drawn his conclusions; he has merely propounded a theory based upon scientific speculation.

The Creationist, as well as the Scientific Creationist, does not believe that the scientist can devise an experiment or experiments to describe the creation process. They are quite correct. The best that they can do is to invent theories about how they think creation might have occurred. However, not all is hopeless!

Scientists and theologians alike agree that there was a time when the universe did not exist, that it appeared suddenly and without precedent. They disagree only in respect to the method by which it came about. The argument is endless. The theologians ask the scientists—"Where did you get the matter for your Big Bang?" The scientists respond that their matter was always there, autonomous, immutable, and eternal. The scientists then ask the theologians—"Where did your God come from?" The theologians respond that God existed before the scientist's matter, that He has always existed, that He is autonomous, immutable, eternal, and that He created the scientist's matter. This type of circular reasoning goes unresolved. The stalemate continues *ad infinitum*.

Nevertheless, among elements that are more liberal, even agnostic and atheistic scientists maintain that there is:

> ". . . astronomical evidence that leads to a biblical view of the origin of the world. The details differ, but the essential elements in the astronomical and biblical accounts of Genesis are the same: the chain of events leading to man commenced suddenly and sharply at a definite moment in time, in a flash of light and energy. Some scientists are unhappy with the idea that the world began this way. Until recently, many... preferred the Steady State theory, which holds that the universe had no beginning and is eternal. But the latest evidence makes it almost certain that the Big Bang did occur many millions of years ago." [14]

Do these more liberal minded scientists believe in God? According to Jastrow,

> "When an astronomer writes about God, his colleagues assume he is either over the hill or going bonkers. In my

case, it should be understood from the start that I am an agnostic in religious matters."[15]

Can the astronomers or the theologians ever "prove" one way or another, the origin of the universe? Can either set up observable scientific experiments that will, finally in time put the argument to rest? Again, there are elements in both disciplines that unequivocally say—no!

According to the Scientific Creationists:

> "**Creation cannot be proved**—Creation is not taking place now, so far as can be observed. Therefore, it was accomplished sometime in the past, if at all, and thus inaccessible to the scientific method. It is impossible to devise a scientific experiment to describe the creation process or even to ascertain whether such a process can take place." [16]

Why is it impossible to devise such an experiment? Jastrow explains.

> ". . . I am fascinated by some strange developments going on in astronomy—partly because of their religious implications and partly because of the peculiar reactions of my colleagues. The essence of the strange developments is that the Universe had, in some sense, a beginning—that it began at a certain moment in time, and under circumstances that seem to make it impossible—not just now, but ever—to find out what force or forces brought the world into being at that moment. Was it, as the Bible says, that 'Thou Lord, in the beginning hast laid the foundations of the earth, and the heavens are the work of thine hands'? No scientist can answer that question; we can never know whether the Prime Mover willed the world into being, or the Creative agent was one of the familiar forces of physics; for the universe was created twenty billion years ago in a fiery explosion, and in the searing heat of that first moment, all the evidence needed for a scientific study of the cause of the great explosion was melted down and destroyed."[17]

What *does* one believe—Big Bang or Divine Fiat? If not one of these theories, what is the alternative? Why not take a middle-of-the-road approach, which combines both?

William F. Dankenbring, in his book *Beyond Star Wars*, suggests that God used the Big Bang as His method in the creation process.

> "Scientific investigation suggests that the original time of creation was between 10 and 15 billion years ago. At that time, evidence suggests, the entire Cosmos was initially created in a great explosion, commonly referred to as the original 'Big Bang'. The Big Bang theory postulates that there once existed a huge primordial cloud composed of matter—this cloud may have contained a 'soup' of all the fundamental particles, which exist in the atom. Hubble's Constant indicates the 'Big Bang' occurred 10,000,000,000 years ago—that was the time when the universe started expanding, with the galaxies flying outward toward the infinite reaches of space. By noting the present observable speed of these far away retreating galaxies, Hubble suggested that about 10,000,000,000 years ago they must have all been closely packed together in a huge primordial cloud. As temperatures in the cloud shot upward, and intense radiation filled the universe, a tremendous explosion rocked the entire mass, creating galaxies, stars, and the various components of the universe, and hurling them outward at fantastic speeds."[18]

Whether the Big Bang was *the* method God used to create the universe is the least important point here. What *is* important is that He created it! However, Dankenbring suggests that even in the Bible there is evidence that points to the Big Bang and an expanding universe. He quotes the prophet Isaiah.

Isaiah makes a rather curious statement in chapter 40 in which he extols God's greatness in comparison to man. In the last part of verse 22 he says that it is God, "that stretcheth out the heavens as a curtain, and spreads them out as a tent to dwell in." This fact, Dankenbring infers, "may be an indication of the *expanding universe.*"[19] Job 9:8 says that it is God "which alone spreadeth out the heavens . . ." In psalm 104:2

David restates this affirmation when he says of God that it is He "who stretchest out the heavens like a curtain."

All three of these words—stretcheth, spreadeth, stretches—are the English renderings of the Hebrew word *natah* (naw-taw'), which means, to stretch or spread out. By implication, the word *natah* can also mean, "to bend away."

Who, then, do we believe—the astronomers who, because they don't believe in a Supreme God, must start with eternally existing matter and laws governing that matter, or the theologians, at least some of which still believe that a Great, All-powerful God created *ex nihilo*? Did God create via the Big Bang, or Divine Fiat? Was it either/or, or was it a combination of both? Did matter, as the astronomers claim, already exist, and, by familiar laws of physics condense, heat up, and explode? These are questions hard to answer.

As for the Big Bang, it is inconceivable to this author, knowing that the condensation of matter stores energy, and that even in an *ex nihilo*, or if you prefer, an *ex Deo* creation, there would not have been some sort of gigantic explosion to start it all off. Therefore, we must consider the possibility that the Big Bang was not necessarily the method that God used to create the universe, but rather, the result.

Dankenbring quotes Lincoln Barnett as saying that:

> "If the universe is running down and nature's processes are proceeding in just one direction (a process called entropy), the inescapable inference is that **everything had a beginning**: somehow and sometime the cosmic processes started . . . most of the clues, moreover, that have been discovered at the inner and outer frontiers of scientific cognition suggest a definite time of creation . . . Every theory rests ultimately on the prior assumption that something was already in existence"[20]

The fact that "everything had a beginning," and that the frontiers of scientific cognition suggest "a definite time of creation," should indicate even to the most recalcitrant scientific mind that matter is not of itself eternal. Science is in agreement with the Bible that there is no past eternity of matter. Entropy supports this beautifully. Radioactivity among the heavy elements confirms it implicitly.

If, as Barnett suggests, "every theory rests ultimately on the prior assumption that something was already in existence," that *something* has to be God. This is as far as anybody can extrapolate backwards in theorizing about the existence of anything!

Therefore, one must conclude that it is the God of the Bible, the Yahweh Elohim, who set the creation process in motion via Divine Fiat, and brought the universe into existence out of nothing (*ex nihilo*), a great explosion or Big Bang notwithstanding.

This leads us logically to a beginning which reveals the history behind the onset of Satan's great deception—Project Apostasy.

Chapter 3
In A Beginning

Genesis 1:1-2 says,

> "In [the] beginning God created the heavens and the earth. The earth was formless and void, and darkness was over the surface of the deep, and the Spirit of God was moving over the surface of the waters."

The first word we need to look at here is the word "God, which is the English rendering of the Hebrew word "Elohim." The word "Elohim" derives from the singular Hebrew word Eloah (el-oah), which means—"a deity or (again with the article, specifically), God . . ."

Trinitarians and Binatarians (e.g., The Worldwide Church of God under Herbert W. Armstrong), because the word is plural, automatically assume that the godhead is composed of more than one person (three), and that all three were active in the creation process. In the case of the Trinitarians these three persons somehow are "one," co-equal and co-eternal. The Binatarians, on the other hand, believe that the Godhead is composed of only two persons, God the Father and God the Son and yet, they too are one, co-equal and co-eternal. Neither the Trinitarians not the Binatarians satisfactorily explain how this is possible. However, scholars agree that although the word is plural in nature, the singular sense prevails.

> "Throughout the Old Testament Scriptures two chief names are used for the **one true divine being**—Eholim, commonly translated *God* in our version . . . Elohim is the plural of

Eloah . . . The etymology is uncertain, but it is generally agreed that the primary idea is that of *strength, power of effect*, and that it properly describes God in that character in which he is exhibited to all men in his works, as the Creator, sustainer and supreme governor of the world. The plural form of Elohim has given rise to much discussion. **The fanciful idea that it referred to the *trinity of persons* in the godhead hardly finds now a supporter among scholars. It is either what grammarians call *the plural of majesty*, or it denotes the *fullness* of divine strength, the *sum of the powers* displayed by God**" (emphasis added).[21]

Hastings' Dictionary of the Bible in one volume says essentially the same thing:

"Elohim, the ordinary Hebrew name [title] for God . . . it is used, as an ordinary plural, of heathen gods, or of supernatural beings (1 Sam. 28:13), or even of earthly judges (Ps. 82:1, 5, cf. Jn. 10:34): **but when used of the One God, it takes a singular verb**" (Emphasis and brackets added).[22]

The above examples are only two of many that define the use of Elohim as the title of the God of the Bible in a singular sense. Elohim is not God's name. His personal name is Yahweh. The word Elohim, as Peloubet states above, is His title and denotes His attributes—the plural of majesty, the fullness of His divine strength, and the sum of the powers He displays. There is no Trinity in this. Why, then, do Trinitarians insist that the use of the plural word Elohim denotes a plurality in the Godhead? It does not make sense and does damage to the monotheistic teachings of the Hebrew Bible.

Another word we need to look at that the Trinitarians misconstrue as indicative of a triune God is the word "Spirit." The word "Spirit" here is the Hebrew *ruach* (roo'-akh). This word is Strong's (H7307), from (H7306) and means: "*wind*; by resemblance *breath*, that is, a sensible (or even violent) exhalation. . ." Again, because the Trinitarians assume the Holy Spirit is the "third person" of the Holy Trinity, they automatically assign activity as evidence for their doctrine. Although the Holy Spirit was obviously present and vigorously active ("the Spirit of God was moving over the surface of the waters") in the Genesis beginning, there is no hint that it is or was the "third person" of a so-called "Holy Trinity." Activity alone is insufficient as proof of personhood. We will discuss the Spirit at length in a subsequent chapter. First, let us continue with the historical account of the creation.

The Super-Angels

We have seen that before the universe existed there was God and that He created immensely powerful creatures they called *Seraphim* (burning or glowing ones), *Cherubim* (bright and shining ones), *Archangels* (chief angels), and *angels* (messengers). The word *"Cherub"* (kerub) apparently is the generic name, if you will, of the first three above.

Just what are these creatures? How do they fit into God's overall plan? Are they real, or merely symbolic and emblematic? *The Companion Bible* says of them:

> "Negatively, we may note: (1) They cannot be the God-head, or Divine in their nature, for [1] likeness of any kind as strictly forbidden (Deut. 4:15-16 etc.): and [2] the Godhead is distinguished from them by being mentioned at the same time. (2) Though heavenly, or celestial and spiritual in their nature and character, they are distinguished from the **Angels** (who, as their name implies, were spirits used as messengers) . . . moreover, they are not dismissed on errands as angels are, and are never seen apart from the throne . . .
>
> "Positively, we may note: (1) that the three root letters of **KeRub**, are the root letters of the word **KaRaB**, which appear in our **GRaB, GRiP, GRasP**. In a passive sense, the notion would be that of *holding* something in safekeeping. (2) (in Gen. 3:24 they are placed to **KEEP** (or guard) the way to the tree of life, and *preserve* the hope of re-genesis (cp. Gen 2:15, where we have the word "keep" in this sense). (3) they are four in number, and four is the number of creation (see Ap. 10). (4) They are represented by the symbolic heads of four great divisions of animate creation: the lion (of the wild beasts), the eagle (of birds), the ox (of tame beasts), man (of humanity) . . ."[23]

If the *Cherubim* are not of the Godhead, exactly what are they, and what do they look like?

A Cherub Is Not

Every year on February 14th millions of school children, teenagers, and adults around the world exchange Valentine's Day cards. Because they have never bothered to research the subject, they never suspect that they are observing and condoning an age-old, time-worn pagan custom that harks back to an era just a few hundred years after the Noachian Flood.

Many of the cards that change hands have printed on them embellished likenesses of naked, pink-bottomed, bow-and-arrow-wielding babies commonly called "*Cherubs.*" But a *Cherub*, contrary to popular concepts and the fanciful, superstitious imaginations of men, is not an impish; pink-bottomed baby whose sole function is to flit about on stubby wings, shooting tiny darts into the throbbing hearts of unsuspecting, would-be lovers.

This whole concept is mere utter nonsense however attractive it may be! Such images and characterizations are vile, blasphemous, pagan adulterations of what *Cherubim* truly are, and what they really represent in God's plan.

A Cherub Is

The *Cherubim*, largely, are intimately associated with God's throne. The Bible uses *Seraphim* and *Cherubim* interchangeably in this association, the term *Cherub* denoting the more generic of the two. The book of Revelation presents a graphic illustration of God's throne. John, who is on the island of Patmos, describes what he saw in a vision.

> "Immediately I was in the Spirit; and behold, a throne set in heaven, and *One* sat on the throne. And He who sat there was like a jasper and a sardius stone in appearance; and *there was* a rainbow around the throne, in appearance like an emerald. Around the throne were twenty-four thrones, and on the thrones I saw twenty-four elders sitting, clothed in white robes; and they had crowns of gold on their heads. And from the throne proceeded lightnings, thunderings, and voices. And *there were* seven lamps of fire burning before

the throne, which are the seven spirits of God. Before the throne *there was* a sea (as it were glassy) of glass, like crystal. And in the midst of the throne, and around the throne, *were* four (different) living creatures full of eyes in front and back. The first creature *was* like a lion, the second living creature like a calf, the third living creature had a face like a man, and the fourth living creature *was* like a flying eagle. And the four (different) living creatures, each having **six wings**, were full of eyes around and within (The A.V. seems to indicate that the eyes were located on the underside of the wings as well as on the upper surfaces). And they do not rest day or night, saying: Holy, holy, holy, Lord God Almighty, who was, and is, and is to come! Whenever the four (different) living creatures give glory and honor and thanks to Him who sits on the throne, who lives forever and ever, the twenty-four elders fall down before the throne and worship Him who lives forever and ever, and cast their crowns before the throne, saying: You are worthy, O Lord, to receive glory and honor, and power; for you created all things, and by your will they exist and were created" (Rev. 4:2-11, NKJV).

Note carefully the characteristics, especially the number of wings, of these four living creatures. (1) Each has a different form (i.e. a different head and face)—one like a lion, one like a calf (ox or bull), one like the face of a man, and one like an eagle. (2) They were in the midst of and around the throne. (3) Each one was full of (covered with) eyes before and behind. (4) Each has **six wings**, covered with eyes on both surfaces: and, (5) they praise and worship God continuously day and night without resting.

The prophet Isaiah saw practically the same thing in vision. He describes it in chapter six.

"In the year that king Uzziah died, I saw the Lord sitting on a throne, high and lifted up (exalted), and the train of His *robe* filled the temple. Above it stood *Seraphim* (the burning ones—indicating brilliance): each one had **six wings**; with two he covered his face, with two he covered his feet, and with two he flew. And one cried to another and said: Holy, holy, holy, is the Lord of hosts: the whole earth is full of His glory" (Isa. 6: 1-3).

The living creatures that Isaiah describes are the same ones John saw in vision. Isaiah calls them *Seraphim*. Each had **six wings**, and in this case, they occupy a superior position to God's throne.

Now, let's take a another look at a description of God's throne in which there is also pictured four living creatures very similar to those in Isaiah and Revelation, but who seem to have a different function or role than the *Seraphim*. In this instance, the four living creatures, composites of those above, the Bible classifies as *Cherubim*. Ezekiel describes them vividly for us. In a startling vision from God, here is what Ezekiel saw.

> "Then I looked, and behold, a whirlwind was coming out of the north, a great cloud with raging fire engulfing (taking hold of) itself; and brightness was all around it and radiating out of its midst like the color of amber (or glowing metal) out of the midst of the fire. Also from within it *came* the likeness of four living creatures. And this *was* their appearance: they (all four) had the likeness (bodily form) of a man. Each one had **four wings**. Their legs were straight (i.e. un-jointed — they did not move by walking), and the soles of their feet were like the soles of calves feet. They sparkled like the color of burnished (highly polished) bronze. *They had* the hands of a man under their wings on their four sides; and each of the four had faces and wings. Their wings touched one another. *The creatures* did not turn (rotate) when they went, but each one went straight forward. As for the likeness of their faces, *each* had the face of a man, each of the four had the face of a lion on the right side, each of the four had the face of an ox on the left side, and each of the four had the face of an eagle. Thus *were* their faces. Their wings *were* stretched upward; two *wings* of each one touched one another, and two covered their bodies. And each one went straight forward; they went wherever the Spirit wanted to go, and they did not turn (rotate) when they went. As for the likeness of the living creatures, their appearance *was* like

burning coals of fire, *and* like the *appearance* of torches. *Fire was going back and forth among the living creatures; the fire was bright, and out of the fire went lightning. And the living creatures ran back and forth, in appearance like a flash of lightning.* (Ezek. 1:4-14).

What an awesome, frightening, nerve-jangling vision! The incredible creatures pictured here are a far cry from the innocent, child-like "*cherubs*" pictured on St. Valentine's Day cards.

Let us look once again at the characteristics of these living creatures and how they differ from those described in Revelation and Isaiah. (1) They came out of the midst of the cloud whose core radiated a metallic glow. (2) Their bodies were formed like a man's body, but each one had four heads (man, ox, lion, and eagle). (3) Each one had only **four wings**, with eyes that covered both surfaces. (4) They rushed in and out of the cloud with lightning-like speed. (5) They went wherever the Spirit commanded them, and, (6) they occupied an inferior position to God's throne, bore it through the heavens, and acted as its guardians.

Anyone witnessing such an awesome spectacle today would surely call it a UFO. The cloud, the strange metallic glow, and the monster-like alien creatures rushing here and there at the speed of light(ning) affecting abrupt 90 degree turns or 180 degree reversals of direction (Ezek. 10:11), would be enough to frighten the wits out of anyone!

Ezekiel was no exception (cf. chap. 1:28). What Ezekiel saw in this dramatic vision was not a UFO, but the awesome, stupendous, frightening **power and glory** of the Almighty, living Creator God of the universe! Not only was what Ezekiel saw a vision of the very throne of God, it was also an amazing eyewitness account of God's throne bearers and advance guard, if you will.

Ezekiel could hardly believe his eyes! He stood entranced, awed, stupefied, and benumbed by the huge, billowing cloud full of "raging fire enfolding upon itself" as it bore down upon him from out of the north. It must have looked, for all practical purposes, like the core of a super-powerful breeder reactor creating more energy than it consumed.

As Ezekiel continued to watch, the cloud boiled intensely, rolling and pulsating, fiercely spitting and crackling as it spewed forth intense, jagged streaks of brilliant lightning, and glowed like the core of a nuclear reactor gone wild with horrendous heat. As the four terrifying composite creatures scurried back and forth, and in and out of the midst of the cloud, powerful, exotic electrical and electromagnetic forces raced up and down and back and forth among them.

It is highly probable that these were the same exotic forces used in the original "Star Wars" for the supremacy of the universe. Whatever these forces were, they badly marred the faces of the planets in our solar system and caused the breakup of one of the planets (q.v. the asteroid belt).

The *Cherubim* though very similar to the *Seraphim*, are not the same. The Bible describes the *Seraphim* as having one head on one body. The *Cherubim* have four heads on one body. The *Seraphim* have **six wings** each, the *Cherubim* only **four**. The *Seraphim* occupy a superior position to God's throne and praise Him continually. The *Cherubim* occupy an inferior position to the throne, and seem to be its transporters and guardians.

A single *Cherub* is a brilliant, shining creature having the form of a man and four heads, one each of a man, an ox or bull, a lion, and an eagle (Ezek. 10:14). Here Ezekiel calls the *Seraph* with the head of an ox a *Cherub*. If the *Seraph* with the head of an ox is included as a member of a group of creatures having the body of a man with four heads on it, it gives its name, that of *Cherub*, to the composite creature.

Apparently, these fierce, composite creatures symbolize the strength, power, and authority of the All-powerful, All-knowing, and All-seeing Creator of the universe in their order of subservience to Him. The ox is the strongest of the domesticated animals; the lion is the king of beasts fearing nothing and having no natural enemies save man; the eagle is the strongest flier among the birds; and the man is the strongest of all by virtue of his intellect, ruling over all of them. The *Cherubim* station themselves beneath God's throne showing that He is supreme in the universal hierarchy.

There is one "species" of *Cherub* yet to consider, the *Archangel*. Where do these creatures fit into the scheme of things, and what do they look like? Keep in mind that a *Cherub* can be a single *Seraph* with the head of an ox, or a composite creature with four heads, which includes the head of an ox.

The remaining "species" of *Cherub*, the *Archangel*, is evidently a higher, more intelligent order of living creature. It is a caste, if you will, of super-angels having humanoid form and the face and head of a man. The *Cherubim* covering the mercy seat on the Ark of the Covenant (symbolic of God's throne), are depicted in this manner.

In addition, the Bible always pictures the *Covering Cherubs* as having only **one pair of wings** as opposed to two pair for the composite creatures specifically called *Cherubim*, and three pair of wings for the *Seraphim*.

The Archangels

After God completed the hard universe, He created a special class of *Cherubs*, a triumvirate (only three are mentioned in the Scriptures) of magnificent and powerful spirit beings called *Archangels*. He named them Lucifer (light-bringer), Michael (one who is like God), and Gabriel (man of God). He gave them great authority over billions upon billions of lesser angels. Each had control over his particular third.

God fitted Lucifer, Michael, and Gabriel for specific tasks—administrator, warrior, and messenger respectively. Lucifer was the Chief Administrator for he possessed a great deal of knowledge about trade and commerce (Ezek. 28:16-18). Michael was the Chief Warrior or General of God's armies (Rev. 12:7; Dan. 10:13, 21; 12:1), and Gabriel was the Chief Messenger (Dan. 9:21-23; Lk. 1:19-26). However, any one of them could have exchanged roles at any given time.

Following the creation of the angelic hosts, God formed and fashioned a very special place called Earth for Lucifer and his third of the angels. But when did He create the earth? Was it immediately after the creation of the angels? We do not know and the Bible does not say. However, there is scientific evidence that points to a 15 billion year gap between the creation of the Cosmos and our solar system.

With this in mind, let us look at Genesis 1:1.

The word "beginning" here is the Hebrew word *réshiyth* (ray-sheeth), and signifies, just as the Greek word *arché* (ar-khay') in John 1:1—a beginning of the first order of rank, time, and place. Although both of these beginnings are of the first order of rank, time, and place, they did not occur at the same time or in the same place. The beginning of Genesis 1:1 apparently occurred much later on our relative time scale than that of John 1:1. We have already seen that conservative estimates place the beginning of the universe at least 10 billion years ago. Referring once again to Dankenbring, we see that:

> "Scientific evidence may be adduced to show that the solar system itself is approximately 5 billion years old. The oldest surface rocks on the earth appear to be 3.5 billion years old. From an abundance of lead isotopes found, it is estimated that the earth, the moon and meteorites have an age of 4.7 billion years"[24]

Whether the creation of the earth occurred 5 or 10 billion years **after** the Cosmic beginning is not the important point. What is important to our understanding is that God created it **after** the creation of the Cosmos and the uncountable billions of angels. The book of Job best illustrates this in chapter 38, verses 4-7.

> "Where were you when I laid the foundations of the earth? Tell Me, If you have understanding. Who determined its measurement? Surely you know! Or who stretched the line upon it? To what were *its* foundations fastened? **Or who laid its cornerstone when the morning stars sang together and all the sons of God (angels) shouted for joy?**"

It is patently obvious from this passage that angels existed prior to, and were therefore present at the creation of the heaven(s) and the earth. The majority of versions in print today includes the definite article in Genesis 1:1, and renders the verse incorrectly. The definite article is not in the original manuscripts. Rotherham's Emphasized bible, in a footnote to Genesis 1:1, explains,

> "The definite article in the rendering, 'In the beginning,' cannot safely be pressed, inasmuch as the phrase may, as preferred by many expositors ancient and modern, be simply construed with what follows: 'In the beginning of God's creating,' etc."[25]

The verse makes more sense if it reads, "In (a) beginning God…" or "In beginning God…" and, in fact, is the better rendering.

Having demonstrated that God (Yahweh) planned, measured, and laid the foundations of the earth at a later date than the creation of the

Cosmos, and certainly long before the advent of man, we can now turn to the story of the one all this has been leading up to—the one who became Satan.

Lucifer Aka Satan

Lucifer tried to destroy God's magnificent, boundless creation by violence and failed. Now he seeks to destroy mankind through deception and a plan that, without qualification, lends itself to the name *Project Apostasy*. First, let us review the events leading up to the real "Star Wars" episode.

Lucifer was probably the first of the archangels created. If so, he most likely watched with childlike awe as the Lord God (Yahweh) created the others. Before He finished, Lucifer knew intuitively that he was the greatest of the angels in power, beauty, and knowledge. These attributes placed him in a very special relationship with his Creator. He was second in authority only to God in the entire universe.

Lucifer was the angelic leader *par excellence*. Conjointly with Michael, he enjoyed the esteemed and prestigious position of covering Cherub (Ex. 25:19-20; Ezek. 28:14). As the chief member of the angelic triumvirate, Lucifer had unlimited access to God's presence and throne. He was closer to his Creators than all the others were and privy to God's total plan for the universe. This intimate knowledge and prestigious position ultimately precipitated his downfall. If ever the adage "familiarity breeds contempt" were true, it was never truer than when it came to the relationship between Lucifer and his Creator.

The Bible describes Lucifer as the most beautiful of all angels. What did he look like in the beginning?

> "Son of man, take up a lamentation against the king of Tyre, and say to him, 'Thus says the Lord God: You *were* the seal of perfection, full of wisdom and perfect in beauty. **You were in Eden**, the Garden of God (Lucifer's governmental seat on the earth before his treasonous rebellion); Every precious stone *was* your covering: The sardius (ruby), topaz, and diamond, beryl (chrysolite), onyx, and jasper, sapphire, turquoise (carbuncle), and emerald with gold . . . '"(Ezek. 28:12-13).

Lucifer was the absolute in beauty and wisdom in the angelic kingdom. There were *none* who could compare with him. As far as his knowledge was concerned, God had "programmed" into him, as it were, every iota of information he would ever need for the proper administration of his responsibilities. God not only gave Lucifer knowledge, He also gave him the consummate ability to use it—wisdom. One thing only was missing—a fully developed, righteous, Godly character. We shall see that Lucifer never developed Godly character, and that this failure led to dire consequences.

A Covering of Stones

Lucifer's form and appearance were beyond compare in the angelic realm. It was a veritable rainbow of colors, splendid, brilliant, scintillating, breathtaking, and covered with "stones" as it were.

A brief study of the stones mentioned in Ezekiel 28 indicates that the covering may not have been of stones (q.v. gemstones) in the ordinary sense of the word. The word "covering" is the Hebrew *MeCukkah* (mes-ook-kaw'), and means—"a covering, i.e., a garnishment or decorative embellishment." MeCukkah is derived from the Hebrew *Sakak* (saw-kak'), which means—"to entwine as a screen." By extension, it is possible that Lucifer's outward appearance was one of a "screen-like decorative embellishment." A screen can be either a coarsely woven structure, or an extremely fine, net-like mesh. This leaves us with two possibilities: (1) Either the covering was a coarsely woven mesh to which cut and/or finely polished gemstones were somehow attached in highly pleasing arrangements: or (2), A fine, net-like mesh woven of the minerals of which the "stones" themselves are composed.

If we could take all of the "stones" mentioned in Ezekiel 28, most of which are a deep, rich, brilliant red in their pure form – and God says that Lucifer was perfect in beauty – melt them down, draw them into minute, hair-like strands, weave them into our fine net-like mesh, and place it on a humanoid form (though composed of spirit matter), we would probably get a pretty good picture of Lucifer's outward appearance. It would be an appearance that would shimmer and glow with glorious and blinding radiance. A rather poor comparison of this sort of effect produced in nature would be the thousands of minuscule, iridescent facets of an insect's compound eye. Intensify this iridescence thousands of times over and you would have the scintillating brilliance of Lucifer's original form.

The gold mentioned in Ezekiel 28 is not the element itself. The word used here is the Hebrew *Zahab'* (zaw-hawb'), and means—"to shimmer" (like gold). Thus, added to the brilliance of the screen-like covering consisting of the "stones," there was a shimmering golden aura that enhanced Lucifer's beauty and luster with a certain deep, rich opulence. No other angelic being in the entire universe could lay claim to such incredible, awe-inspiring beauty.

Thus far, we have seen that Lucifer possessed awesome power, incredible strength, high rank, supreme angelic authority, consummate wisdom befitting his office and position, a profound knowledge and understanding of the requirements of his office, unparalleled beauty, executive privilege, and the reverential respect of his peers and underlings. Who could have or desire more? Incredible as it may seem, it was not enough! Because of this mighty *Cherub's* inordinate desire to possess one more thing—the very throne of God and all its sovereign powers—he lost even that which he had. The celestial battle that ensued altered the perfect state of the universe beyond comprehension. How did it all come about?

Pride and Prejudice

God says of Lucifer: "... you *were* perfect in your ways from the day you were created, till iniquity was found in you" (Ezek. 28:15). Iniquity is synonymous with lawlessness and anarchy. However, why would Lucifer resort to anarchy when he had so much going for him? With his supreme angelic authority, he commanded a vast empire unrivaled by any that would follow except the soon coming Kingdom of God.

> "Your heart," God continues, "was lifted up because of your beauty; you corrupted your wisdom (his ability to make right decisions based on sound principles) for the sake of your splendor" (Ezek. 28:17).

Lucifer became haughty, proud, and arrogant to the point that he could no longer make sound judgments. Despite repeated warnings, Lucifer's pride in his beauty and splendor, and his corrupt and deteriorating attitude, continued to grow out of all proportion. Not only did he flaunt his pride in himself and his great administrative and leadership abilities before his angelic subjects, he used them in direct defiance of the Godhead. Unwittingly trapped by the lure of infinite riches and boundless power and glory, Lucifer became so enamored and impressed with his own pomp and circumstance that he assumed a posture of self-deification. So vain were his imaginations that soon nothing short of universal conquest and rulership would satisfy his evil desire for gain.

Once Lucifer had mastered the subtle art of deception, he used it to persuade his angelic charges that God was unfair (see Genesis 3:1-6), and that He was no longer capable of ruling the universe in justice and righteousness. To implement his nefarious plan of rebellion this great angel of light fell into the habitual habit of lying, and in lying he committed gross character assassination and spiritual libel against his Creator. Thus, as God says:

> ". . . he (Satan) was a murderer from the beginning, and *does not* stand in the truth, because there is no truth in him, when he speaks a lie, he speaks from his *own resources*, for he is a liar and the father of it" (John 8:44, NKJV).

In his demented, twisted state of mind, Lucifer began to look upon God as a tyrant and a malevolent dictator. His rancor finally got the best of him. He could not shake off the interminable desire to have his own way! Lucifer could not quench his overwhelming desire to usurp God's authority and seize His throne. The great light-bringer who sealed up the sum of wisdom, and who was once perfect in beauty, rebelled. However, his pride was not the only cause of his rebellion. There was yet another, often overlooked factor—his prejudice against man although God had not yet created him.

But how, you say, can one be prejudiced against something that does not exist? In Lucifer's case, it was very simple. God had revealed His universal plan to all His angels, including the fact that man would ultimately *judge* and *rule* over them in his immortalized state (Heb. 2:5-8; I Cor. 6:3). This knowledge, coupled with Lucifer's sour and bitter attitude, became the proverbial straw that broke the camel's back. "*After all*," Lucifer must have surmised, "*why should I allow myself to be subjected to the utter humility of allowing puny man with all his foibles,* limited intelligence, and human weaknesses, to judge, rule over, and tell **me** what to do?" He must have overlooked the fact that man, in his capacity as ruler and judge, would no longer be flesh and blood, but immortal. He was unable to cope with such a concept. It must have tasted like bile in his mouth. The idea that man—immortal or not—would someday rule over him, was a fatal blow to his super-human, super-angelic ego.

Having conceived and initiated his plan of rebellion, there remained no doubt in Lucifer's mind about how he would accomplish his objectives. He cajoled, wheedled, and persuaded the angels under his command with promises and visions of power, glory, and co-rulership—a piece of the action as it were—until they succumbed, unaware of the consequences. They were gently brow beaten by Lucifer's silver-tongued blandishments until, before they knew it, they were victims of his grandiose, evil machinations. With his angels' support, Satan readied himself for his greatest blunder. Finally, the moment arrived when Lucifer said in his heart:

> "**I will** ascend into heaven, **I will** exalt my throne above the stars (angels) of God; **I will** sit on the mount of the congregation on the farthest sides of the north; **I will** ascend above the heights of the clouds, **I will** be like the most high" (Isa. 4:13-14).

The die was cast, the decision irreversible. Lucifer's fate was sealed. It was in that tense moment that Lucifer launched his unwinnable "Star Wars" for the supremacy of the universe. Born of corruption and nurtured by an overwhelming desire for power, he executed his plan with ruthless abandon without thought or consideration of the utter finality of the consequences. Lucifer's consummate evil brought about his absolute defeat. God, with Michael and his angels were gloriously and unequivocally triumphant. God cast Lucifer and his angels headlong back to the earth (Rev. 12:7-9).

These seditious, rebellious angels became demons (Rev. 12:4). From the very day and hour that Lucifer fell, he has vented his wrath and anger against mankind with undying vengeance (Lk. 10:18). Jesus Christ, who saw him fall in a prophetic vision, warned:

"Woe to the inhabitants of the earth and the sea! For the devil has come down to you, having great wrath, because he knows that he has (but) a short time" (Rev. 12: 12).

Satan

The once distinguished and majestic covering angel Lucifer became, for all time, Satan the Devil, archenemy and consummate adversary of God and man. From the moment he fell he began to formulate diverse and deadly plans to destroy humanity. Lucifer's obdurate bitterness and hatred transformed him into the opposite of what he had been. Where once he had been the beauty, he now became the beast; where once he had been the transcendent prince of angels, he became the prince of darkness, and the cowardly, picayunish god of this world (II Cor. 4:4).

As the evil god of this world, Satan is categorically responsible for injecting his hostile, bitter, and rebellious attitude into human minds through a vast variety of means. How does he do this, and how does he appear to man when he does it? The Bible says that he goes around like a roaring lion seeking whom he can devour (1 Pt. 5:8). Does he look like a lion? Hardly! Modern society popularly and comically depicts him as a pointed-tailed, red-suited villain with a Van-dyke beard and two horns, wielding a trident and sporting a lascivious grin. But does he really look like this? No! Satan is much too subtle for that. He represents himself as he appeared in the beginning—an angel of light. He successfully palms himself off as the bearer of truth, wearing many different religious hats, as it were. Satan's chief method of operation is the art of deception, and he uses it extremely well.

Take Heed That You Be Not Deceived

From the very beginning of modern man's existence Satan has persistently dispatched a multitude of false prophets throughout the world to spread his perverse brand of idolatrous, apostate religion. It comes in various forms and guises, but in the western world its most subtle form is "Christianity" so-called. Satan's "Christianity" is the result of the adoption and assimilation of Gnosticism and pagan rites, customs, and practices by the Christian church beginning with the first century A.D. This syncretistic "Christianity" is a far cry from God's truth.

The Apostle Paul was very concerned about this takeover of the Christian churches by paganism. In 2 Thessalonians, he talks about the great apostasy that crept into the Church unawares.

> "Now, brethren, concerning the coming of our Lord Jesus Christ and our gathering together to Him, we ask you, not to be soon shaken in mind or troubled, either by (an evil) spirit, or by word or by letter, as if from us, as though the day of Christ had come. **Let no one deceive you by any means;** *for that day will not come unless the* **falling away** *comes first,* and the man of sin is revealed, the son of perdition, who opposes and exalts himself above all that is called God or that is worshipped, so that he sits as God in the temple of God, showing himself that he is God. Do you not remember that when I was still with you I told you these things? And now you know what is restraining, that he may be revealed in his own time. For the **mystery of lawlessness** is already at work; only He who now restrains *will do so* until He is taken out of the way. And then the lawless one will be revealed, whom the Lord will consume with the breath of His mouth and destroy with the brightness of His coming. The coming of the *lawless one* is according to the working of Satan, with all power, signs, and lying wonders, and with all **unrighteous deception** among those who (are perishing), because they did not receive the love of the truth, that they might be saved. And for this reason God will send them strong delusion, that they should believe **the lie**, that they may be condemned (judged or punished) who did not believe the truth but had pleasure in unrighteousness" (II Thess. 2:1-12, emphasis mine).

Everywhere Paul established congregations, he warned them against paying heed to the false prophets who crept in unawares among them as ravening wolves dressed in sheep's clothing (Mt. 7:15). However, *Paul* was not deceived. He *knew* what was going on, what was going to happen before it happened, every time he established a new congregation and moved on to another city. The church at Ephesus is a good example.

Ephesus was a thoroughly paganized city and the capitol of the Roman province of Asia. Its most famous building was the illustrious temple of Diana, which stood conspicuously at the head of the harbor. The temple's magnificence was known all over the civilized world, and the Ephesians were devotedly attached to it. Their devotion was such that they called the city itself the "warden" or keeper of Diana. Because of the worship of Diana, the manufacture of silver idols and other religious paraphernalia flourished there. Most significant of these trinkets were the portable shrines, which devotees and strangers purchased and carried to their homes. It is not difficult, then, to understand why Paul said what he said to the elders of the church there.

Having completed his journeys in Greece, he and his companions sailed from Philippi to Troas and then to Miletus. While he was in Miletus, he called for the elders of the church at Ephesus. When they came to him, he warned them to watch carefully over the flock that he had left in their care.

> "Therefore," he admonished, "take heed to yourselves and to all the flock, among which the Holy Spirit has made you overseers, to shepherd the Church of God which He purchased with His own blood. For I know this, that after my departure savage wolves will come in among you, not sparing the flock. Also from among yourselves men will rise up, speaking perverse things, to draw away the disciples after themselves. Therefore watch, and remember that for three years I did not cease to warn everyone night and day with tears" (Acts 20:28-31).

To the Corinthian church, Paul defended himself against the false prophets and apostles because he was deeply concerned about their faithfulness. He talks about his godly jealousy toward them and his fear for their spiritual safety.

> "I wish that you would bear with me in a little foolishness; but indeed you are bearing with me. For I am jealous for you with a godly jealousy; for I betrothed you to one husband, so that to Christ I might present you *as* a pure virgin. But I am afraid that, as the serpent deceived Eve by his craftiness, your minds will be led astray from the simplicity and purity

of devotion to Christ. For if one comes and preaches another
Jesus whom we have not preached, or you receive a different
spirit which you have not received, or a different gospel
which you have not accepted, you bear *this* beautifully. For I
consider myself not in the least inferior to the most eminent
apostles. But even if I am unskilled in speech, yet I am not *so*
in knowledge; in fact, in every way we have made *this* evident
to you in all things. (2Co 11:1-6)

Paul calls preachers who preach another (false) Jesus, who preach a different (false) gospel, whose real intent is not to edify the name of Christ but to corrupt the simplicity that is in Christ by their flatteries and subtleness of speech, and who, by boasting of their godliness, pass themselves off as righteous men of God:

". . . **false apostles**, deceitful workers, transforming
themselves into apostles of Christ. And no wonder! For
Satan himself transforms himself into an angel of light.
Therefore, it is no great thing if his ministers also transform
themselves into ministers of righteousness, whose end will
be according to their works" (2 Cor. 11:13-15).

As mentioned earlier, Satan, disguised as an angel of light, is responsible for every perversion of God's truth, for every false doctrine extant today. **He has deceived the vast majority of mankind**—the many—into believing the very opposite of the true nature and character of the Godhead. Most today do not understand the beautifully simple truth of God's word because it is, and always has been, deliberately hidden from them by Satan and his false ministers.

"... it is veiled to those who (are perishing), whose minds the
god of this world (Satan) has blinded, who did not believe,
lest the light of the gospel of the glory of Christ, who is the
image of God, should shine on them" (2 Cor. 4:3-4).

Because they are blinded, they think the truth of God is foolishness (1 Cor. 1:18), and reject it in order to cling to the fables taught them by false ministers. Jesus Christ warned:

"Take heed that no man deceive you. For many will come in My name, saying, 'I am the Christ, (i.e. not that they themselves are the Christ—though a few might claim this—but that *Christ* is the Christ), and will **deceive the many**'" (Mt. 24:4-5).

If it is the many who are deceived; if Satan can transform himself into an angel of light; and if Satan was a liar from the beginning; how does he go about his great deception—by lying or telling the truth? If he is a liar and the father of lies, can he *tell* the truth? Of course he can (Job 2:2)! However, he would rather tell the lie. Okay, how often does he tell the truth? He tells the truth just as often as he needs to get you to the place where you will not check up on him anymore. If you go that far he has you! He will tell you the big lie, and he will tell it so often that he will have you believing it, or believing that you believe it.

In the following chapters, we will lay bare Satan's treacherous and cunning deceptions. We will also show how his false religious teachings have inundated the world with a flood of false doctrines, and how they have been responsible for a plethora of malodorous and vile crimes against humanity. Most importantly, we will show how Satan duped the world into believing the Trinitarian Doctrine, that blasphemous, satanic lie against the true nature and character of God that has led millions upon millions into rank, pagan idolatry.

Chapter 4
THE BEGINNINGS OF APOSTASY

Lucifer fell (Isa. 14:12; Lk. 10:18; Rev. 12:2, 9), became Satan. The indomitable will and superlative power of God and His holy angels completely shattered his dreams of conquest and universal rulership.

Undaunted by this tragic reversal of fortune, Satan skulked about his fragmented empire in silent rage. Resolutely, he rose from the ashes of defeat like a great Phoenix, pulled together the broken shards of defeat and began to formulate a subtle, nefarious plan of revenge. However, he had to wait patiently, like it or not, until the right moment for its implementation. He had to wait until God created the target of his intended wrath.

The World That Once Was

The solar system lay in ruins. It was tragically battered, torn, and scarred. It reeled and smoldered under the aftermath of the destructive onslaught of unimaginably powerful, exotic forces.

The earth was awash in a globe-girdling sea of murky, foreboding waters. Gigantic tidal waves raged undiminished and uncontrollably to crash thunderously against the shores and beaches of the continents. However, they did not stop there. They left their natural boundaries to roil and foam across the hills, valleys, and mountains, covering everything until the earth was, literally, a water planet. Thousands of years later, after the *second destruction* of the earth by water (Noah's Flood); God set impassable limits upon the oceans promising that He would never again destroy the earth with a flood (Gen. 9:11, 15).

Now the waves that broke over the entire surface of the globe abated. The surface waters brooded quiescently. The earth lay enshrouded in a cumbersome, ominous, thick black layer of clouds, impenetrable and impervious to the light of the sun, moon, and stars.

Once, millennia ago, the sons of God (angels) shouted for joy when He first created *the* heavens and *the* earth (Job 38:7). It was utterly breathtaking, a flawless, sparkling blue and green jewel hung on nothing among the stars (Job 26:7). Now, it lay ruined, chaotic, and void (Gen. 1:2). After countless eons, God began His work of restoration.

The First Family

By sundown the fifth day, the work of re-shaping and re-forming the earth's surface was all but completed. That which remained was the creation of the beasts of the field, and, most importantly, man.

In the early dawn light of the sixth day the Lord God stooped beside a cold, clear running stream (the River Jordan?), and began to scoop up handfuls of the miry red clay that lined its banks. He proceeded rapidly and meticulously to sculpt the body of the man He would call Adam (red clay). When the sculpting was finished, the Lord God leaned over and breathed the breath of life into the nostrils of the inert, lifeless form. The man Adam *became a living soul* (Gen. 2:7).

The events that follow are familiar to all of us. God saw that Adam needed someone to help him and to be a companion to him. He caused Adam to fall into a deep sleep, took one of his ribs, created woman, and brought her to Adam. Satan's opportune moment had arrived.

Satan's Plan Unfolds

It was time to begin to draw man away from his Creator. With Adam and Eve, Satan inaugurated the malodorous deception that, by about 1500 years later, brought about the destruction of the surface of the earth once again by water.

Satan approached Eve in the guise of a fantastically beautiful "serpent" that could apparently walk upright and speak (Gen. 3:1, 14). The word "serpent" is the Hebrew *nachash'* (naw-khawsh'), and means— a snake (from its hiss):—Serpent. This word, however, is derived from the Hebrew *nachash* (naw-khash'), and is a primary root; properly, to hiss, i.e. *whisper* a (magic) spell; generally, to prognosticate:—. . . (a) divine enchanter, (use) enchantment . . . etc. (Strong 5172).Whether it was actually a serpent that appeared to Eve, it is implied here that there was "magic" or enchantment used to deceive her. That the Bible refers directly to Satan as the enchanter is obvious.

We have already seen that Satan works his deceptions by presenting himself as an "angel of light." It is likely he used the same ruse on Eve. If so, he appeared to her in his *Cherubic* form and brightness. Such is indicated by *The Companion Bible* on page 24 of the appendices.

> "The *Nachash*, or serpent, who beguiled Eve (1 Cor. 11:3) is spoken of as an "angel of light" in v. 14. Have we not, in this, a clear intimation that it was not a snake, but a being of glorious aspect, apparently an angel, to whom Eve paid such great deference, acknowledging him as one who seemed to possess superior knowledge, and who was evidently a being of a superior (not of an inferior) order?...We cannot conceive of Eve holding converse with a snake, but we can understand her being fascinated by one, apparently "an angel of light" (i.e. a glorious angel), possessing a superior and supernatural knowledge."[26]

If we can believe *The Companion Bible*, we see Satan appearing as an "angel of light" (not as a literal serpent), "hissing," "muttering", "peeping," and enchanting Eve with his corrupted *and* corrupting wisdom. Through subtle innuendo, he convinced her that God, not he, was a liar. She ate the forbidden fruit of the tree of the knowledge of good and evil, gave some to Adam, and he ate it also—but not without knowing that he was wrong in doing so.

Because they took Satan at his word and followed his advice, they deferred to him instead of obeying God, and cut themselves off from their source of life. God expelled them from the garden and placed *Cherubs* at the entrance to bar the way. He never allowed them to return to eat of the tree of life, the symbol of God's Holy Spirit, which imparts eternal life to all who receive it.

It is highly probable that the *Cherubs* that God stationed at the entrance to the Garden of Eden were the source of bull-worship in the ancient post-diluvian world. If you recall the description of a *Cherub* given in chapter 2, you saw that one of the four heads of the *Cherubim and the Seraphim* was that of an ox or a bull. E. A. Wallace Budge declares:

> "Man in all ages seems prone to believe in the existence of composite animals and monsters, and the most cultured of the most ancient nations, e.g., the Egyptians and Babylonians, form no exceptions to the rule"[27]

It is not surprising that centuries earlier, even in ante-diluvian times, we see mankind comfortably established in bull worship, and bull-worship was connected to the Apostasy and the Trinitarian doctrine of the Babylonians and the Egyptians.

The late Evangelist Garner Ted Armstrong observed about the times of Seth, and the Sethites:

> "They knew God, and they knew something else. They knew of a forbidden area that was possible to reach by a laborious trip across a desert-like arabah, over some very precipitous rock mountains in the Anatolian Peninsula, over one of the deepest rift valleys in the world. . .but the way was barred. And so, for millennia, for generations, for hundreds of years, for centuries, literally millions of little children, now speaking all sorts of dialects and languages were told a story of a land they might have called Uz, or Oz . . . a land very, very distant toward the (Mediterranean) sea, reached by a very tortuous route across a blazing desert, across a river (the River Jordan) and up very steep mountains, guarded by dragons . . .the dragons would come roaring out at some intrepid voyagers, and they would seem to be actually capable of spewing fire, like napalm, out of their mouths. . . they would make horrible sounds and would have a shining sword that would appear to be like a laser beam flashing in the air. "When Adam and Eve lost their first home, God set *Cherubim* (at the entrance of the Garden). And *Cherubim* look like what? . . . they looked like men, lions, bulls, and oxen, or like an aggregate of all four. And if you see the bulls of Bashan and some of the great monuments of Egypt and Babylon, you will see these great creatures that were actually reproduced by eye-witnesses. But these pagans began to worship these creatures instead of realizing their place in the plan of God. "No doubt real *Cherubim* were placed to

guard the way of the tree of life, or God's Garden of Eden which remained intact until the time of The Flood. But no man was allowed in there..." (parentheses mine).[28]

In post-diluvian times the stories, legends, and descriptions of the fierce, composite "monsters" came down to the children of Noah's sons, for, as we shall see, both Egypt and Babylon worshipped the winged bulls.

Budge says of Pepi I, a Pharaoh of Egypt, that:

> "In the text of Pepi I (line 419) we have a reference to a god with four faces in the following words: – Homage to thee, O thou who hast four faces which rest and look in turn upon what is in Kenset." [29]

Kenset was the first Nome of Egypt which included the first cataract and its islands Elephantine, Sahel, Philae, Senmut, etc., and in which the Egyptian Trinity of Osiris, Isis, and Horus, was worshipped. Of the god Her-shef, or Ra, Budge declares:

> "In a figure of the god reproduced by Lanzone, he has four heads; one is the head of a bull..."[30]

Cain

After God expelled Adam and Eve from the Garden of Eden, Adam knew Eve, and she conceived and bore Cain (Gen. 4:1). Did Cain look like his parents? Did he have the same skin color or the same hair? Some do not think so. If one reads very carefully about what happened between Cain and Abel, and very carefully about the birth of Seth, one might well conclude that Cain was black, or at least that he was much darker than his parents were. Again, the late Evangelist Garner Ted Armstrong observed:

> "When Cain is born, Eve does not seem necessarily pleased. She says, 'Oh, it's a boy!' She says, 'I've gotten a man-child from the Eternal'. But when the next boy is born, it says they begot a child who was made in their image, and looked like the parents.

> "Every baby girl that is born has as a microscopic life form, every egg she will ovulate for the remainder of her natural life . . . Mother Eve, at her creation, had inside her body the capacity to produce every spectrum of the color range of the human race . . . finally it filtered down into three basic color groups and then dozens of varieties in between. Adam and Eve had the capacity to produce a child that was quite dark, another who appeared to be coppery-skinned or yellowish in caste, another one who might have appeared like. . .*they* appeared, which would be basically Caucasian, that is to say, Mediterranean, not at the other end of the spectrum. Cain very likely was a black man, Abel lighter skinned than his parents."[31]

Jack Randolph Conrad speaks of an account in the pseudepigraphal *Book of Enoch* in which Enoch tells his son Methuselah about a dream he has had. In it Enoch describes the creation of Adam and Eve, and the births of Cain, Abel, Noah, Shem, Ham, and Japeth. In the dream each one appears as a cow or heifer.

> Of *Adam*: "And behold, a cow sprung forth from the earth; And this cow was white." Of *Eve*: "Afterwards a female heifer sprung forth." Of *Cain* and *Abel*: "The black heifer then struck the red one, and pursued it over the earth." Of *Noah* and his *sons*: "Then the white cow, which became a man, went out of the ship, and the three cows with him." Of *Shem*, *Ham*, and *Japhet*: "One of the cows was white, resembling that cow, one of them was red as blood; and one of them was black."[32]

If any credibility can be given to the pseudepigrapha we see that Cain, as well as Ham, was black. Since Adam is described as a white cow, he and Eve were probably very close to the middle of the color spectrum between a deep ebony skin color and the blond-haired, blue-eyed, light-skinned Nordic races. This would place them among the peoples, as Mr. Armstrong speculates, of the Mediterranean castes (q.v. the Italians and Spaniards).

If Adam and Eve produced the first black child, it must have been very perplexing. Probably neither of them understood that what happened was the result of a mere chance combination of genes. They may have felt that it was a part of the curse that God pronounced upon them for their disobedience. Nevertheless, they did not reject the child, but tried to rear him according to God's ways. What happened next obviously negated their efforts.

What Price Lifestyle?

The birth of Abel compounded Adam and Eve's perplexity over Cain. Abel was more like them, though probably lighter skinned. He most likely became the immediate favorite. Thus, there was evinced very early on, a sibling rivalry between Cain and Abel for their parents attention and affections. As they grew older, it intensified until it culminated in the death of Abel Let's look at the story in Genesis 4.

> "Now the man had relations with his wife Eve, and she conceived and gave birth to Cain, and she said, "I have gotten a man-child with *the help of* the LORD." Again, she gave birth to his brother Abel. And Abel was a keeper of flocks, but Cain was a tiller of the ground. So it came about in the course of time that Cain brought an offering to the LORD of the fruit of the ground. Abel, on his part also brought of the firstlings of his flock and of their fat portions. And the LORD had regard for Abel and for his offering; but for Cain and for his offering He had no regard. So Cain became very angry and his countenance fell. Then the LORD said to Cain, "Why are you angry? And why has your countenance fallen? "If you do well, will not *your countenance* be lifted up? And if you do not do well, sin is crouching at the door; and its desire is for you, but you must master it." Cain told Abel his brother. And it came about when they were in the field, that Cain rose up against Abel his brother and killed him. Then the LORD said to Cain, "Where is Abel your brother?" And he said, "I do not know. Am I my brother's keeper?" He said, "What have you done? The voice of your brother's blood is crying to Me from the ground. "Now you are cursed from the ground, which has opened its mouth to receive your brother's blood from your hand. "When you cultivate the ground, it will no longer yield its strength to

you; you will be a vagrant and a wanderer on the earth." Cain said to the LORD, "My punishment is too great to bear! "Behold, You have driven me this day from the face of the ground; and from Your face I will be hidden, and I will be a vagrant and a wanderer on the earth, and whoever finds me will kill me." So the LORD said to him, "Therefore whoever kills Cain, vengeance will be taken on him sevenfold." And the LORD appointed a sign for Cain, so that no one finding him would slay him. Then Cain went out from the presence of the LORD, and settled in the land of Nod, east of Eden" (Gen 4:1-16).

Notice that in verse 4 it says, "Abel on his part **also** brought of the firstlings of his flock." The phrase "also brought" infers that Abel, in addition to bringing "of the firstlings of his flock," brought "of the fruit of the ground" just as Cain did. Abel, then, brought a complete sacrifice as required by God, but Cain brought only a portion of the required sacrifice. Consequently, God rejected Cain's sacrifice.

Cain apparently murdered Abel because God accepted Abel's sacrifice and rejected his. This hardly seems a serious enough event to cause one man to murder another in cold blood unless the murderer suddenly lost control in a fit of malicious anger. And that is exactly what happened!

However, if you look deeply enough you will find that it was not that single event itself that precipitated the murder of Abel. God's rejection of Cain's sacrifice was just the final blow in a long series of disappointments, which finally crushed Cain's oversized ego.

God commanded an animal sacrifice, but Cain, the father of Deism, thought he could worship God in his own way, and offered Him only the "fruit of the ground." The murder itself was just the natural consequence of years of bitter resentment, an attitude obviously egged on by Satan, the great arch rebel himself. It was a calculated ploy to further the apostasy he had so effectively set in motion in the Garden.

Genesis 4:5 says that Cain became "very angry" and that "his countenance fell." Cain succumbed to a deep, melancholy fit of depression aided and abetted by uncontrolled hatred and resentment that sprang from wrong thinking and the harboring of wrong attitudes toward his parents, his brother, and most importantly, his God. What really happened?

At the End of Days. . .

God commanded a sacrifice, but neither Cain nor Abel decided when to give to God. The time was predetermined. According to some, the sacrifice came at the conclusion of an agricultural harvest season. "In the process of time" (Gen. 4:3) should be rendered "at the end of days." The presumption that Cain's sacrifice came at the conclusion of an agricultural season is plausible, but weak. The term "at the end of days" does not necessarily indicate the end of an agricultural season. Keil and Delitzsch identify the phrase as *"In process of time"* (lit., at the end of days, i.e., after a considerable lapse of time)," without assigning to it the conclusion of an agricultural season.[33] Clark thinks that it is most probably the Sabbath and that the "gifts" and "offerings" were a part of the worship of the true God.

> "This worship was," Clarke declares, "in its original institution, very simple. It appears to have consisted of two parts:
>
> 1. Thanksgiving to God as the author and dispenser of all the bounties of nature, and oblations indicative of that gratitude.
>
> 2. Piacular [atoning for sin] sacrifices to his justice and holiness, implying a conviction of their own sinfulness, confession of transgression, and faith in the promised Deliverer. "If we collate the passage here with the apostle's allusion to it, Heb. 11:4, we shall see cause to form this conclusion (brackets added)."[34]

The command to Cain and Abel was to bring all of what was required for the sacrifice at a particular time. We learn further from Keil, Delitzsch and Clarke that Cain did indeed leave out the part of the sacrifice that pertained to the blood sacrifice that looked forward to the sacrifice of God's Messiah. Notice that the KJV rendering of Gen. 4:3 uses the word "gift" instead of "offering" for the *minchah* (Strong

H4503—From an unused root meaning to *apportion*, that is, *bestow*; a *donation*; euphemistically *tribute*; **specifically a sacrificial offering (usually bloodless and voluntary)**:—gift, oblation, (meat) offering, present, sacrifice.).

According to Kiel and Delitzsch:

> "Cain brought of the fruit of the ground a gift...to the Lord; and Abel, he **also** brought of the firstlings of his flock [in addition to the minchah of fine flour, oil and frankincense], and indeed (vav in an explanatory sense, vid., Ges. §155, 1) of their fat," i.e., the fattest of the firstlings, and not merely the first good one that came to hand. מיבלח [richest or choice parts] are not the fat portions of the animals, as in the Levitical law of sacrifice. This is evident from the fact, that the sacrifice was not connected with a sacrificial meal, and animal food was not eaten at this time. That the usage of the Mosaic law cannot determine the meaning of this passage, is evident from the word minchah, which is applied in Leviticus to bloodless sacrifices only, whereas it is used here in connection with Abel's sacrifice. "And Jehovah looked upon Abel and his gift; and upon Cain and his gift He did not look"...The reason for the different reception of the two offerings was the state of mind towards God with which they were brought, and which manifested itself in the selection of the gifts ... Abel offered the fattest firstlings of his flock, the best that he could bring; whilst Cain only brought a portion of the fruit of the ground, but not the first-fruits...The sacrifices offered by Adam's sons, and that not in consequence of a divine command, but from the free impulse of their nature as determined by God, were the first sacrifices of the human race. The origin of sacrifice, therefore, is neither to be traced to a positive command, nor to be regarded as a human invention (brackets added)."³⁵

Clarke interprets verse four giving an explanation that makes a great deal of sense:

> "Dr. Kennicott contends that the words he also brought, אוה םג איבה hebi gam hu, should be translated, Abel brought

it also, i.e. a minchah or gratitude offering; and beside this he brought of the first-born (תורכבמ mibbechoroth) of his flock, and it was by this alone that he acknowledged himself a sinner, and professed faith in the promised Messiah. To this circumstance the apostle seems evidently to allude, Heb. 11:4: By Faith Abel offered πλειονα θυσιαν, a More or Greater sacrifice; not a more excellent, (for this is not the meaning of the word πλειων), which leads us to infer, according to Dr. Kennicott, that Abel, besides his minchah or gratitude offering, brought also θυσια, a victim, to be slain for his sins; and this he chose out of the first-born of his flock, which, in the order of God, was a representation of the Lamb of God that was to take away the sin of the world; and what confirms this exposition more is the observation of the apostle: God testifying τοις δωροις, of his Gifts, which certainly shows he brought more than one. According to this interpretation, Cain, the father of Deism, not acknowledging the necessity of a vicarious sacrifice, nor feeling his need of an atonement, according to the dictates of his natural religion, brought a minchah or eucharistic offering to the God of the universe. Abel, not less grateful for the produce of his fields and the increase of his flocks, brought a similar offering, and by adding a sacrifice to it paid a proper regard to the will of God as far as it had then been revealed, acknowledged himself a sinner, and thus, deprecating the Divine displeasure, showed forth the death of Christ till he came. Thus his offerings were accepted, while those of Cain were rejected; for this, as the apostle says, was done by Faith, and therefore he obtained witness that he was righteous, or a justified person, God testifying with his gifts, the thank-offering and the sin-offering, by accepting them, that faith in the promised seed was the only way in which he could accept the services and offerings of mankind.

"If Dr. Kennicott is correct, and I believe he is, the "part that Cain left out" or failed to "rightly divide" was the blood sacrifice of the firstlings, the best part of Abel's flock, which Cain could have obtained from his brother to add to his *minchah*, and which looked forward to the blood sacrifice of Jesus the Messiah. Abel saw Jesus' day in his mind's eye. Cain did not; therefore, his sacrifice was a mere ploy to gain God's continued favor without the benefit of faith."[36]

From what we have seen above, it was the fact that Cain did not bring the proper sacrifice and approached the worship of God with a cavalier attitude. His brother brought a sin-offering (the fat portions of his firstlings); he did not. Clarke's paraphrase and explanation of Gen. 4:7 sheds a lot of light on what God might really have said to Cain. There is no indication in explanation that God accused Cain of being a sinner. Rather, He informed him that there was still space for Cain to "repent," so to speak, and do the right thing.

> **If thou doest well** - That which is right in the sight of God, shalt thou not be accepted? . . . But if thou doest not well, can wrath and indignation against thy righteous brother save thee from the displeasure under which thou art fallen? On the contrary, have recourse to thy Maker for mercy; לפתח חטאת רבץ lappethach chattath robets, *a sin-offering lieth at thy door*; an animal proper to be offered as an atonement for sin is now couching at the door of thy fold (emphasis mine).

> "The words חטאת chattath, and חטאה chattaah, frequently signify sin; but I have observed more than a hundred places in the Old Testament where they are used for sin-offering, and translated αμαρτια [*hamartia*] by the Septuagint, which is the term the apostle uses, 2Co. 5:21: He hath made him to be sin (αμαρτιαν, A Sin-Offering) for us, who knew no sin. *Cain's fault now was his not bringing a sin-offering when his brother brought one, and his neglect and contempt caused his other offering to be rejected*. However, God now graciously informs him that, though he had miscarried, his case was not yet desperate, as the means of faith, from the promise, etc., were in his power, and a victim proper for a sin-offering

was lying (רבץ robets, a word used to express the lying down of a quadruped) at the door of his fold."³⁷

It is not surprising that he murdered his brother in a fit of jealous rage! When God confronted Cain and asked him where his brother was, Cain retorted, "I don't know! Am I my brother's keeper" (Gen. 4:9)? There was no remorse for what he had done. Because of his unrepentant attitude, God pronounced a curse upon him, set a mysterious "mark" upon him, and banished him from the land.

Cain's lament over God's severe pronouncements was that his punishment was greater than he could possibly bear. However, he referred to neither the curse nor the banishment, nor did he object to the fact that he was to be forever a fugitive upon the face of the earth. His all consuming fear was that the heinous crime he committed was of such magnitude that not even God could forgive him. Cain's response to God indicates that his mind was already made up, for he says:

> "Surely You have driven me out this day from the face of the ground; I shall be hidden from Your face; I shall be a fugitive and a vagabond on the earth, and it will happen *that* anyone who finds me will kill me" (Gen. 4:14).

When Cain said to God, "I shall be hidden from your face," he did not mean that God would withdraw Himself, but quite the opposite. The Hebrew word for "hidden" is *Cathar* (saw-thar'), and means, literally or figuratively, "to hide" (the self). Remember—Cain showed an unrepentant attitude for what he did. God would have forgiven him immediately if only he had repented and asked for that forgiveness. What Cain was really saying was, because of the murder he had committed, because of his unrepentant attitude, and because he thought God's punishment unfair and too harsh, he was choosing to withdraw *himself* from the face of God to go his own way, or rather, Satan's way. When he turned away from the true God, Satan became his god. His unfortunate choice plunged him farther into his already well developed, idolatrous leanings. Genesis 4:16 states: "Cain went out from the presence of the Lord and dwelt in the land of Nod on the east of Eden."

Flavius Josephus gives this account:

"And when Cain had traveled over many countries, he, with his wife (one of his sisters), built a city, named Nod, which is a place so called, and there he settled his abode; where he also had children. However, he did not accept of his punishment in order to amendment, but to increase his wickedness; for he only aimed to procure everything that was for his own bodily pleasure, though it obliged him to be injurious to his neighbors. He augmented his household substance with much wealth, by rapine and violence; he excited his acquaintance to procure pleasures and spoils by robbery, and became a great leader of men into wicked courses" (parenthesis added).[38]

Cain gave himself over to Satan, perhaps to the point of possession, and apostatized himself with that false god's wickedness. In John 3:12 we read:

". . .Cain *who* was of the wicked one murdered his brother. And why did he murder him? Because his works were evil. . ."

Cain was under Satan's direct influence long before he murdered Abel, for it says in Genesis 4:7:

"If you do what is right, will you not be accepted? But if you do not do what is right, sin is crouching at your door; it desires to have you, but you must master it" (NIV).

Sadly, Cain did not heed God's advice. Neither did his descendants. *Project Apostasy* was well under way!

Lamech

The violence, the rapine, the robberies, and the murders did not stop with Cain; nor did the apostate beliefs and teachings he spawned in their wake. Each was passed on to succeeding generations until, by the time of Noah, they filled the whole earth. We see that even Cain's great-great-great-great grandson Lamech was a man of considerable violence. Genesis 4:23, 24 say of him:

> "Then Lamech said to his wives: 'Adah and Zillah, hear my voice; O wives of Lamech, listen to my speech! For I have killed a man for wounding me, even a young man for hurting me. If Cain shall be avenged seven-fold, then Lamech seventy-sevenfold" (*NKJV*).

This is a significant statement. It shows that at least four generations removed from Cain, his descendants were still keenly aware of the curse that would fall upon anyone who killed him. The curse became so ingrained in their minds that Lamech believed that anyone who killed *him* would be avenged by an eternal vendetta. It was almost as though Cain's descendants believed that as a race they were invincible, and that the curse pronounced upon their father concerning his enemies was actually a blessing in disguise. Josephus declares:

> "... because he (Lamech) was so skilled in matters of divine revelations (or divinations?), that he knew he was to be punished for Cain's murder of his brother, he made that known to his wives (the first stated case of bigamy). Nay, even while Adam was alive, it came to pass that the posterity of Cain became exceeding wicked, every one successively dying one after another more wicked than the former. They were intolerable in war, and vehement in robberies; and if anyone were slow to murder people, yet was he bold in his profligate behavior, in acting unjustly, and in doing injuries for gain"[39]

When Adam was 130 years old, Eve gave birth to Seth, who was like them in every way. Seth grew to manhood a righteous man before God. According to Josephus, he and his descendants were the inventors of astronomy.

> "Now this Seth, when he was brought up, and came to those years in which he could discern what was good, became a virtuous man; and as he was himself of excellent character, so did he leave children behind him who imitated his virtues. They were the inventors of that wisdom which is concerned with the heavenly bodies, and their order."[40]

There is no doubt that Josephus means astronomy here. However, Cain's descendants perverted even this, turning it into the pseudo-scientific art of astrology. Astrology in post-diluvian times developed rapidly into a cultic form of worship in which it was believed the heavenly bodies controlled the destinies of men. Out of this cultic worship arose the deification of the idolatrous Nimrod and his mother-wife Semiramis. As Nimrod's consort and the "Queen of Heaven," the Babylonians later incarnated her as the third member (Holy Spirit) of the blasphemous Babylonian "Holy Trinity." This, largely, was the crowning point of her licentious reign.

The Egyptians

The Egyptians did not regard Seth or his descendants as the inventors of astronomy, or any of the other sciences for that matter. The credit for these inventions goes to their god Thoth. Thoth was the same as the Greek Hermes, and Hermes, as we shall see, is connected with Cush, the father of Nimrod. He was known by the names Bel, Hermes, and Mercury. Budge says of the Egyptians:

> "They described him (Thoth) as the inventor of astronomy and astrology, the science of numbers and mathematics, geometry and land surveying, medicine and botany; he was the first to found a system of theology, and to organize a settled government in the country; he established the worship of gods, and made rules concerning the times and nature of sacrifices; he composed the hymns and prayers which men addressed to them, and drew up liturgical works; he invented figures, and letters of the alphabet, and the arts of reading, writing, and oratory in every branch of knowledge, both human and divine."[41]

One might wonder how Thoth could be the author of so diverse a list of subjects, but the answer is simple. He was regarded by the Egyptians as the heart, mind, reason, and understanding of Ra, the supreme deity of all deities. Ra was the same as Osiris who was none other than the Babylonian Nimrod who inherited all of his father's characteristics and abilities, even down to his names. We shall see later that Cush and Nimrod were possessed and controlled by Satan himself. Thus, we see the real reason for the intelligence behind the extraordinary mind of the Egyptian god Thoth. He was the personification *par excellence* of the mind of the Egyptian god Ra who was the all-pervading, governing, and directing power of heaven and earth!

This was, and still is, Satan's all consuming desire. It is one of the very reasons he rebelled against God. Satan is the inventor of false religion and all of its accoutrements. He is the driving force behind the Great Apostasy.

Noah and the Last Days

About 1400 years after the creation of Adam, when Noah was 480 years old, the earth and all that were in it became so corrupt and violent that God decided to destroy it. We find the description of the prevailing conditions in Genesis 6:1-5.

> "Now it came to pass, when men began to multiply on the face of the earth, and daughters were born to them, that the sons of God (angels) saw the daughters of men, that they were beautiful; and they took wives for themselves of all they chose. And the Lord said, 'My Spirit shall not strive (abide) with man forever, for he *is* indeed flesh (wicked, carnal); yet his days shall be one hundred and twenty years'. There were giants on the earth in those days, and also afterwards, when the sons of God came into the daughters of men and they bore *children* to them. Those *were* the mighty men who were of old, men of renown. Then the Lord saw that the wickedness of man was great in the earth, and *that* every intent of the thoughts of his heart *was* only evil continually [daily]" (NKJV).

The earth experienced a burgeoning population explosion! If this population, for the most part, was confined to the area known as the Fertile Crescent, it must have engendered tremendous social and economic problems, not to mention a diverse assortment of political and religious ones that were unprecedented in the history of the world even by today's standards.

Albert M. Rehwinkle has calculated that, given the conditions for long life spoken of in the Bible, there were at least 15 generations from Adam to Noah; and that if the average family numbered 10 members, there could have been in excess of 11 billion people on the earth by Noah's time!"[42] Were this population not necessarily confined to the Fertile Crescent, but dispersed over the face of the earth (though gathered into large metropolitan areas as Rehwinkle suggests), there still could have existed staggering social, economic, political, religious, and moral problems. One has only to witness our present day dilemmas with a world population of only about 6 billion.

Sons of God and Daughters of Men

Who were the "sons of God" and the "daughters of men"? There is much speculation and more than enough controversy about Genesis 6:4. Many theologians maintain that the phrase "sons of God" refers to angels, and that these angels came down and co-habited with the daughters of men. But, is such a theory tenable?

According to Keil and Delitzsch, the theory is plausible but not probable.

> "Three different views have been entertained from the very earliest times: the "sons of God" being regarded as (*a*) the sons of princes, (*b*) angels, (*c*) the Sethites or godly men; and the "daughters of men," as the daughters (*a*) of people of the lower orders, (*b*) of mankind generally, (*c*) of the Cainites, or of the rest of mankind as contrasted with the godly or the children of God. Of these three views, the first, although it has become the traditional one in orthodox rabbinical Judaism, may be dismissed at once as not warranted by the usages of the language, and as altogether unscriptural. The second, on the contrary, may be defended on two plausible grounds: first, the fact that the "sons of God," in Job 1:6; Job 2:1,

and Job 38:7, and in Dan 3:25, are unquestionably angels (also ינב םילא in Psa 29:1 and Psa 89:7); and secondly, the antithesis, "sons of God" and "daughters of men." Apart from the context and tenor of the passage, these two points would lead us most naturally to regard the "sons of God" as angels, in distinction from men and the daughters of men. But this explanation, though the first to suggest itself, can only lay claim to be received as the correct one, provided the language itself admits of no other. Now that is not the case."⁴³

Keil and Delitzsch deny that the sons of God are angels because there are many other passages which refer to the son's of God as other than angels (Ps. 73:15; Deut 32:5; Hos. 1:10; Ps. 80:17, etc.).⁴⁴

"The question whether the "sons of *Elohim*" were celestial or terrestrial sons of God (angels or pious men of the family of Seth) can only be determined from the context, and from the substance of the passage itself, that is to say, from what is related respecting the conduct of the sons of God and its results. That the *connection* does not favour the idea of their being angels, is acknowledged even by those who adopt this view. "It cannot be denied," says *Delitzsch*, "that the connection of Gen 6:1-8 with Gen 4 necessitates the assumption, that such intermarriages (of the Sethite and Cainite families) did take place about the time of the flood (cf. Mat 24:38; Luk 17:27); and the prohibition of mixed marriages under the law (Exo 34:16; cf. Gen 27:46; Gen 28:1.) also favours the same idea." But this "assumption" is placed beyond all doubt, by what is here related of the sons of God. In Gen 6:2 it is stated that "the sons of God saw the daughters of men, that they were fair; and they took them wives of all which they chose," i.e., of any with whose beauty they were charmed; and these wives bare children to them (Gen 6:4). Now השׁא חקל (to take a wife) is a standing expression throughout the whole of the Old Testament for the marriage relation established by God at the creation, and is never applied to πορνεία, or the simple act of physical connection. This is quite sufficient of itself to exclude any reference to angels."⁴⁵

Those who hold to the theory that the sons of God were the line of Seth, i.e., mere human beings, point to Mark 12:20-25; Matt. 22:25-30; and Luke 20:29-36 as proof that Angels are spirit beings and neuter in gender. Therefore, their reasoning is, they possess no reproductive capabilities. If it is true, they maintain, that "giants" were produced by human/angelic unions, how then does one explain Mark 12:20-25; Matt. 22:25-30; and Luke 20:29-36?

Let us use Luke 20:27-36 as an example of their reasoning. The Sadducees approached Him with a hypothetical doctrinal question relating to the resurrection, which they did not believe in to begin with. They presented the following scenario.

> "Now there came to Him some of the Sadducees (who say that there is no resurrection), and they questioned Him, saying, "Teacher, Moses wrote for us that if a man's brother dies, having a wife, and he is childless, his brother should marry the wife and raise up children to his brother." Now there were seven brothers; and the first took a wife and died childless; and the second and the third married her; and in the same way all seven died, leaving no children. "Finally the woman died also. "In the resurrection therefore, which one's wife will she be? For all seven had married her." Jesus said to them, "The sons of this age marry and are given in marriage, but those who are considered worthy to attain to that age and the resurrection from the dead, neither marry nor are given in marriage; for they cannot even die anymore, because they are like angels, and are sons of God, being sons of the resurrection" (Lk. 20:27-36 NASB).

When Jesus stated that "they neither marry nor are given in marriage, for they cannot die anymore, but they are like the angels, and are sons of God, being sons of the resurrection," he was not referring to sexual ability but simply to the fact that those who are resurrected have no need or desire to procreate, and are like the angels in this respect. Christ says nothing in this passage about the sexual ability of angels. He neither admits nor denies that they are capable of reproduction. In addition, he neither admits nor denies that the resurrected are capable of reproduction. The main thrust of his answer is that they both live forever, that like the angels; they are sons of God and sons of the resurrection. In the resurrection, then, it does not matter whose wife the woman will be because the resurrected do not marry.

> "While it is also true for the general resurrection that individual identity persists in spite of death, so that men will stand before God in their complete being, a fuller language is used for believers. They will be 'equal to angels [*isangeloi*]' (Lk. 20:36), free of all impulses of the *psychē*, including sexual ones (Matt. 22:30; 24:38)."[46]

Contrary to Keil and Delitzsch's view, no less an authority than the *International Standard Bible Encyclopedia* in the article Sons of God (OT), James Crichton declares of the line of Seth- line of Cain theory,

> "Most scholars now reject this view and interpret "sons of God" as referring to supernatural beings in accordance with the meaning of the expression in other passages. They hold that Dt 14 1, etc., cannot be regarded as supporting the ethical interpretation of the phrase in a historical narrative. The reference to Jer 32 20, etc, too is considered irrelevant, the contrast in these passages being between Israel and other nations, not, as here, between men and God. Nor can a narrower signification (daughters of worldly men) be attached to "men" in ver 2 than to "men" in ver 1, where the reference is to the human race in general. This passage (Gen 6 1-4), therefore, which is the only one of its kind, is considered to be out of its place and to have been inserted here by the compiler as an introduction to the story of the Flood (vs. 5-8). The intention of the original writer, however, was to account for the rise of the giant race of antiquity by the union of demigods with human wives. This interpretation accords with En chess 6-7, etc, and with Jude vs. 6f, where the unnatural sin of the men of Sodom who went after 'strange flesh' is compared with that of the angels (2 Pet 2 4ff)."[47]

In accordance with the above view, Josephus declares,

> ". . .for many angels of God accompanied with women, and begat sons that proved unjust, and despisers of all that was good, on account of the confidence they had in their own strength: for the tradition is, that these men did what resembled the acts of those whom the Grecians call giants."[48]

In the pseudepigraphal *Book of Enoch*, translated from the Ethiopian by R.H. Charles, Enoch gives a detailed account of the co-habitation that took place between the angels and daughters of men in chapter six.

> "And it came to pass when the children of men had multiplied that in those days were born unto them beautiful and comely daughters. And the angels, the children of the heaven (sons of God), saw and lusted after them, and said to one another: 'Come, let us choose wives from among the children of men and beget us children.'"[49]

Enoch further describes the dilemma brought about by the offspring of the angelic/human unions.

> "And all the others (the remainder of the two-hundred mentioned on page 15) together with them took unto themselves wives, and each chose for himself one, and they began to go in unto them and to defile themselves with them, and they taught them charms and enchantments, and the cutting of roots, and made them acquainted with plants. And they became pregnant, and they bare great giants, whose height was three thousand ells: Who consumed all the acquisitions of men. And when men could no longer sustain them, the giants turned against them and devoured mankind. And they began to sin against birds, and beasts, and reptiles, and fish, and to devour one another's flesh, and drink the blood."[50]

Anthony Buzzard, in his book *Our Fathers Who Aren't in Heaven*, mentions the activities of these evil angels who wantonly disobeyed God and messed with the genetics, probably not only of humans, but also of the animals mentioned in the quote from the *Book of Enoch* above. There is a hint here that they may have been engaged in genetic engineering and experimentation (cf. the Minotaurs and Centaurs of Greek mythology). On page 19, speaking of man's continued rebellion, Buzzard states,

> "According to Genesis 6 a ghastly disruption of human affairs occurred when evil angelic beings interfered with the human biological chain by uniting sexually with chosen women (Gen. 6:4). The result was the production of a race of terrifying giants (Gen. 6:5) who dominated the earth and became the legendary heroes remembered in Greek mythology."[51]

On page 147, Buzzard discusses the continuing rebellion from the outset of its development, a rebellion that I have dubbed *Project Apostasy*. Says he of Satan's plot to destroy mankind:

> "A coherent "plot" runs throughout the Scriptures. Adam is created with divine office. He "sells out" to Satan after being outwitted by the cunning of the Devil (the arch villain of the drama). The first pair thus "vote for" the evil ruler, and this tendency to submit to Satan is perpetuated in subsequent generations. The accumulating rebellion reaches a crisis in Genesis 6, where evil angelic beings (fallen "Sons of God")[52] interfere with the human genetic system to produce a race of giants. This terrible condition on earth calls for a world catastrophe at the Flood...The descendants of Noah do no better than their predecessors. A second race of tyrants is born of the hybrid angelic-human "marriages" (Gen. 6:4; Num. 13:33; see also Jude 6)."[53]

Regardless of whether it was evil angels or the line of Seth who "married" the daughters of the line of Cain, by the time Noah was 480 years old the practice of taking these women as wives was rampant. The statement, "of all whom they chose," could be construed to mean that divorce and remarriage were very common practices among men, or that the women really had no choice in the matter as to whom they were to have as a husband, or both. The word "took" in this particular setting is the Hebrew *laqach* (law-kakh'), and can mean not only to take, accept, or receive voluntarily more than one (wife), but also to take more than one (wife) forcibly or by seizure. The latter fits nicely into the scheme of things if one considers the unbelievable rapine and violence that were the norm in that day and society.

Socially and religiously the world descended into a cesspool of moral depravity. It was entangled in a web-like morass of rape, murder, robbery, divorce, polygamy, and idolatry. Crime, violence, and disobedience to God's laws and way of life were the norm rather than the exception. They were its gods!

There Were Giants in the Earth

The Bible calls the "giants" mentioned in Genesis 6:4 *Nephil* [im] (nef-eel'). The Hebrew means—properly, a *feller*, i.e. a *bully* or *tyrant*:—giant. Nephil is derived from the root word *na-phal* (naw-fal') which means, to fall or ... (cause to, let, make, ready to) fall (away) ... overthrow, overwhelm ... slay ... etc.

That these Nephilim were of giant stature there is no doubt. However, their stature was not necessarily their main claim to fame. It is evident from the above that the proper use of the word is *bully* or *tyrant*, and that the root word from which *nephil* is derived connotes those who cause or make others fall (away) from something by overthrowing, over-whelming, or slaying them. By extension, it can be said that these "giants" were instrumental in drawing the masses away from the worship of God through intimidation and violence. They were later the "mighty ones," the Titans used by Nimrod to establish his dictatorial empire. They were the over-throwers, the over-whelmers, and the slayers of mankind in Satan's plan to establish his apostate religion and his Trinitarian Doctrine worldwide. They were men of renown, i.e. men of great physical prowess and fame. However, the word "renown" can also mean—to be renamed or take a different name often. *The Companion Bible* says that they were men of name, i.e. the "heroes" of the Greek mythology (p.7).Later, it is clear that with the intermarriage of these angels with the daughters of men they began to rename themselves by or after the names associated with the Satanic system of worship that had rapidly infiltrated the Patriarchal system. History, and especially

Babylonian history, bears this out. We shall learn more about who these "giants," connected to Nimrod were in the next chapter.

After the Flood

That Satan's plan for the destruction of the human race was imminently successful the Bible confirms by the fact that it reveals that the entire ante-diluvian society was corrupt beyond saving (Gen. 6:11-12). God, because of the rampant evil that prevailed throughout the earth chose Noah, a just and perfect man (Gen. 6:9), to witness to the world for 120 years (Gen. 6:3) about the coming worldwide destruction, and told him that he, along with his family, would be saved out of it.

That society's stubborn, stiff-necked rebellion went too far, and God, as it were, had had enough. For 120 long years, even in the face of impending doom, the people continued to go about their collective everyday life, business-as-usual routine until the very day that Noah and his family entered the Ark (Gen. 7:11), the fountains of the deep were broken up, and the rains began to fall.

Noah and his family rode out the storm in the Ark he prepared and built according to God's instructions (a vessel that was of the 40,000 to 60,000 ton class). In the Ark with Noah were his wife, his three sons—Shem, Ham, and Japeth—and their wives.

Little is said concerning Noah's sons, or their wives, about their belief in God and God's laws. They were saved because of Noah's righteousness. The only information we have from the Bible is what happened to them after the Flood, especially of Shem, and the descendants of Ham.

Concerning Ham and his descendants, we find our first clue in Genesis 9:20-25. It is here that there is described a scene in which Noah's son Ham commits an act so scandalous that Noah pronounces a curse on him and his descendents, and in particular, his son Canaan.

> "And Noah began *to be* an husbandman, and he planted a vineyard: and he drank of the wine, and was drunken; and he was uncovered within his tent. And Ham, the father of Canaan, saw the nakedness of his father, and told his two brethren without. And Shem and Japeth took a garment, and laid *it* upon their shoulders, and went backward, and they saw not their father's nakedness. And Noah awoke from his wine, and knew what his younger son had done

unto him. And he said, 'cursed *be* Canaan; a servant of servants shall he be unto his brethren'".

What happened in that tent? The narrative simply reveals that Ham entered the tent and "saw his father's nakedness." This phrase is a Hebrew idiom or euphemism. Webster's 1828 Dictionary says that "*To uncover nakedness, in Scripture, is to have incestuous or unlawful commerce with a female.*" The latter is the usage of Lev. 18:19 in which God gives the purity laws to Moses. To "uncover" a woman's nakedness in this case simply means to have sex with her. However, the usage in Gen. 9:22 is slightly different and a little hard to grasp, but apparently is another euphemism. The meaning here concurs with the first part of Webster's definition as being incestuous. Thus to "see" or "uncover" the father's nakedness means to have an incestuous relationship with his wife or one's mother. The Scripture says simply that Ham "saw" his father's nakedness. We must remember that in Gen. 9:21, Noah uncovered himself. We can conclude from this that whatever happened, Ham did not come into physical contact with his father, i.e., he did not commit a homosexual act. If it was an incestuous act, it had to have happened with his mother, the Red Matriarch and royal wife of Noah. This monstrous crime against his father was his contemptible way of claiming the Red Matriarch, his mother, for himself in his attempt to usurp his father's authority and right to make laws, i.e., his Anship. The fact that Ham came out of the tent and reported to his brothers that he had seen his father's nakedness was a ploy to divert their attention away from the fact that he had lain with his mother and claimed her as his own wife. They were unaware at the time that he had usurped his father's Anship and claimed the right to rule. Evidently, there was no child produced from this illicit union. Why, then, did Noah curse Canaan, who was not even born yet, instead of Ham?

Pilkey clarifies the background behind the curse as it relates to the White Matriarch, Ham's royal wife. Says he,

> ". . .the ultimate target of Noah's hierarchic curse was Canaan's mother, the White Matriarch, who had broken the law against mother-son incest by bearing Sidon to Canaan."[54]

Pilkey explains further,

"The punishment for Ham's misbehavior fell on his royal wife as though she had instigated Ham's actions. Her motive was to supplant the Red Matriarch as Noah's royal wife and "Mahadevi," empress of Greater Arabia (including India and Egypt). Ham witnessed his father's nakedness as a ritual step toward breaking the law against filial incest by claiming his mother, the Red Matriarch, as his own royal wife. In doing so he claimed Noah's Anship [his right to rule and enact laws] for himself. . .One of the purposes of the Abrahamic war narrative of Genesis 14 is to reject Ham's claim by showing that Melchezedek (Shem), rather than Bera (Ham), claimed the legitimate Anship after Noah's death."[55]

We see from this that the curse was politically motivated. Ham alienated himself from Noah and Shem (who would naturally inherit the Anship) immediately when he committed his misdeed, for that was what it was designed to do. According to Pilkey,

"As Hislop and all Christian separatists recognize, the Mesopotamian world order became alienated from the God of Shem and, presumably, from Shem himself. We have found that the source of this alienation lay in the curse-blessing event of Genesis 9:26: a theocratic revolution favoring Shem and based on Noah's alienation from Ham. The revolution split the Noahic world into two warring factions: and the opposition faction (headed by Canaan, Sidon, and Nimrod) gained the upper hand in shaping the traditions of Mesopotamia."[56]

Satan worked diligently to break up Noah's family and set them at war with one another, especially in the case of Ham against Noah and Shem. Within 200 years after the Flood, Project Apostasy was alive and well upon planet earth. Even righteous Noah, who was perfect in all his generations, could not escape being included, albeit indirectly, in the rampant idolatry of his day. His and his son's progeny began almost immediately to worship him as a god! Hislop declares:

"Noah, as having lived in two worlds, both before the flood and after it, was called 'Diphues', or 'twice-born', and was represented as a god with two heads looking in opposite directions, the one old, and *the other young*"[57]

Ham, Father of the Trinitarian Concept

Ham, as legend has it, is the father of the black races. Whether he was black, or just dusky as the Egyptians, we do not know. The *International Standard Bible Encyclopedia* states:

> "As Shem means 'dusky', or the like, and Japeth 'fair', it has been supposed that Ham meant, as is not improbable, 'black'. This is supported by the evidence of Heb and Arab, in which the word *hamam* means 'to be hot', and 'to be black', the latter signification being derived from the former."[58]

We do know that Cush, the oldest son of Ham, was black and the father of the Cushites, or more properly, the Ethiopians. It is through the descendants of Ham that the idolatrous concept of a "Holy Trinity" came into being. It was the brainchild of Cush's wife Semiramis, the Babylonian "Queen of Heaven," and later the mother-wife of Nimrod.

All of them—Noah, his wife, his sons and their wives—witnessed the wickedness and violence of the antediluvian world, and the results that wickedness brought about. Some of them did not learn the lesson. With the memories of the great destruction wrought by God still fresh in their minds, they set about anew to plunge humanity headlong into the same cesspool of idolatry and moral depravity. Satan laughed with glee at the prospect!

Chapter 5
NIMROD THE MIGHTY HUNTER

Some years after The Flood, the descendants of Noah's sons migrated to the plains below the Mountains of Ararat and settled, in particular, in the Plain of Shinar, the fertile, alluvial tract of land lying between the Tigris and Euphrates rivers. God told them not to congregate into crowded, sprawling urban centers as before (cp. Isa. 5:8), but to spread out and colonize the whole earth.

True to their ancient fathers' stubborn, rebellious ways, they adamantly refused. According to Josephus:

> "...they were so ill-instructed (in God's ways) that they did not obey God; for which reason they fell into calamities, and were made sensible, by experience, of what sin they had been guilty: for when they flourished with a numerous youth, God admonished them again to send out colonies; but they, imagining the prosperity they enjoyed was not derived from the favor of God, but supposing that their own power was the proper cause of the plentiful condition they were in, did not obey Him. Nay, they added to this their disobedience to the divine will, the suspicion that they were therefore ordered to send out separate colonies, that being divided asunder, they might the more easily be oppressed."[59]

God knew that if they congregated into large, overcrowded urban centers their decision to do so virtually fixed their chances of oppression. Nevertheless, Satan still lurked in the background, cajoling, harassing, and persuading by innuendo, muttering, hissing, peeping as ever, and making God out to be a liar.

Having persuaded them that God was mistaken about the possibility of oppression if they massed together. Satan in order to advance *Project Apostasy*, chose as his instruments of oppression *par excellence* the prophet Cush, and the son of the prophet Cush—Nimrod.

Cush

Historically, Cush was the eldest son of Ham (Gen. 10:6), but he was also known as Bel, (the "Confounder"), Hermes (son of Ham), or Mercury, and Chaos (the god of Confusion). Under the laws of Chaldaic pronunciation, "Chaos" is just an established form of Chus or Cush. As "Bel the Confounder," His symbol was a club, denoting that he was responsible for "breaking up" the previously united earth.

> "How significant, then, as a symbol, is the club as commemorating the work of Cush, as Bel, the 'Confounder'? . . . when the reader turns to the Hebrew of Gen. 11:9. . . (he) finds that the very word from which a club derives its name is that which is employed when it is said, that in consequence of the confusion of tongues, the children of men were 'scattered abroad upon the face of the earth.' The word there used for scattering abroad is Hephaitz, which, in the Greek form becomes Hephaizt, and hence the well known but little understood name of Hephaistos, as applied to Vulcan, 'the father of the Gods.' Hephaistos is the name of the first ringleader in the first rebellion, as 'The Scattered Abroad,' as Bel is the same individual as the 'Confounder of tongues.' Here, then, the reader may see the real origin of Vulcan's Hammer, which is just another name for the club of Janus or Chaos, 'The God of Confusion;' and to this, as breaking the earth in pieces, there is a covert allusion in Jer. 50:23, where Babylon, as identified with its primeval god is apostrophized: 'How is the hammer of the whole earth cut asunder and broken!'"[60]

In Egypt Cush was known as Meni, Mene, or Menes. The name Meni meant "The Numberer." It was a synonym for Cush or Chus and signified "to cover," or "to hide," but it also means "to count or number." The true or proper meaning of the name Cush is . . . The Numberer" or "Arithmetician." While Nimrod, as the "mighty one," was the great propagator of the Babylonian system of idolatry by force and violence, Cush, as Hermes, was the real author of that system. He was the original prophet of idolatry after the Flood. He was known by the ancient pagans as the originator of their religious rites and the interpreter of the gods. He is said to have "taught men the proper mode of approaching the Deity with prayers and sacrifice." Hermes or Cush was the first to discover numbers, and the art of reckoning. He developed geometry, astronomy, and the games of chess and hazard. The name Meni is just the Chaldean form of the Hebrew "Mene," the "Numberer." The Chaldean (i) often takes the place of the final (e).

We have already seen in chapter four that the Egyptian god Thoth was the same as the Greek Hermes, and the inventor of science, theology, and the alphabet. Cush, as Her-mes, is also Thoth-Hermes, the son of Ham and Egypt's first king.

That Cush, or Bel, should be known as the "interpreter of the gods" at a time when the whole world spoke the same language seems incongruous. However, it was not until after God stopped the building of the Tower of Babel and confounded the language that Bel, or Cush, became known as the interpreter. The tower story is found in Genesis 11:1-9. However, our main interest here is verse 1. "Now the whole earth used the same language and the same words" (Gen 11:1 NASB). The word "earth" here is the Hebrew *eretz*—Strong H776—From an unused root probably meaning to *be firm*; the *earth* (at large, **or partitively a *land***):—X common, country, earth, field, ground, **land**, X nations, way, + wilderness, world (emphasis mine). The use of the word "earth" in vs. 1 is misleading. It should read "the whole land" meaning Egypt. In referring to Genesis 10:31 we see an apparent contradiction. "These are the sons of Shem, according to their families, according to their **languages**, by their lands, according to their nations. (Gen 10:31 NASB, emphasis mine). Notice that vs. 31 uses the word "languages" (plural). If, as stated in Genesis 11:1, the "whole earth" spoke the same language (singular), then Gen. 10:31 cannot be true or Gen. 11:1 is mistranslated. How, then, do we resolve this dilemma?

John Pilkey explains it most satisfactorily.

> "Talmudic tradition accurately interprets the Tower of Babel as an Egyptian phenomenon, not because the Hamitic stock was solely responsible for the Tower scheme, but because

the Hamitic tongue of the Utuship was supposed to have been the universal imperial language of mankind. The divine judgment on the Tower of Babel did not generate but confused languages. Noah's adversaries, coming to formal power a century and a half after the Flood, succeeded in a scheme to impose the Hamitic tongue on all mankind in celebration of a new Imperial Age. They completed the Tower a decade later and experienced the confusion of tongues a year later in 2357 B.C."[61]

We see from Pilkey, then, that the Hamitic stock had conquered and enslaved the Semitic stock and were forcing them to learn the Hamitic language. Consequently, the reason for the reading of Gen. 11:1 is that the conquered peoples, who spoke a different tongue (see Gen. 10:31), needed to learn the language of their conquerors in order that they would be able to communicate with them clearly. Else, how could the Tower-building progress efficiently?

After God came down and confused the languages, it is most logical that Mercury or Hermes (Cush) needed to interpret the speeches of mankind. In the language of the Mysteries, the word Peresh in the Chaldean means, "to interpret." It was often pronounced by the ancient Egyptians and Greeks, and often by the Chaldeans themselves *aseres*, which means, "to divide." Mercury or Hermes (Cush), who was the son of Ham, was the "divider of the speeches of men." In reality, God was the divider, but Cush was responsible. In building the Tower of Babel, he was guilty of open rebellion against God.

> "As the tower building was the first act of open rebellion after the flood, and Cush, as Bel, was the ringleader in it, he was, of course, the first to whom the name Merodach, 'The great Rebel', must have been given, and, therefore, according to the usual parallelism of the prophetic language, we find both names of the Babylonian god referred together, when the judgment on Babylon is predicted: 'Bel is confounded: Merodach is broken in pieces'" [Jer. 1:2][62]

Cush was the first after the flood to carry on the apostasy by openly rebelling against God and building a tower whose top "reached the heavens." The tower-building was Cush's attempt to make a name for himself and his subjects (Gen. 11:4), and to rally them to his cause. However, it was contrary to the direct command of God to spread out and colonize!

The tower itself was most likely a ziggurat. Pilkey describes it in these words:

> "There is little question that the Tower of Babel was a prototype of the Mesopotamian ziggurat and Egyptian pyramid, a numinous form symbolic of the cosmos of the third heaven."[63]

It was a marvelous technical achievement of great magnitude far ahead of its time in design and workmanship. In its day, it was comparable to the Great Pyramid at Giza. We read of God saying:

> "Indeed the people *are* one and they all have one language, and this is what they begin to do; now *nothing* that they propose to do will be withheld from them" (Gen. 11:6).

Cush wanted fame and recognition. He wanted to draw the people to himself and his son Nimrod so he could establish control over them and force upon them the most oppressive of governments. He knew that the tower would be a magnificent drawing card. It would attract thousands, perhaps millions to it to thwart God's plan for them to spread out and colonize. However, God's plan was not to be laid aside. He came down, stopped the tower-building by confusing or dividing the people's language, and scattered them over the face of the earth. To allow them to continue would have skewed God's prophetic time scale. He was not about to let that happen!

Cush founded Babylon, but his son Nimrod finished building it. Cush established a government, but Nimrod was its first real king. We do not even find Cush's name in the Chaldean king lists. That which Cush caused to be scattered, Nimrod managed somehow to reassemble and consolidate into one of the greatest nations on the face of the earth. Thus, the scion of the prophet Cush carried Project Apostasy, Satan's grand design for deception, forward.

A Mighty Hunter against the Lord

The name "Nimrod" means "tamer" or "subduer of the leopard." He was the son of Cush the prophet as we have already seen. However, he was more. He was also the son, and later, the husband of his mother Semiramis. Like his father, Nimrod was dark skinned or black. His bent for despotism was unparalleled, exceeding both that of his father and his mother.

Feigning concern for the safety and well-being of his countrymen, Nimrod was the first after the flood to gather successfully into highly organized units, others for the purpose of "self-protection." However, his ultimate and evil purpose was to bring upon them the onerous yoke of despotic, dictatorial oppression.

According to Genesis 10:9, Nimrod was "a mighty hunter before the Lord." However, the word "before" is more correctly translated "against," for he was anti-God in all his manners, customs, and beliefs. That he was a "mighty hunter" was the result, perhaps, more of necessity than of the love of the hunt.

By the time Nimrod reached manhood, wild animals were multiplying faster than humanity. These beasts ravaged the land, attacked the unfortified towns and villages, and mauled the inhabitants. The people had no certain defense against these marauding beasts or the terrors of frequent and often fatal attacks. The situation was similar to that brought about by Israel's captivity hundreds of years later, or what would have occurred if Israel had invaded Canaan immediately following the Exodus, and wiped out its inhabitants. As Hislop comments:

> "By the time he (Nimrod) appeared, the wild beasts of the forest multiplying more rapidly than the human race, must have committed great depredations on the scattered and straggling populations of the earth, and must have inspired great terror into the minds of men. The danger arising to the lives of men from such a source as this, when population is scanty, is implied in the reason given by God Himself for not driving out the doomed Canaanites before Israel at once, though the measure of their iniquity was full (Exod. Xxiii. 29, 30): 'I will not drive them out from before thee in one year, lest the land become desolate, and the beasts of

the field multiply against thee' . . . The exploits of Nimrod, therefore, in hunting down the wild beasts of the field, and ridding the world of monsters, must have gained for him the character of a pre-eminent benefactor of his race."[64]

Rollin writes of Nimrod's hunting skills:

> "In applying himself to his laborious and dangerous exercise, he had two things in view; the first was to gain the peoples affection, by delivering them from the fury and dread of wild beasts; the next was, to train up numbers of young people, by this exercise of hunting, to endure labor and hardship, to form them to the use of arms, to inure them to a kind of discipline and obedience that at a proper time after they had been accustomed to his orders, and habituated to arms, he might make use of them for other purposes more serious than hunting."[65]

There is no question that Nimrod had every advantage in these pursuits. He had previously tamed the horse and used it in the chase or the hunt. Employing the horse, he also managed to subdue the leopard, which he then utilized in formidable combination with the horse, to hunt down and capture or kill other wild beasts. His very name means "subduer of the leopard," or "leopard tamer." He dressed himself in the skins of the leopards he slew as a trophy of his skill. His appearance deeply impressed those who saw him. Consequently he was called not only the "subduer of the spotted one," but Nimr (the spotted-one) himself. Thus, Nimrod used his incomparable skills as a hunter to gain the adoration, confidence, and dependence of the people. He quickly became their hero. Hislop writes that:

> "In the Hebrew, or Chaldee of the days of Abraham, 'Nimrod the Shepherd', is just 'He-roe'; and from this title of the 'mighty hunter before the Lord', have no doubt derived, both the name Hero itself, and all that hero-worship, which has since overspread the world."[66]

Once Nimrod gained the people's confidence, once he gave them protection, once he taught them the use of arms and the skills of the hunt, once he had convinced them that there was nothing to fear, their dependence upon him followed automatically. Having obtained their fidelity and loyalty, Nimrod set about to turn the people's minds farther from God than even his father had dared. He persuaded them that it was he, not God that saved them and brought them their happiness. Having accomplished this, he changed the government to tyranny because he saw no other way of turning the people from God and bringing them into constant dependence upon his power.

Men of all ages have rallied around their heroes in hopes of gain no matter the price. The ancient Babylonians were no exception. They were enthralled by Nimrod's great abilities and persuasive powers. They flocked to his side like flies to the sweet savor of honey. They hung on every felicitous word of promise of a better, more magnanimous life and the hope of eternal happiness. The world has witnessed many such "Nimrods," q.v. Alexander the Great, the most despicable of the Roman Caesars, and in our century the cruel and demoniacal Adolph Hitler.

After Nimrod fully persuaded the Babylonians that it was an act of cowardice to call upon the name of God, he began to institute the perverse system of idolatrous worship that has persisted to this day. It remains as strong as ever though much modified and infinitely more subtle. It remains virtually hidden in modern times because so much of it is included under the name of Christianity.

Nimrod set an excellent precedent in the art of deception, an art that he learned extremely well from the master of all deceivers.

> ". . . by setting (himself) up as king, Nimrod invaded the Patriarchal system, and abridged the liberties of mankind, yet he was held by many to have conferred benefits upon them, that amply indemnified them to the loss of their liberties, and covered him with glory and renown."[67]

It is no wonder that the ancient Babylonians allowed themselves to be drawn inexorably into the most bastardized religious system of all time. It was a system whose very foundations were laid in pagan hero-worship. But of course, this has always been the case. The masses, largely, have never been able to make up their minds about how they should conduct their lives whether religiously or governmentally, and especially governmentally. It has ever been their wish not to be bothered with the drudgeries of government, taxation, the feeding of the socially deprived, or the maintenance of standing armies for the protection of their liberties. It has always been so much easier to let the bureaucrats see to these things until the very freedoms they live and die for are slowly, piece by piece, bit by bit, disappear. They live for the promises of tomorrow but having piled up a multitude of tomorrows, they are left holding nothing but a lot of empty yesterdays. Such was the case with those who followed Nimrod, and much to their eternal chagrin, they suffered unbearably for their indiscretions and lack of wisdom.

Nimrod the Conqueror

Having accomplished the purposes he had in mind for his countrymen, i.e. of delivering them from the ravenous attacks of wild beasts and of habituating them to the use of arms and warfare, Nimrod marched against the Assyrians.

> "The country of Assyria, in one of the prophets (Micah vs. 6)", declares Rollin, "is described by the particular character of being the land of Nimrod . . . It derived its name from Assur, the son of Shem, who without doubt had settled himself and his family there, and was probably driven out, or brought under subjection, by the usurper Nimrod."[68]

As with all greedy, evil men, the euphoria brought about by the success of so bold a stroke as subjugating another people served only to whet Nimrod's appetite for further conquest. As Ninus, the king of the Assyrians, Nimrod engineered a drastic change in those ancient people's manners and customs. They no longer lived contentedly because their king did not live contentedly. His new passion, the desire for conquest, constantly provoked his craving for more. He was the first after the Flood who utilized organized warfare against his neighbors. He conquered every nation from Assyria to Libya. It was an easy task because they were as yet unacquainted with the arts of warfare on a large scale.

There was not a nation on the face of the earth that could withstand Nimrod's swift and decisive victories. From Assyria, he crossed the great desert wastelands of Arabia. He conquered the Canaanites who derived their name from his uncle Canaan, and advanced speedily upon Egypt and Libya, easily subduing the descendants of his grandfather Ham.

Unas

During the V Dynasty, the Egyptians called one of their kings Unas. Upon his death, as was their custom after the Babylonians, the Egyptians deified him. In his deified state, he assumed many of the characteristics of the god Osiris.

According to Budge:

> ". . . Unas is declared to be the son of Tem, and has made himself stronger than his father . . . He is considered to have been a mighty conqueror upon the earth, for those whom he has vanquished are [pictured] beneath his feet."[69]

It is not revealed in the Egyptian texts who this Unas was, but if Unas is so closely equated to Osiris who was the Egyptian Nimrod, Tem can be no other than Cush, the father of Nimrod. It is remarkable that the text exactly parallels the case of Nimrod and his father, for Nimrod did indeed make himself stronger than his father did.

Tradition states that Cush was the father of the Ethiopians who dwell in Africa. However, there was another Ethiopia, which the ancient Greeks called "White Ethiopia," supposedly situated in the area of Arabia Felix or western India, or both.

William Steuart McBirne declares:

> "Socrates said that Matthew was allotted Ethiopia in the Apostolic comity agreement . . . Ambrose connects him with Persia, Paulinus of Nola with Parthia, Isidore with Macedonia."[70]

The Greeks included the name Ethiopia under the name "India," as well as Arabia, Parthia, Persia, and the territories of the Medes.

> "The difficulty in knowing for certain the countries which Matthew probably visited lies," according to McBirne, "in the identification of the country called 'Ethiopia'. The Ethiopia in Africa is well known to all of us, but there was also an Asiatic 'Ethiopia' which was south of the Caspian Sea in Persia."[71]

If Nimrod conquered Assyria and waged war on his neighbors, he must have also conquered India (White Ethiopia), Arabia Felix, Parthia, Media, Persia, Canaan, Egypt, Libya, and black Ethiopia as well. His vast empire stretched from western India to the Nile Valley and beyond.

Among the hundreds of Egyptian gods was one who was renowned for his great valor and mighty deeds of war. His name was Heru-Behutet. He was a form of the god Osiris whose Babylonian counterpart was Nimrod.

> "All the facts indicate that we are not dealing entirely with mythological events, and it is nearly certain that the triumphant progress ascribed to Heru-Behutet is based upon the exploits of some victorious invader who established himself in Edfu in very early times, and then made his way with his followers northwards, beating down all opposition as he went. It is pretty clear that he owed his success chiefly to the superiority of the weapons with which he and his men were armed, and to the material of which they were made..."[72]

The material of which Heru-Behutet's weapons were made is not known, but it could have been copper, bronze, or even iron. It is extremely likely that it was the latter. The refining of metals was known and practiced long before the advent of the Noachian flood (cp. Gen. 4:22). These invaders knew the art of smelting ores. Once they firmly established themselves in Edfu, they conquered the remainder of Lower Egypt. Afterwards they built a foundry at Edfu and began to manufacture more weapons.

> "The place where metalwork was done, i.e. where the ore was smelted and weapons were forged", writes Budge, "was called *mesnet*, the 'foundry'; and the worshipers of Horus of Behutet [Heru-Behutet] never tired of describing their god as the 'lord of the forge-city', i.e. Edfu, the place where tradition declared he first established himself as the great master blacksmith."[73]

Budge states that we cannot know the identities of this master blacksmith and his followers, and yet, he himself furnishes the clues whereby we may know. Says he:

> "It is, of course, impossible to say who were the blacksmiths that swept over Egypt from south to north, or where they came from, but the writer believes that they represent the invaders in pre-dynastic times, who made their way into Egypt, **from a country in the east**, by way of the Red Sea, and by some road across the eastern desert . . . They brought with them the knowledge of working in metals and of brick-making . . ." (emphasis mine).[74]

It is difficult to understand how Budge could have overlooked so obvious a reference to the ancient Babylonians. If these mysterious invaders came from a country in the east; if they came across the eastern desert (Arabia, or Arabia Felix); if they came by way of the Red Sea bringing with them the knowledge of the smelting, refining, and forging of metals; and if they knew brick-making; there can be no doubt as to who they were. The key to the mystery lies not in the fact that they were forgers of metal, but in the making of (fire-hardened) brick. The ancient Babylonians were the first after the flood who worked in brick (Gen. 11:3), and it is likely the same was true for metals. The "blacksmiths" were just Nimrod's armies, or more specifically, a special contingent of his armies known as the "mighty-ones," his elite corps of "storm troopers" as it were. More will be said of these blacksmiths later.

Fire Worship

Having tamed the horse and perfected the art of warfare and, therefore, the means by which he was able to invade and conquer the known world, it was no great task for Nimrod to establish his perverse brand of religion wherever he went.

If the adage "misery loves company" is true, it was never truer as it relates to Satan. After he lost his position of prestige and power in his abortive war against God, he determined to drag all of mankind down with him by appealing to the basest aspects of human nature. His plan was a masterstroke of evil genius. It has succeeded in deceiving the world beyond, perhaps, even *his* wildest dreams. It was, and is, truly a "mystery of iniquity."

> "It is indispensable that we know", writes Hislop, "and continually keep before our eyes, the stupendous nature of that mystery of iniquity . . . It can trace its lineage far beyond the era of Christianity, back over 4,000 years, to near the period of the flood and the building of the Tower of Ba-bel. During all that period its essential elements have been nearly the same, and have a peculiar adaptation to the corruption of human nature . . . Every statement in the Scripture shows that it was truly described when it was characterized as 'Satan's master-piece'—the perfection of his policy for deluding and ensnaring the world"[75]

Satan's masterpiece of deception was inaugurated in earnest when Nimrod, demon-possessed, and under Satan's ever watchful eye, set up the false religious system based on fire-worship and the adoration of a fiery serpent, a symbol of Satan himself. In practically every case history singles out Nimrod as the author of fire-worship. The sun was considered the great source of light and heat and was worshipped under the name of Baal. This fact alone demonstrates the audacious character of the beginnings of this great apostasy. Of the fiery serpent as a symbol of Satan, Hislop writes:

> "The 'serpent of fire' in the plains of Shinar seems to have been the grand object of worship. There is the strongest evidence that apostasy among the sons of Noah began in fire-worship and *that* in connection with the symbol of the serpent"[76]

However, the fiery serpent was not just a symbol of Satan. It was also the symbol of the pagan idea of the resurrection. It is common knowledge that the serpent sloughs its skin every year. To the ancient Assyrians this symbolically represented a renewing of youth. This was a ready-made excuse for idolatry. It was seen as an emblem of the sun which was considered the "great regenerator" who every year regenerates the face of the earth. When Semiramis and the Babylonians deified

Nimrod, they worshipped him as the Great Fire-god and identified him with the serpent.

We will see later that Nimrod, as the representative of the great fire-god, was worshipped in Egypt under the name of Ra, and Osiris, the Egyptian god of the resurrection.

> "In Egypt, one of the commonest symbols of the sun, or sun-god, is a disc with a serpent around it. The original reason of that identification seems just to have been that, as the sun was the great enlightener of the physical world, so the serpent was held to have been the great enlightener of the spiritual, by giving mankind the 'knowledge of good and evil'"[77]

Of Human Sacrifice

It was not long until Nimrod, under the control and tutelage of Satan, the original "fiery serpent" and the "bright and burning one," became as depraved and despotic as his evil mentor. Not only did Nimrod *teach* the Assyrians fire worship, he *completely embroiled* and *immersed* them in it; so much so in fact, that he caused them to "pass through" it, i.e. he sacrificed multitudes in the name of the great fire-god Moloch.

> "The power, the popularity, and skill of Nimrod, as well as the seductive system itself, enabled him to spread the delusive doctrine far and wide, and he was represented under the well-known name of Phaethon, as on the point of 'setting the world on fire', or (without the poetic metaphor) of involving all mankind in the guilt of fire-worship"[78]

Nimrod was the representative of the devourer Satan. As he played out this role, he sacrificed untold numbers of victims, especially children. In this regard, his followers knew him universally as Saturn, the "Great Child Devourer." He sacrificed to the god Moloch, a god of bloody barbarity. The term "Moloch" signifies "king," and Nimrod was the first after the flood that maliciously violated the Patriarchal system, setting himself up as king over his countrymen.

He was worshipped as a revealer of truth and goodness at first but that worship was later transformed to conform to his dark and forbidding complexion. Nimrod was known, among a multitude of other names, by the name Zer-Nebo-Gus. Zer-Nebo-gus was a black, ill-omened, malevolent divinity with horns and hooves. He was the exact counter-part of the Devil. The name is almost pure Chaldean and seems to denote "the seed of the prophet Cush." Cush, as we have seen, was the father of Nimrod and was black, i.e. a Negro.

Where did the idea of a black Devil with horns and hooves originate? Hislop supplies the answer in reference to a woodcut found in *Layard's Nineveh and Babylon*, p. 605.

> "In the woodcut referred to, first we find 'the Assyrian Hercules', that is, 'Nimrod the giant', as he is called in the Septuagint version of Genesis, without club, spear, or weapon of any kind, attacking a bull. Having overcome it, he sets the bull's horns on his head, as a trophy of victory and symbol of power; and thenceforth the hero is represented, not only with horns and hoofs above, but from the middle downwards, with the legs and cloven feet of the bull . . . This in all likelihood, is intended to commemorate some event in the life of him who first began to be mighty in war, and who, according to all ancient traditions, was remarkable also for bodily power, as being the leader of the Giants that rebelled against heaven"[79]

Hislop quotes Plutarch as saying that there was a tradition in ancient Egypt that Osiris was also black. This must have been out of the ordinary in a land where the general complexion was dusky (see *The Two Babylons*, p. 43). It is significant that there were two gods in such distant countries whose lives paralleled each other so closely.

Nimrod involved all of mankind in idolatrous fire worship. Everywhere, and under myriad names, we see him in the forefront of vile, depraved, evil practices and teachings of the most injurious kind. More than any other of Nimrod's idolatrous institutions, human sacrifice seems to have excited the imaginations of the more barbaric of ancient men to a frenzy. In times of calamity, the Carthaginians progressed far beyond a state of frenzy to that of the depths of a seemingly uncontrollable blood lust.

> "The . . . deity particularly adored by the Carthaginians," says Rollin, "and in whose honor human sacrifices were offered, was Saturn, known in Scripture by the name of Moloch; and his worship passed from Tyre to Carthage. Philo quotes a passage from Sanchoniathon, which shows, that the kings of Tyre, in great dangers, used to sacrifice their sons to appease the anger of the gods; and that one of them, by his action, procured himself divine honors, and was worshipped as a god, under the name of the planet Saturn: to this doubtless was owing the fable of Saturn devouring his children . . ."[80]

However, adults were also profusely given in sacrifice for the appeasement of the gods. If the sacrificing of adults was a tragedy beyond imagination, the burning of innocent children to appease the gods was doubly so.

Rollin further states:

> "At first children were inhumanly burned, either in a fiery furnace, like those in the Valley of Hinnom, so often mentioned in Scripture, or enclosed in a flaming statue of Saturn. The cries of these unhappy victims were drowned by the uninterrupted noise of drums and trumpets"[81]

The Carthaginians, who were the heirs apparent of the bloody sacrificial rites of the kings of Tyre, if it were possible, were even more depraved than either Nimrod (Saturn) or the kings of Tyre. The rulers of Carthage seemingly used any excuse they could find to justify sacrificing their children and the children of their subjects.

> "In times of pestilence", Rollin continues, "they used to sacrifice a great number of children to their gods . . . Diodorus relates an instance of cruelty . . . At the time Agathocles was just going to besiege Carthage, its inhabitants, seeing the extremity to which they were reduced, imputed all their misfortunes to the just anger of Saturn, because that, instead of offering up children nobly born . . . he had been fraudulently put off with the children of slaves and foreigners. To atone for this crime, two-hundred children

of the best families in Carthage were sacrificed to Saturn . . . Diodorus adds that there was a brazen statue of Saturn, the hands of which were turned downwards, so that, when a child was laid on them, it dropped immediately into a hollow, where was a fiery furnace"[82]

Frazer says essentially the same thing.

"When the Carthaginians were defeated and besieged by Agathocles, they ascribed their disasters to the wrath of Baal; for whereas in former times they had been wont to sacrifice to him their own children, they had latterly fallen into the habit of buying children and rearing them to be victims. So, to appease the angry god, two hundred children of the noblest families were picked out for sacrifice . . . They were sacrificed by being placed, one by one, on the sloping hands of a brazen image, from which they rolled into a pit of fire."[83]

To say the least, it is incredible that the human mind can devise and stoop to such miserable atrocities. One could ascribe it to the barbarity or near savagery of these ancient peoples with their overwhelming penchant for superstition, witchcraft, sorcery, necromancy, and black magic in general. However, that would be a rash conclusion because these peoples were neither barbarians nor savages. Largely, it was not only the so-called primitive peoples who assimilated such practices into their societies and religions, but also those peoples, nations, and societies who considered themselves to be highly civilized, sophisticated, intelligent, and wise in their own ways and their own eyes, q.v. Egypt, Rome, Greece, etc. The Apostle Paul said of such people that they were without excuse.

"Because that, when they knew God, they glorified *Him* not as God . . . but became vain in their imaginations, and their foolish heart (mind, personality, emotional make up) was (spiritually) darkened. Professing themselves to be wise, they became fools, and changed the glory of the incorruptible God into an image made like unto corruptible man, and to birds, and four-footed beasts, and creeping things. Wherefore God also gave them up to uncleanness through the lusts of their own hearts, to dishonor their own bodies between themselves: who changed the truth of God into a lie, and worshipped and served the creature more than the Creator, who is blessed forever. Amen." (Rom. 1:21-25).

If you think that "modern" man with all his intelligence, sophistication, and advanced technology (which in too many cases has become his surrogate savior), cannot resort to such vile behavior as the ancients were guilty of, witness the example of Adolph Hitler in the "enlightened" Twentieth Century. What common bond so many thousands of years removed from the Babylonians, Egyptians, Tyrenians, Carthaginians, and Romans, etc., inspired Hitler to gas and burn millions of Jews, to "sacrifice" them, as it were, in gas chambers and "fiery furnaces" just as the ancient Assyrians had done, though not for the same reasons? Simply this: Hitler, like Nimrod and others of his ilk, was just another pawn in a centuries-long list compiled by the Master Deceiver himself.

William L. Shirer says that:

> ". . . without Adolf Hitler, who was possessed of a demonic personality, a granite will, uncanny instincts, a cold ruthlessness, a remarkable intellect, a soaring imagination there almost certainly would never have been a Third Reich.[84]

Hitler was just another victim of Satan's greatest deception ever— **Project Apostasy.** Why did both the ancients and the moderns allow it to happen? For the very reason that was mentioned before; the masses never did know what they wanted. Additionally, there was the unfortunate fact that they were never able to recognize the subtle deceptions of Satan for what they were. Instead of relying on their God, and their God-given intelligence, they resorted to sentimental emotionalism, always seeking the ultimate "spiritual" experience.

Rollin says that it was just that:

> "Sentiments, so unnatural and barbarous and yet adopted by whole nations, and even by most civilized, as the Phoenicians, Carthaginians, Gauls, Scythians, and even the Greeks and Romans, and consecrated by custom during a long series of ages, can have been inspired by him only who was a murderer from the beginning, and who delights in nothing but the humiliation, misery, and perdition of men"[85]

If the system of fire-worship and human sacrifice instituted by Nimrod abridged and subsequently abrogated their most precious liberties, and brought about so much humiliation, suffering, and misery, why did they not revolt and put the system down? In so many words, **human government!**

Marilyn Ferguson has hit upon a principle that very closely approximates what must have been the result of the very first highly organized government set up by man.

> "Government itself is an awesome strategy for avoiding pain and conflict. For a considerable price, it relieves us of responsibilities, performing acts that would be as unsavory for most of us as butchering our own beef. As our agent, the government can bomb and tax. As our agent, it can relieve us of the responsibilities once borne face to face by the community: caring for the young, the war-wounded, the aged, and the handicapped. It extends our impersonal benevolence to the worlds needy, relieving our collective conscience without uncomfortable firsthand involvement. It takes our power, our responsibility, our consciousness"[86]

In the beginning, Nimrod's newly formed government relieved the Babylonians of the pain and conflict they suffered from the attacks of ravaging beasts. The community no longer had to meet the danger face to face. That responsibility was naturally transferred to the established standing army, which was more than capable of handling the task of subduing the wild animal population. Nevertheless, the people paid the "considerable price" of which Ms Ferguson speaks. Not only did they concede to Nimrod their liberties and freedoms, they relinquished their power as a collective bargaining unit, their consciousness of the true

God, and eventually, their very lives for the "privilege" of worshipping a "fiery serpent" and the system it represented.

Nevertheless, let us not forget the element of hero-worship, yet another reason why they did not rebel against such dehumanizing hardships. For within that system of hero-worship there lay sequestered the delusion and deception that made them unwitting victims of the able disciple of the Master Deceiver. God let them have their own way. He "gave them over to their own lusts." He blinded their minds to the truth.

Man is, by nature, a God-seeking creature. He possesses an innate desire to worship—whether the true God, man, machine, animal, tree, stick, stone, fish, insect, bird, or heavenly host. A relatively modern example comes to us from India, a nation undeniably ensnared in the deadly web of paganism.

> ". . . To this day in India," says Frazer, "all living persons remarkable for great strength or valor or for supposed miraculous powers run the risk of being worshipped as gods. Thus, a sect in the Punjab worshipped a deity whom, they called Nikkal Sen. This Nikkal Sen was no other than the redoubted General Nicholson, and nothing that the General could do or say damped the enthusiasm of his adorers. The more he punished them, the greater grew the religious awe with which they worshipped him" [87]

It was no different with the worshipers of Nimrod. He was idolized almost universally despite a multitude of heinous crimes against his subjects. As with the Punjabis and their General Nicholson, the more Nimrod punished the Assyrians, the more they adored and worshipped him.

There was no end to the extent of Nimrod's depravity. He thrived on human suffering, standing ghoulishly by as the sacrificial victims screamed, cried, and begged for their lives. He grew to relish the groans and wailings of his human sacrifices. They were sweet music to his ears and a delight to his heart.However, Nimrod did not stop with these malodorous crimes against God and humanity. His appetite for the bizarre, the weird, and the incontinent was insatiable. In addition to human sacrifices, he also established one of the most detestable cultic practices ever devised by the ungodly human mind.

Cahna-Baal

Nimrod was not just the king of the Babylonians and the Assyrians, he was also the high priest of the apostate religion that he founded and perpetuated. He required those lesser priests under him to eat the flesh of sacrificial victims or of the enemies his armies defeated and slew. According to Hislop:

> "... the priests of Nimrod or Baal were necessarily required to **eat of the human sacrifices**; and thus it came to pass that 'Cahna-Bal', 'the priest of Baal', is the established word in our own tongue for a devourer of human flesh" (emphasis mine).[88]

This most abhorrent of all human practices was not confined to Babylon. It was exported to all the lands that Nimrod warred against and conquered. We do not know when cannibalism was introduced into Egypt, but it must have been prior to or during dynastic times. Budge alludes many times in his works to predynastic times and the traditions, customs, and socio-religious mores that were "possibly" extant in those days. However, despite all sources available to him he seems never to have been able to connect events in the predynastic periods with those of Nimrod or his Mystery of Iniquity. Nevertheless, it is evident that there are too many parallels for them to have developed independently.

The Egyptian texts that have been translated from the dynastic period speak of a god called Unas, to whom we have already alluded. This Unas, says Budge in quoting a hymn dedicated to the god:

> "... is the master of the offering and he tieth the knot, and provideth meals for himself; **he eateth men** and he liveth upon gods, he is the lord of offerings, and he keepeth 'count of the lists of the same'" (emphasis mine).[89]

This god, like all the gods of Egypt, possessed many of the characteristics attributed to Osiris or Saturn, whom, we have seen, were just different forms of Nimrod, the great child devourer. Was the hymn just a mythical account of a god who utterly defeated whatever enemy came against him, or was the fact that he "ate men," meant to be taken literally? According to Budge, it was a literal statement of fact.

> "The statement here that Unas ate men is definite enough, and it is not easy to give any other than a literal meaning to the words; we can only assume then that this portion of the text has reference to some acts of cannibalism of which a tradition had come down from pre-dynastic times."[90]

This pre-dynastic tradition was based upon the mistaken belief that if one ate the flesh of strong and mighty men, or drank their blood, one absorbed, as it were, their life, nature, and strength into one's body. It was a belief that came out of, and was perpetuated by, the priests of the Babylonian Mystery Religion.

Were it not for the fact that God has His servants who, in every age have defended His righteous laws and principles, Nimrod might have plunged every man, woman, and child on the face of the earth into the fiery depths of Satan's treacherous attempt to stamp out God's true religion. But even in those early days men of God looked forward to the coming of Messiah and God's kingdom on earth, and they knew that no amount of evil, whether Satanically or humanly devised, could ever prevail against God's church, or long suppress God's truth.

The Death of Nimrod

The establishment and spread of Satan's system of fire-worship was not without its detractors. The most prominent of these was Noah's son Shem. Like his father before him, he was a preacher of righteousness, a devout follower of God, and a leader of the patriarchal system, which Nimrod so blasphemously rejected.

We have already seen that Nimrod was known as the Babylonian Hercules, but Shem was also called Hercules by the ancient pagans. He was the leading spokesman against the atrocities of the apostasy. Who, then, among all peoples, would be the most likely to lead the opposition against the apostasy? One of the most ancient names of the primitive Hercules in Egypt was Sem.

This Hercules was supposed to have fought and defeated the "giants." It is interesting to note that the word "giant" can mean, literally, giant (*nephil* [nef-eel']), or a *feller*, i.e. a *bully* or *tyrant* (Strong 5303). It has been shown that there were "giants in the earth" in ante-diluvian times who were the progeny of the union between the sons of God (fallen angels) and the daughters of men, and that Nimrod, as the Assyrian or Babylonian Hercules (see *The Two Babylons*, p. 38), was called a giant because of his great physical prowess, his skill in the hunt, his renown for valor, and because he was the most notorious tyrant of the times.

These giants, or tyrants, as a race died out with the flood! Notice, however, the phrase "and also afterward" inserted almost as an afterthought in Genesis 6:4. A second time the fallen angels mated with the daughters of men and the seeds of that race of giants were once again in evidence in Noah's and Shem's day within 200 years after the flood. It is likely that these "giants" are the Titans associated with Nimrod and Greek mythology. It is they whom Nimrod used to conquer and subdue the nations of the post-diluvian world.

Shem, aka Hercules Ogimus

We have previously alluded to the possibility that the master "blacksmith" and his followers who invaded Egypt in pre-dynastic times (who were also known as "black-smiths"), was none other than Nimrod and his "mighty ones" or Titans.

A *smith* is a forger of metals, but there is no clue in that name from which one could deduce that any should be called "black" smiths. Why, then, regardless of the color of their skin, are forgers in metals called by that name? If the blacksmiths who invaded Egypt in predynastic times were Nimrod's armies, the answer becomes rather obvious. They were called "blacksmiths" because: (1) they derived their name from the master blacksmith, i.e. Nimrod, who was himself black, or, (2) they were themselves black, or, (3) both. Thus, by whatever name one wishes to call them, the "mighty ones," the "Titans," and the "blacksmiths" were the same.

The primitive Hercules who defeated these Titans was worshipped by the Celts, a strange and pagan horde about whose origins, until recent times, was little is known. The Hercules of the Celts was known as *Hercules Ogimus*. In the Chaldean tongue, the name means "Hercules the lamenter."

Shem, as a man of God and a preacher of righteousness, bore a tremendous burden of grief and sorrow seeing the establishment and spread of the Apostasy by Nimrod and the dastardly crimes committed by him in the name of religion against both God and man. He aspired to redress these great wrongs and set about with his followers to seek Nimrod's life. It was by the power of God's Holy Spirit that Shem defeated Nimrod and his "mighty ones" and put them to flight. Where did their ill-fated flight take them?

> "According to tradition," declares Dr. Herman Hoeh, "Saturn (Nimrod) fled from his pursuers to Italy. The Apennine Mountains of Italy were anciently named the mountains of Nembrod or Nimrod. Nimrod briefly hid out at the site where Rome was later built. The ancient name of Rome before it was rebuilt in 753 B.C., was Saturnia—the site of Saturn's (Nimrod's) hiding. There he was found and slain for his crimes"[91]

After Shem slew Nimrod, he cut his body into several pieces and sent each one to a different province throughout Nimrod's empire as a warning that whoever continued to practice fire worship openly would likewise perish. In Egypt, the same calamity was traditionally celebrated concerning the death of Osiris. His slayer was Set or Typhon.

> "A statement in Plutarch's *De Iside et Osiride* (article 62)", declares Budge, "informs us that Typhon was called Seth (this information is of considerable interest, for it makes) the identity of Set and Typhon, and it is, moreover, supported by the evidence of the inscriptions. The name Seth is, of course, Set..."[92]

This Set, or Seth, cannot have been the Seth of the Bible for he lived before the flood. We have already seen that in Egypt Shem was called Sem, but there can be little doubt that Sem, Set, and Typhon are the same irrespective of the differences in spelling between Sem and Set.

The Egyptian Set was supposed to be the brother of Horus (the elder), or Osiris in the earliest times. Although Shem and Nimrod were not brothers, they were grand-uncle and grand-nephew respectively—not a close family tie, but a family tie nevertheless. Later on Set (Shem) became the enemy of Osiris (Nimrod), as well as the type and symbol of all evil, because he slew Osiris. Legend has it that there was a time when Osiris (Nimrod) ranged throughout the world bestowing upon the people the "blessings" of civilization. It is a reference to the fact that Osiris (Nimrod), as he was conquering the known world, was not only organizing those vanquished peoples into governments and teaching them the arts of warfare and building with fire-glazed brick, but was also teaching them the nuances of serpent and fire-worship. It was for this reason that Set (Shem) conspired to kill him.

When he returned from his campaigns, Osiris was met by Set and seventy-two co-conspirators. They slew him, sealed him in a coffin, and cast him into the Nile. Years later, as the story goes, Set was hunting by moonlight and came across the coffin quite by accident. Recognizing it, he tore the body into fourteen pieces, and scattered it about the land.

Although there are certain discrepancies between these two accounts, they are not serious enough to negate the fact that both refer to the same person and event. The parallels are unmistakable.

That Set, or Shem, became the Egyptian symbol of evil is quite understandable in light of the aims and purposes of the Babylonian Mysteries. It was necessary that Shem be made a symbol of evil if the deified Nimrod was to be represented as the "great enlightener," the sum total of all that was good. Moreover, it is consistent with Satan's methods of deception (Genesis 3:5).

With Nimrod's death *Project Apostasy* was apparently dealt a fatal blow. However, it survived and eventually grew stronger. In death, Nimrod emerged a hero and a martyr. He was later deified as the "father of the gods" through the efforts of his mother-wife Semiramis. It was she who convinced his followers that he gave his life voluntarily for the good of mankind; a "messiah", as it were, who defeated death by sacrificing himself only to be reincarnated or resurrected in the form of a son named Ninyas.

The Apostasy Goes Underground

Under the circumstances, continued worship of the deified Nimrod could not remain an overt activity.

> "It seems to have been now ... that the secret mysteries were set up ... (for) now it was evidently felt that publicity was out of the question ... when that Apostate's dismembered limbs were sent to the chief cities, where no doubt his system had

been established, it will be readily perceived that if idolatry was to continue—if above all, it was take a step in advance, it was indispensable that it should operate in secret. The terror of an execution, inflicted on one so mighty as Nimrod, made it needful that, for some time to come, at least, the extreme of caution should be used. In these circumstances, then, began . . . that system of 'mystery'; which, having Babylon for its center has spread over the world. In these mysteries, under the seal of secrecy and the sanction of an oath . . . men were gradually led back to all the idolatry that had been publicly suppressed, while new features were added that made it still more blasphemous than before."[93]

By going underground, the Apostasy did not just take a step in advance, it advanced by rapidly as though it were shod in seven-league boots. As Hislop indicates, Semiramis added many new features of a blasphemous nature. One of these new features, as we shall see, was the Trinitarian Doctrine as supposed to be the true make up of the Godhead. The Trinity she espoused was composed of Nimrod, herself as the Mother-of-God, and Ninyas, the "white" son who was born to Nimrod after his death.

We shall see that the Trinitarian Doctrine portrays a very erroneous picture of God's true nature and character. It has been, in fact, one of the prime movers that have caused the majority of modern day Christianity to remain unknowingly within the slavish grasp of Satan's great apostatizing system.

Chapter 6
SEMIRAMIS QUEEN OF THE MYSTERIES

The establishment of the Babylonian Mysteries did not immediately follow the death of Nimrod. It could not for we have seen that the idolatrous system of fire-worship established by Nimrod that so bastardized the Patriarchal system, was forced underground. There it remained for some time, its disciples fearful of further reprisals by Shem and his followers.

With the systems apostate leader dead, and Semiramis temporarily out of the picture, there was only token adherence to its principles. Indeed, history records that Shem was instrumental in turning the hearts of men back to God, if only for a brief interlude of time. This he accomplished through the sword of the Spirit.

Flight for Life

Semiramis' enemies forced her to flee for her life in order to avoid a similar fate as her husband.

> "When her husband for his blasphemous rebellion against the majority of heaven, was cut off, for a season it was a time of tribulation also for her. The fragments of history that have come down to us give an account of her trepidation and flight, to save herself from her adversaries" [94]

The sudden alarm she must have felt upon learning of her husband's death and dismemberment quickly subsided after she was out of the grasp of her enemies. History does not reveal where Semiramis' flight took her, but there are indications that it was Egypt. Most likely it was to the delta city of Sais where she was worshipped under the name of the goddess Neith prior to the establishment of the very early part of the First Dynasty. The use of the name as a component part of royal names dates to the first half of the Archaic period, and long predates the theological system of Heliopolis.

During this period of exile, Semiramis did not waste her time agonizing over the death of Nimrod, or lamenting her fate. Moreover, she did not indulge in self pity. Her evil disposition and her plans for her subjects would not condone it. It was a time for cold, hard logic and analysis; a time of increasingly deep, unforgiving hatred of Shem and the Patriarchate; a time devoted to a totally new concept in religious beliefs and practices; and a time of scheming, planning and dreaming of the day she would return to her native Babylon to wreak havoc and vengeance upon those who had so mercilessly attempted to snuff out the apostate system set up by her late husband. Her success was so unexpected, and her plan so subtle, that it caused the defection of even those who had returned to the right worship of the true God under the persuasive powers of the Patriarch Shem.

There is no questioning that Semiramis returned triumphantly to Babylon to fulfill her evil machinations. The Chaldean Mysteries can be clearly traced to the days of Semiramis who is said to have impressed upon the Babylonians the image of her own demented nature. And why not? She had been in full accord with her husband in every aspect of the false, idolatrous, fire-worship system. Fully aware that she could not overtly continue in the system's evil practices, Semiramis quietly returned to her throne feigning utter denial of her former beliefs while she covertly re-established them, though much modified. It was a ridiculously simple task despite the fact, at least superficially, that the old system had been smashed. The rigors and chaste demands of the Patriarchal system were hard pressed to compete with the sensual pleasures of the new Mysteries.

Subtlety and More

Where Nimrod had gained the confidence, obedience, and adoration of the people through sheer force of arms, Semiramis accomplished the same through subtlety. She captured the hearts and minds of her subjects with her incomparable beauty and feminine wiles.

This eternally beautiful and abandoned queen of Babylon was a paragon of unbridled lust and licentiousness. In the Mysteries, of which she was the chief architect, she was worshipped as Rhea, the great "mother of the gods." This is exactly how she presented herself as part of the blasphemous Babylonian "Holy Trinity" after the death of Nimrod and the alleged virgin birth of Ninyas. Hislop says that her beauty was such that she quelled a riot by merely making a timely appearance when the situation was on the verge of getting completely out of hand.

> "The beauty of Semiramis is said on one occasion to have quelled a rising rebellion among her subjects on her sudden appearance among them; and it is recorded that the memory of the admiration excited in their minds by her appearance on that occasion was perpetuated by a statue erected in Babylon, representing her in the guise in which she had fascinated them so much. This Babylonian queen was not merely in *character* coincident with Aphrodite of Greece and the Venus of Rome, but was, in point of fact the historical original of that goddess that by the ancient world was regarded as the very embodiment of everything attractive in female form, and the perfection of female beauty . . ."[95]

Semiramis was just as depraved as her former husband was and just as capable as he of the heinous crimes that he committed against God and man. Her behavior was never propitious. She was the ultimate incarnation of the most decadent sort of licentiousness.

How did she appear to her subjects at the time she quelled the rebellion spoken of above? Exactly as she appeared in representations of her, i.e. statues of her hundreds of years later— in the nude or nearly so! She is alleged to have been in her dressing room at the time the riot occurred, and not taking time to finish applying her make-up or properly dress, she fled quickly to the scene. How else could she have affected their minds as to cause them immediately to cease from their rioting? One can almost hear the cat-calls and wolf-whistles, or imagine every man straining to catch a glimpse of her voluptuous form. Their reasons for inciting riot and rebellion were forgotten for the moment, lost amid their inordinate desire to see their queen, as it were, *aux naturale*!

The Vestal Virgins

In addition to her shameless displays of feminine pulchritude, Semiramis was guilty of a multitude of whoredoms by which it is said she conceived and bore several children. Not only did she engage in acts of prostitution herself, she coerced others among the women of her kingdom to do the same in the name of religion. Herodotus tells us that:

> "The Babylonians have one most shameful custom. Every woman born in the country must once in her life go and sit down in the precinct of Venus, and there consort with a stranger . . . the larger number seat themselves within the holy enclosure with wreaths of string about their heads,— and here there is always a great crowd, some coming and others going; lines of cord mark out paths in all directions among the women, and the strangers pass along them to make their choice. A woman who has once taken her seat is not allowed to return home until one of the strangers throws a silver coin into her lap, and takes her with him beyond the holy ground. When he throws the coin he says these words— 'The goddess Mylitta prosper thee'! Venus (Semiramis) is called Mylitta by the Assyrians. The woman goes with the first man who throws her money, and rejects no one. When she has gone with him, and so satisfied the goddess, she returns home . . ."[96]

These women, largely, formed the core of what became the Vestal Virgins, or temple prostitutes. Semiramis passed this shameful practice was on to the rest of the empire and it was just as lewd and licentious elsewhere as it was in Babylon.

Budge says that:

> "On a stele in the British museum . . . we see the goddess, who is here called 'Kent, lady of heaven', standing on a lion between Amsu, or Min, and Reshpu, and with these gods she appears to form a Semitic **triad. . .**Qetesh (Semiramis-Kent-Isis) must have been worshipped as a nature goddess, and it was probably the licentiousness of her

worship, at all events in Syria, which gave to the Hebrew word (ked-ay-shaw', a female devotee, i.e. a *prostitute*, harlot, or whore) the meaning which it bears in the Bible"—Gen. 38:21-22; Deut. 23:18; Num. 25:1; Hosea 4:4.[97]

Auguries, Oracles, and Divinations aka That Old Black Magic

Semiramis' beauty and feminine wiles notwithstanding, she successfully employed yet another method of persuasion. It was, perhaps, more powerful in its effects than all of the seductiveness of the Vestal Virgins. It was the art of black magic.

That Semiramis learned black magic from Cush (he was known as a prophet and a diviner) is self-evident. Within the discipline of black magic is found such practices as augury, oracles, divination, sorcery, and necromancy. For the most part the auguries, oracles, and divinations did not originate with Semiramis or Cush. They were corruptions of God's divine oracles given to men before the Noachian Flood.

> "Nothing is more frequently mentioned in ancient history than oracles, auguries, and divinations. No war was made, or colony settled; nothing of consequence was undertaken, either public or private, without the gods being first consulted. This was a custom established among the Egyptian, Assyrian, Grecian, and Roman nations; which is no doubt proof... of its being derived from ancient tradition, and that it had its origin in the religion and worship of the true God. It is not to be questioned but that God before the deluge did manifest His will to mankind in different methods, as He has since done to His people, sometimes in His own person (as Yahweh), and *viva voce*, sometimes by the ministry of angels, or of prophets inspired by Himself, and at other times by apparitions or in dreams. When the descendants of Noah dispersed themselves into different regions, they carried this tradition with them, which was everywhere retained, though altered and corrupted by the darkness and ignorance of idolatry"[98]

These corrupted, pagan practices so intrigued mankind that their spread was very rapid, until the whole world observed them from the most primitive to the most sophisticated societies. However, the one was just as ignorant, rash, and superstitious in its passions as the other.

Augury and soothsaying were undoubtedly the unavoidable result of profound ignorance, uncontrollable rashness, insatiable curiosity, and the stumbling, blind passions of demonically inspired men. These men, and women, who presumed to interrogate God about practically everything, were so naive that they believed that God would be obliged to answer every idle imagination and unjust enterprise.

The oracles, for the most part, were conducted in dark places in the earth, i.e. caves, grottos, and caverns. The Greeks were especially fond of the use of oracles, and hundreds of years after the inauguration of the Mysteries we find them worshipping Apollo (Nimrod, see *The Two Babylons*, footnote, p. 32) at Delphos under the name of Pythian. It was here that a priestess called a Pythia served as the intermediary or medium for the oracle.

> "The Pythia, before she reached the tripod, was a long time preparing for it by sacrifices, purifications, a fast of three days, and many other ceremonies . . . The Pythia could not prophesy till she was intoxicated by the exhalation of the sanctuary . . . as the divine vapor, like a penetrating fire, had diffused itself through the entrails of the priestess, her hair stood upright on her head, her looks grew wild and furious, she foamed at the mouth, a sudden and violent trembling seized her whole body, with all the symptoms of distraction and frenzy. She uttered at intervals some words almost inarticulate . . . after she had been a certain time upon the tripod, she was re-conducted to her cell . . ."[99]

Often as not, according to the ancient historian Lucan, after the priestess uttered her oracular words under the influence or possession of the demon that acted as the oracle at Delphos, she was rewarded with death. Hers was hardly an envious position. Unlike the oracle at Delphos, God has **never** spoken in dark holes in the earth, or in secret places (Cf. Isa. 55:19). Semiramis instituted just such a practice for the allurement of men into her idolatries that long antedate the Pythia.

"Now the secret system of the Mysteries," declares Hislop, "gave vast facilities for imposing on the senses of the initiated by means of various tricks and artifices of magic. Everything was contrived as to wind up the minds of the novices to the highest pitch of excitement, that, after having surrendered themselves implicitly to the priests, they might be prepared to receive anything. After the candidates for initiation had passed through the confessional, and sworn the required oaths, 'strange and amazing objects . . . presented themselves'. Sometimes the place they were in seemed to shake around them; sometimes it appeared bright and resplendent with light and radiant fire (the divine fire of the oracle at Delphos), and then again covered with black darkness, sometimes thunder and lightning, sometimes frightful noises and bellowings, sometimes terrible apparitions astonished the trembling spectators" [100]

It is no wonder that the initiates were prepared to accept anything after such frightening experiences. These apparent miracles, just as those at Delphos, were ready-made for the pagan, superstitious mind. Under the control of crafty priests, this magic was very powerful. The sheer intimidation of such displays served to bring the initiates solidly under the control of the Mysteries. Most of them were still averse to the holiness and sanctity of the Patriarchal system. They still yearned for the sensualities and pleasures of the Mysteries.

Not only were the initiates of the Mysteries fooled by all of this nonsense, the general populace likewise allowed themselves to be taken in. They never questioned the source of these mysterious goings on however fraudulent they might have appeared at the time. They were actually convinced, for example, that the oracular voices they heard were the voices of gods. Frazer says that:

"Certain persons are supposed to be possessed from time to time by a spirit or deity; while the possession lasts, their own personality lies in abeyance, the presence of the spirit is revealed by convulsive shiverings and shakings of the man's whole body, by wild gestures and excited looks, all of which are referred, not to the man himself, but to the spirit which has entered into him; and in this abnormal state all his utterances are accepted as the voice of the god or spirit dwelling in him and speaking through him"[101]

This temporary inspiration or possession by the spirit or god was brought about in one of several ways.

"One of these modes of producing inspiration is by sucking the fresh blood of a sacrificed victim. In the temple of Apollo Diradiotes at Argos, a lamb was sacrificed by night once a month; a woman, who had to observe a rule of chastity, tasted the blood of the lamb, and thus being inspired by the god she prophesied and divined"[102]

It was no different in India which was invaded by Nimrod, proselytized by Semiramis, and which still boasts of devil-worship cults to this day.

"In southern India a devil-dancer drinks the blood of the sacrifice, putting the throat of the decapitated goat to his mouth. Then, as if he had acquired a new life, he begins to brandish his staff of bells, and to dance with quick but wild unsteady steps. Suddenly the afflatus (inspiration) descends. There is no mistaking that glare, or those frantic leaps. He snorts, he stares, he gyrates. The demon has now taken bodily possession of him; and, though he retains the power of utterance and of motion, both are under the demon's control, and his separate consciousness is in abeyance . . . The devil-dancer is now worshipped as a present deity, and every bystander consults him respecting his disease, his wants, the welfare of his absent relatives, the offerings to be made for the accomplishment of his wishes, and, in short, respecting everything for which superhuman knowledge is supposed to be available" (parenthesis mine).[103]

It is a sad commentary on man's intelligence that he allows himself to be duped by the god of this world into believing that he is worshipping the true God, especially when it can be shown beyond a reasonable doubt that the supernatural forces he is dealing with are nothing more than spiritual shams.

> "A thousand frauds and impostures, openly detected at Delphos, and everywhere else, had not opened men's eyes, nor in the least diminished the credit of the oracles, which subsisted upwards of two thousand years, and was carried to an inconceivable height even in the minds of the greatest men, the most profound philosophers, the most powerful princes, and generally among the most civilized nations, and such as valued themselves most upon their wisdom and policy."[104]

By the time Semiramis instituted the Mysteries, the whole system—the secrecy, the apparent miracles, the rites and ceremonies, the oracles, auguries, and divinations—were dedicated to the glorification of the dead Nimrod. Those who rejected God, and who preferred to have a visible object of worship, were more than delighted to be able to hear a voice, intoned by an unseen priest from behind the scene, purporting to be that of their dead hero Nimrod, while the aforementioned manifestations were taking place.

The moment arrived for Semiramis to deal the final card in her deck of spiritual trickery. It was a move, which would immortalize her as the greatest benefactress, who ever lived. Her plan was to elevate herself to a position that would place her on a par with all other gods so-called, as the "Mother of God," (i.e. the deified Nimrod), and a goddess in her own right. It was a subtle lie instigated by Satan some 2500 years before the birth of Christ. It was a lie, which was picked up centuries later and included as a major doctrine of the Church of Rome. The doctrine, which arose from that remote lie, is known in the Catholic religion as "Mariolatry."

Boettner says that:

> "The titles given to Mary are in themselves a revelation of Roman Catholic sentiment toward her. She is called: Mother of God, Queen of the Apostles, Queen of Heaven, Queen of the Angels, The Door of Paradise, The Gate of Heaven, Our Life, Mother of Grace, Mother of Mercy, and many others which ascribe to her supernatural powers." All

of these titles are false . . . And the title, 'Queen of Heaven,' is equally false, or even worse. Heaven has no 'queen'. The only references in scripture to prayers to the 'queen of heaven' are found in Jeremiah 7:18; 44:17 -19, 25, where it is severely condemned as a heathen custom practiced by some apostate Jews. This so-called 'queen of heaven' was a Canaanitish goddess of fertility, Astarte (plural, Astaroth) (Judges 2:13)"[105]

Not only are these titles false, they are blasphemous! God does not have a mother! To imply that just because Mary gave birth to Jesus, (whom orthodox believers believe is God incarnate) she is the Mother of God is not justified.

Again, according to Boettner:

"When we say that a woman is the mother of a person we mean that she gave birth to that person. But Mary certainly did not give birth to God . . . She was not the mother of our Lord's divinity, but only of His humanity. . . At first glance the term 'Mother of God' may seem comparatively harmless. But the actual consequence is that through its use Roman Catholics come to look upon Mary as stronger, more mature, and more powerful than Christ. To them she becomes the source of His being and overshadows Him. So they go to her, not Him" (parenthesis mine).[106]

This is exactly what Semiramis intended when she elevated herself to deity and procured for herself a place among the gods as the "Mother of God"! The scheme was skillfully formed and implemented. She gained her glory from the dead and deified Nimrod. Before long both of them were worshipped under the names of Rhea and Nin, Goddess-Mother and son. Their statues were set up and adored everywhere and the people worshipped them universally with incredible enthusiasm and adoration.

The Stage Is Set

It is now, after the years of planning, scheming, and setting in motion the rites and ceremonies of the Mysteries, that we get our first glimpse of Semiramis' ultimate goal. The worship of the goddess-mother and son was the culmination of the establishment of the Babylonian Holy Trinity. However, before the Trinity could become a reality in the minds of the people; before the mother-son worship could be given any credibility, one last obstacle had to be overcome—what to do about the fact that Nimrod was black, and that Semiramis and her son Ninyas were apparently white or at least of much fairer complexion than her dead husband. Who, after all, would be inclined to worship such a threesome? In all likelihood, what was touted an impossible situation by Semiramis' advisors was cunningly and quickly dispatched by that evil queen.

> "Wherever the Negro aspect of Nimrod was found an obstacle to his worship, this was very easily obviated. According to the Chaldean doctrine of the transmigration of souls, all that was needful was just to teach that Ninus (Nimrod) had reappeared in the person of a posthumous son, of fair complexion, super-naturally borne by his widowed wife after the father had gone to glory"[107]

It is beyond the scope of the imagination that anyone could accept the protracted virginity of a woman who had been twice married and who was guilty of a multitude of whoredoms of the vilest sort. But unbelievably millions upon millions did just that! The implications of the doctrine of the transmigration of souls, as it applied to the dead Nimrod and his posthumous, fair complexioned son were far reaching. In this application we see the subtle beginnings of the Satanic counterfeit of the virgin birth of Christ. It was the first case, as far as we know, in which the birth of a child supposedly occurred parthenogenetically. In Egypt this was reputed to have been the exact method by which the goddess Net gave birth to the sun-god Ra.

> "The statements of Greek writers, taken together with the evidence derived from hieroglyphic texts, prove that in very early times Net (Isis/Semiramis) was the personification of the eternal female principle of life which was self-sustaining and self-existent, and was secret, and unknown, and all-pervading; the more material thinkers, whilst admitting that she brought forth her son Ra (Ninus/Nimrod) without the

aid of a husband were unable to divorce from their minds the idea that a male germ was necessary for his production, and finding it impossible to derive it from a power or being external to the goddess, assumed that she herself provided not only the substance which was to form the body of Ra but also the male germ which fecundated it. Thus Net was the prototype of parthenogenesis"[108]

With the dissemination and teaching of the doctrine of the transmigration of souls, Semiramis successfully established Nimrod, or Ninus "the son" as the rival of Christ the Messiah.

The plan was almost complete. Semiramis had now claimed convincingly that the fair complexioned Ninus, or Ninyas (who was just Nimrod reincarnated) had been born of a virgin, making her the "Mother of God the Son." Indeed, Ninyas was called by almost every name attributed to the true Messiah.

The Specter of Reality

At long last the departed father, the mother, and the "virgin born" son were deceptively melded into a "Holy Trinity," deified, and worshipped as one. The culmination of Semiramis' plans and schemes, the long dreamed of fulfillment of her grandiose evil machinations, became reality. The Holy Trinity was indeed fact in the minds of millions, and the principal doctrine of the pagan and wholly idolatrous Babylonian Mysteries.

The original triad may have been two males and a female but it did not always remain so. In later times it was viewed as consisting of two females and one male.

> "In Babylon, the statement of Diodorus (lib. ii, p. 69) shows the Triad there at one period was two goddesses and the son—Hera, Rhea, and Zeus; and in the capitol at Rome, in like manner, the Triad was Juno, Minerva, and Jupiter; while when Jupiter was worshipped by the Roman matrons as 'Jupiter-puer', or 'Jupiter the child', it was in company with Juno and the goddess Fortuna (Cicero, *De Divinatione*, lib. Ii, Cap. 41, Vol. iii, p. 77). This kind of divine Triad seems to be up to very ancient times among the Romans; for

it is stated both by Dionysius Halicarnassius and by Livy, that soon after the expulsion of the Tarquins, there was at Rome a temple in which were worshipped Ceres, Liber, and Libera"[109]

Symbols

After Semiramis was exalted to her divine position as the Queen of Heaven, she took as her symbol the dove, which represented the Holy Spirit incarnate. When she was represented as the dove, it was just a means of identifying her with the Spirit of all grace. In many sculptures found at Nineveh the wings and tail of the dove stood for the third member of the idolatrous Babylonian Trinity.

The idea of a triune God, with the third member a female representing the Holy Spirit incarnate, was spawned in the stygian spiritual darkness of ancient paganism. Regardless of what the majority of modern day Christianity chooses to believe, the Holy Trinity that they adoringly worship is a product of the Babylonian Mysteries whose high priest and priestess were depraved, evil pawns of Satan, the most evil master of deception of all time.

It is patently obvious from the quotations above that the concept of the Holy Spirit as the third person of the Babylonian Trinity was **not that of a force or power** as conceived of by the Patriarchal system (and throughout the New Testament for that matter), but of a "person" incarnated in female form! The Holy Spirit of the Mysteries was looked upon as the very embodiment of the evil Semiramis herself. She *was* the Holy Spirit incarnate, a concept to which the Bible gives no credence!

The various symbols used to depict the pagan Holy Trinity throughout the centuries have changed little. History records that the dove—as well as its wings and tail (a triad), the equilateral triangle (often formed by three fishes placed head-to-tail at the apices), and even air, were employed. The unity of the only god of the Babylonians was symbolized by the equilateral triangle. It is the same Trinitarian symbol that is today pictured in like manner by the Romish Church.

But what about the air? What could air possibly have to do with depicting the Holy Spirit as the "third person" of the Trinity? Just this. The air was identified with Juno. Her symbol was that of the third person of the Assyrian Trinity. The Chaldean word for air is the same word that means "Holy Spirit." Thus we see that the air—which acts as a **force** or **power** though it cannot be seen—is associated with Juno (Semiramis), who palmed herself off as the Holy Spirit incarnate.

There was yet another Trinitarian symbol that came to prominence during the reign of Semiramis. It was the horn, or tusk. Shem, the eldest son of Noah, was anciently shown or pictured as having tusks protruding from his mouth. They symbolized his power of persuasion concerning the things of God.

> "As a 'horn' means power, so a tusk, that is, a horn in the mouth, means 'power in the mouth'; in other words, the power of persuasion; the very power with which 'Sem', the primitive Hercules, was so signally endowed"[110]

Nimrod was **never** pictured in this manner for his was not the power of persuasion, but of barbaric force. As his symbol of power he utilized the bull's horns under the name Kronos.

> "The name Kronos . . . signifies 'The Horned One'. As a horn is a well known Oriental emblem for power and might, Kronos, 'The Horned One', was, according to the mystic system, just a synonym for the scriptural epithet applied to Nimrod—viz. Gheber, 'The Mighty One' (Gen. 10:8), 'He began to be mighty on the earth'", and, "The meaning of the name Kronos, 'The Horned One', as applied to Nimrod, fully explains the origin of the remarkable symbol, so frequently occurring among Nineveh sculptures, the gigantic **horned** manbull (see Bulls of Bashan, p. 15a), as representing the great divinities of Assyria. The same word that signified a bull, signified a *ruler* or *prince*. Hence, the 'Horned Bull' signified 'The Mighty Prince', thereby pointing back to the first of those 'mighty ones', who, under the name of Guebres, Gabras, or Cabiri, occupied so conspicuous a place in the ancient world . . ."[111]

Thus, at first there were only two horns symbolizing the power and might of the head of the Babylonian system, and these were *always* associated with royalty. Semiramis was not content with this. In order to consolidate further her position in the Babylonian Trinity, she added a third horn to the cap or crown of her royal power and authority.

> "As sovereignty in Nimrod's case was founded on physical force," declares Hislop, "so the two horns of the bull were the symbols of that physical force. And, in accordance with this, we read in 'Sanchuniathon', that, 'Astarte (Semiramis) put on her own head a bull's head (as Thoth did for Isis in Egypt) as the ensign of Royalty'. By-and-by, however, another and higher idea came in, and the expression of that idea was seen in the symbol of the three horns . . . In Assyria the three horned cap was one of the *sacred emblems*, in token that power connected with it was of *celestial* origin—the three horns evidently pointing at the power of the Trinity"[112]

In summary, the "Holy Trinity," anciently, was not the teaching of the True God or of the Patriarchate, but of the pagan, idolatrous system of Satan-worship known as the Babylonian Mysteries. The third horn of the regal crown was just a representation of Semiramis, the "mother of God the son," and "the Holy Spirit incarnate" in the form of a dove. The wings and tail of the dove—a pattern of three—showed:

> "blasphemously, the unity of the father, seed, or son, and Holy Ghost. While this had been the original way in which pagan idolatry had represented the triune god . . . there is evidence that at a very early period an important change had taken place in the Babylonian notions in regard to the divinity; and that the three persons had come to be, the Eternal Father (Nimrod), the Spirit of God incarnate in a human mother (Semiramis), and a divine son (Ninus or Ninyas), the fruit of that incarnation"[113]

So successful was Semiramis that this blasphemous, evil concept of a "Holy Trinity" has borne fruit down to and including the present era. Today, the Trinitarian Doctrine is widely believed by millions.

Chapter 7
THE PROMISED LAND

Despite the fact that Nimrod was pursued to the uttermost limits of his vast empire and slain; that the "Titans" or "Giants" were defeated and slain with him; that Semiramis was forced to flee for her life; that the Mysteries were forced underground; despite all these persecutions by Shem and the Patriarchate, the Apostasy refused to be destroyed. It grew, rather, in scope, power, and popularity.

For those who felt they needed a material object to inspire their worship and to remind them constantly to whom they gave their allegiance, Satan's success in seducing the masses into his perverted, blasphemous system of serpent and fire-worship was incredible. Thus we have seen that the Babylonian system with its human sacrifices, cannibalism, sorcery, and secret, ritualistic practices incited the unsuspecting masses worldwide to a blood frenzy that, even down to the times of the Inquisition and beyond, witnessed the massacre and martyrdom of thousands in the name of religion. All of recorded history down to the present has witnessed the incredible lengths to which the many will go to believe **The Lie** rather than embrace the uncomplicated, common-sense truth of God Almighty.

One need look no farther than the morass of confusion that is today called Evangelical or Orthodox Christianity to know that Satan is still alive, and very active. He has not relinquished his dream of universal conquest or his plan for the physical and spiritual destruction of mankind.

But what about the Mysteries? How did they continue to influence the world in order to draw man away from God?

Following Semiramis' death, her son Ninyas—supposedly virgin-born, said to have been the Babylonian "messiah", and, through the doctrine of transmigration of souls, one and the same with his father Nimrod—began gradually to bring into the open once again all the licentiousness of the Mysteries excepting those practices still held in strictest secrecy (q.v. human sacrifices, cannibalism, initiatory rites, etc.). But even these eventually surfaced once again, and by the time of the death of Shem, were ubiquitous throughout the Babylonian system.

There was never a time that God's people did not encounter the Mysteries in one form or another, or a time that the system did not prosper and flourish in all its wickedness. Although there were occasional attempts to put the system down throughout the centuries following the death of Shem, it was never permanently abolished among God's people (Cf. Judges 6:25, 28-30; 2 Kings 3:2; 10:19, 27-28; 11:18, etc.).

This fact, coupled with the Israelite's stubborn, stiff-necked penchant for ignoring God's dire warnings against idolatry, eventually precipitated their downfall. Where they were once a holy, separate, called-out nation, they became a stigma, and their eventual captivity under the Babylonians and Assyrians stripped them of their God-given identity. With the exception of Judah, Benjamin, and Levi, they became known as the "Lost Ten Tribes" because they flagrantly disregarded God's command not to learn the way of the heathen (Jer. 10:2). Their story begins with the Patriarch Abraham.

Abraham, Friend of God

The smashing successes of the Apostasy and its tenacious hold over the masses notwithstanding, there were those among the Babylonians who refused to be taken in for all time by the lying deceitfulness of the Mysteries. It was by the grace of God that they revised their thinking and came out of the Babylonian system into the freedom that is Christ.

One such person who lived, worked, and worshiped in the midst of it all was Abraham. When he saw the error of his ways and the fallacies of that false religious system, he resolved not only to change *his* ways, but the ways of his fellow citizens as well. His enthusiasm for his newfound beliefs almost cost him his life. Although he was unable to persuade those around him to change their religious beliefs, he was, with the help of God, imminently successful concerning his own efforts. So successful was he that he became known as the Father of the Faithful, and the Friend of God.

Ur of the Chaldees

As a boy, Abraham probably played on the steps of the idolatrous temples (Ziggurats) in Ur of the Chaldees. *The International Standard Bible Encyclopedia* says that Ur (Urima) was possibly the center of Nannar-worship, i.e., moon-god worship.[114] It is likely that, with his parents, he even attended and participated in the festivals of Nannar and Ishtar. As Abraham grew to manhood he was schooled in mathematics and astronomy. These disciplines assured him of a position among the elite of his generation and he became one of "Magi" or "Chaldeans," if you will, the wise men and priests who were the presiding religious leaders of the day.

> "It was not in the restricted sense, but as a synonym of Babylonian, that the name Chaldean obtained the signification of 'wise man'. That the Chaldeans in the restricted sense were more learned than, or even as learned as, the Babylonians in general is unlikely. Moreover, the native inscriptions give no indication that this was the case. The Babylonians in general . . . were enthusiastic students from early times. From their inscriptions it is certain that among their centers of learning may be classed Sippar and Larsa, the chief seats of sun-worship; Nippur . . . Borsippa . . . Ur of the Chaldees, and Erech . . . wherever an important temple existed there was . . . a priestly school. 'The learning of the Chaldeans' (Dan. 1:4; 2:2; 4:7; 5:7, 11) comprised . . . some knowledge of Astronomy and Astrology; mathematics . . . and a certain amount of natural history"[115]

Although the *ISBE* says the Chaldeans were probably no more learned that the average Babylonian, the term "Chaldean" seems to have evolved from just a synonym for Babylonian in earlier times to a specific appellation by the time of Abraham. Peloubet says that:

> "We find the term Chaldeans used as the name for a caste of wise men, learned in literature and science, a member

of which Daniel became (Dan. 1:4). They were priests, magicians, or astronomers . . ."[116]

Further, according to Josephus:

> "In the tenth generation after the flood, there was among the Chaldeans a man righteous and great, and skillful in the celestial sciences"[117]

As a scientist (q.v. a Chaldean in the restricted sense) Abraham proved through scientific experimentation and observation, i.e. through application of the scientific method, that there was but one Supreme, All-powerful, Creator God. Abraham's upbringing, however, had acquainted him with many gods and goddesses, particularly the two gods and one goddess of the Babylonian Holy Trinity. Now, his experiments concluded, his proofs congealed his thinking into an uncompromising mental and spiritual stand against the Babylonian system with its pagan, polytheistic beliefs and practices, and especially its blasphemous Trinitarian Doctrine. Consequently, Abraham began to speak out boldly against the system, which had nurtured him to manhood. He openly denied the power of the Babylonian pantheon to be of any benefit to himself or his fellow citizens and co-workers.

Josephus relates that:

> "He (Abraham) was a person of great sagacity, both for understanding all things and persuading his hearers, and not mistaken in his opinions; for which reason he began to have higher notions of virtue than others had, and he determined to renew and change the opinion all men had concerning God; for he was the first (after the Flood among the Chaldeans) that ventured to publish this notion, That there was but one God, the Creator of the universe . . . This his opinion was derived from the irregular phenomenon that were visible both at land and sea, as well as those that happen to the sun, and moon, and all the heavenly bodies, thus: 'If (said he) these bodies had power of their own, they would certainly take care of their own regular motions; but since they do not preserve such regularity, they make it plain, that in so far as they co-operate to our advantage, they do it

not of their own abilities, but as they are subservient to Him that commands them, to whom alone we ought justly offer our honor and thanksgiving'. For which doctrines, when the Chaldeans, and other people of Mesopotamia, raised a tumult against him, he thought fit to leave that country; and at the command and by the assistance of God, he came and lived in the land of Canaan"(parenthesis mine).[118]

It is apparent that Abraham did not decide suddenly or without precedent to challenge the Babylonian system. To observe the various phenomena of nature and the motions of the heavenly bodies would have required, at the very least, one year. It would have taken perhaps another year to correlate all the information and draw the correct conclusions. If Abraham was as wise as Josephus says he was, he must have given considerable thought to his conclusions before he presented them to the Chaldeans. It follows that he must also have considered the ramifications of such controversial doctrines.

God did not just as suddenly appear to Abraham, and command him to escape for his life (Amos 3:7)! Abraham had come to a full knowledge of who God was by the time He appeared to him in Babylon. *The JFB Commentary* says that Abraham's being brought to the knowledge and worship of the true God had probably been a considerable time before he was called.[119]

If Abraham tried to change the Chaldean's minds about their gods; if he tried to convince them that they were indulging in rank foolishness; and if he tried to persuade them that there was only *One True God* (Yahweh Elohim, The Lord God, God the Father), who was the **Master** of all things, can anyone deny that his arguments were designed to discredit *their* belief concerning their Holy Trinity as though *it* was the only true God? I think not!

The Chaldeans adhered to a false concept of the true God and that in itself constituted idolatry. As a logically-thinking scientist Abraham would not go to the trouble to discredit the entire Babylonian pantheon and incite the Chaldeans, and all of Mesopotamia, to anger and violence against himself without including their Holy Trinity. In fact, it was probably just this that inflamed the Chaldeans so greatly. Their jealous regard for their Trinitarian beliefs had been suddenly breached by one of their own who had become a vile heretic in their eyes. Their belief in a triune god was held, after all, to be most sacred.

The Chaldeans became so enraged over Abraham's new and revolutionary doctrine of one true God that they immediately conspired to kill him. They could not stand to hear the righteous truth! In this respect they were no different than the religious hierarchy of Jesus' day. The Scribes and Pharisees engineered the bloody and brutal death of Jesus Christ because He exposed them for what they were—hypocrites and religious charlatans who had laid a heavy and grievous yoke of legalism and religious bondage upon the people—and because He, like Abraham, came teaching and preaching the truth!

The Lord God could have allowed Abraham to be martyred for his beliefs, but that was not in The Plan. God commanded Abraham to leave the country (Gen. 12:1). Evidently Abraham's parents were also threatened although Terah his father was an idol worshiper. We read in Genesis 11:31 that Terah took Abraham, Abraham's wife Sarah, and his nephew Lot from Ur of the Chaldees and started for the land of Canaan. However, Terah was not quite ready to relinquish his polytheistic beliefs. Apparently he never did, for he settled in Haran. Haran was the city of Abraham's brother by the same name. It was located in northern Mesopotamia about 60 miles midway up the River Balikh, a tributary of the Euphrates at its northern end. Haran was also the center of worship of the moon-god Sin, and had an impressive Ziggurat.

Abraham and his family remained there until the death of his father who was then 145 years old. It had been 25 years since Abraham had left Ur of the Chaldees and now, with no reason to remain in Haran, he moved on to the land of Canaan.

But why Canaan? The religious climate there was no different than that of Babylon, Ur, or Haran. We have already seen that Nimrod and Semiramis had managed to spread their perverse brand of religion throughout the known world, which certainly included Canaan. Why would God throw Abraham out of the frying pan into the fire, so to speak? What did He have in mind? For the answer we must relate back to the very beginning.

The land of Canaan was, credibly, the site of the original Garden of Eden with its center probably situated in the area of Mt. Zion, and the environs of Mt. Moriah, the Mt. of Olives, and present-day Jerusalem.

Jerusalem is the focal point of all end-time prophecy and the locale to which Jesus will return at His second coming (Zech 14:4). It will be God's headquarters on earth during the Millennium. The land of Canaan was also to be a proving ground, as it were, for Abraham and his descendants to see whether they would follow God or the Babylonian system.

Mount Moriah was the site where the sacrifice of Isaac was to take place and where Solomon later built his temple, although not on the present-day Temple Mount. The sacrifice of Isaac was to be a type of the sacrifice of Jesus Christ for the sins of mankind. What better place, then, for God to send Abraham in order to institute His plan for the nation Israel?

Canaan

Who were the Canaanites, and what were conditions like in Canaan when Abraham entered it? The Canaanites, largely, were the descendants of Noah's grandson Canaan. They were an admixture of several different peoples of Semitic origin, speaking a Semitic language, and occupying the region of the Mediterranean coast of Asia south of Asia Minor. They were culturally related to the peoples of the Tigris-Euphrates region, i.e. the Babylonians and Assyrians. By the time Abraham arrived the Canaanites had been introduced to metal-working (by Nimrod) many centuries before, and the culture, known as the Middle Bronze Age, was drawing to a close.

Abraham's first impression of Canaan must have been one of having merely traded geographical locations, for what he found culturally, politically, religiously, and militarily was much the same as what he had left in Babylon. Leon Wood describes what he thinks Abraham might have encountered in the following manner:

> "Canaan had been a progressive land during the prior centuries. Excavation reveals that Early Bronze people had effected remarkable urban development. Cities like Meggido, Bethshan, Shechem, Ai, Jericho, and Lachish . . . already existed and were well built, boasting strong fortifications . . . Later in the third millennium, however, still before Abraham's appearance, Canaan experienced a major change at the hands of a semi-nomadic people pushing into

the land. Many of the fine Early Bronze cities (Meggido, Jericho, Ai, etc.) were destroyed and abandoned, beginning about 2200 B.C. . . . The cultural level of Palestine before Abraham's arrival had been high, comparing favorably with that of any part of the world with the exception of Abraham's native Sumeria or Egypt . . . Abraham would have found the cities that remained well made, boasting fine houses. Pottery would have manifested numerous shapes and sizes, displaying intricate, attractive decoration"[120]

Werner Keller describes it differently.

"About 1900 B.C. Canaan was but thinly populated. Properly speaking it was a no-mans land. Here and there in the midst of ploughed fields a fortified keep could be seen. Neighboring slopes would be planted with vines or with fig trees and date palms. The inhabitants lived in a state of constant readiness. For these widely scattered little townships, like veritable islands, were the object of daring attacks by the desert nomads. Suddenly, and when least expected, these nomads were upon them, with indiscriminate butchery, carrying off their cattle and their crops. Just as suddenly they would disappear again into the vast recess of the desert plains to the south and east. There was endless war between the settled farmers and cattle breeders, and these plundering hordes who had no fixed abode, whose home was a goat's hair tent somewhere out under the open skies of the desert. It was into this restless country that Abraham made his way with his wife Sarah, his nephew Lot, his kinfolk and his flocks"[121]

And again:

"The Canaanite towns were fortresses, places of refuge in times of danger, whether it was from sudden attack by nomadic tribes or civil war among the Canaanites themselves. Towering perimeter walls built of . . . great boulders invariably enclose a small area, not much bigger than St. Peter's square in Rome. Each of these town-forts had a water supply, but they were not towns in which a large population could have made a permanent home. Compared with the palaces and great cities in Mesopotamia or on the Nile they look tiny. Most of the towns in Canaan could have gone into the palace of the kings of Mari comfortably ... Bitter feuds between tribal chiefs were the order of the day. There was no supreme authority. Every chieftain was master in his own territory. No one gave him orders and he did what he pleased. The Bible calls the tribal chieftains 'kings'. As far as power and independence were concerned that is what they were"[122]

If we are to believe both Keller and Wood, we see that Abraham entered a land that was at the same time culturally advanced and barbaric, a seemingly incongruous situation. Wood has the Canaanites living in fine houses while Keller has them holed up in stark fortresses utilized only for defense, not as permanent residences. It hardly seems feasible, if what Keller says is true, that the Canaanites would have had time to indulge in the art of fine pottery making and the building of fine houses.

According to the Bible, conditions in the land of Canaan were quite different from the way Keller describes them when Abraham finally arrived there. We read in Genesis 13:10 that the plain of Jordan was well watered and like the garden of the Lord, (i.e. Eden), rich, lush, and verdant. This could hardly be a picture of a no-mans land in which there was a sparse population living, as it were, in an occasional keep that dotted the landscape.

There is only mention here of a single battle, and that was not waged between or among tribal chieftains and desert nomads, but between certain kings of the east under Chedorlaomer and certain kings of Canaan because the kings of Canaan had rebelled against their subservience of thirteen years to that eastern king. The description of Canaan given by Keller is cleared up by Wood. Says he:

"Later in the third millennium, still before Abraham's appearance, Canaan experienced a major change at the hands of a semi-nomadic people pushing into the land. Many of the fine Early Bronze cities ... were destroyed and abandoned, beginning about 2200 B.C. Those first affected lay west of the Jordan, but later (after 2000 B.C.) the same happened on the east. Cities thus became few in number and population scarce. The people who brought the change clearly were Amorite... Amorites are known to have moved similarly into other parts of the Near East at this time..."[123]

Abraham was born around 2000 B.C. He left Ur of the Chaldees when he was 75 years old, stayed in Haran about 25 years, and entered Canaan when he was just short of 100 years of age. Keller's description of conditions in Canaan at the time of Abraham's arrival is simply two to three hundred years too late!

By the time Abraham arrived, peace was the order of the day, and the Canaanites had managed to rebuild and regain the culture they had lost to the Amorites. Herein may lie the reason for Abraham's 25 year delay in coming into the land of Canaan. God surely would not have had the old Patriarch expose himself and his family to the dangers of warring tribes but would have waited until things settled down, as it were, in order to give them the fairest chance at survival. Abraham entered a relatively peaceful domain in which the inhabitants were pursuing the "good life" and practicing the religion that had been handed down to them by the Babylonians. Wood says that:

> "Canaanites he (Abraham) would have encountered would have been deeply religious, as witnessed by temples and altars uncovered in various excavations; but if their religion was like that represented later at Ugarit, which is likely, it was morally based in employment of fertility rites"[124]

Of course it was based on the employment of fertility rites! It was the same religion that was invented and spread by Nimrod and Semiramis. The Canaanites worshiped the same gods that Babylon and Egypt worshiped—Baal, Astoreth, Astarte, Ashera, El, Anath, Baalath, etc.—and believed the same stories, legends, and myths that had been perpetuated about their gods and goddesses through the ages.

> "There is secular evidence for what the Bible calls 'the abominations of the heathen'... At the head of the baals of

Canaan was the god El. His wife was Asherah, a goddess who is also mentioned in the Bible. El married his three sisters, one of whom was Astarte. She is frequently referred to in the Old Testament as Ashtaroth (Judges 10:6 etc.). El not only kills his brother but also his own son: he cuts off his daughter's head, castrates his father, castrates himself and compels his confederates to do the same . . . in Canaan in those days the cult of sensuality was regarded as the worship of the gods, men and women prostitutes ranked as 'sacred' to the followers of the religion, the rewards for their 'services' went into the temple treasuries as 'offerings for the god'"[125]

The El of the Canaanites was a Bull-god associated with fertility rites. His consort was Astarte, the goddess of fertility and war, who was often depicted as a cow. The Canaanite El, like the Israelite El, was the supreme deity and was considered to be the father of Baal or Adad. He was noted as being a rather remote being that supposedly inhabited the lofty mountainous regions of the remote northern heavens. He is said to have transferred his dynamic bull-like qualities to his son Baal in much the same way that Cush transferred his powers of magic, his authority, and his names to his son Nimrod. Leon Wood describes the connection between El, Baal, and Anath.

> "The most significant deity of the Canaanites was Baal, for he controlled rain and storm . . . Though El (not the El of the O.T.) was theoretically the chief deity, Baal received the greater homage. The extensive epic literature found at Ras Shamra sets forth many other gods also, with Baal always being central in importance. Mot, god of death, is described as annually effecting Baal's death, but Anath, goddess of war and both sister and consort of Baal, is able as often to effect his resurrection. Ashera, though presented as wife of El at Ras Shamra, in lower Canaan appears as consort of Baal; and her carved pole is mentioned in the O.T. as standing beside his altar (Judg. 6:25-28; I Kg. 15:13). Ashtaroth, goddess of fertility, love, and war, is also frequently linked with Baal in the O.T. (Judg. 2:13; 10:6; I Sam. 7:3-4; 12:10).

The concepts of all three female deities, Anath, Ashera, and Ashtaroth, were somewhat fluid, tending to change and merge into one another, so that clear distinctions were not always maintained. Prescribed worship of these deities involved religious prostitution, and the mythology includes stories of extreme brutality and immorality. Child sacrifice and snake worship were also observed" [126]

R.K. Harrison says that:

". . . the religion of the Canaanite peoples was a crude and debased form of ritual polytheism. It was associated with sensuous fertility-cult worship of a particularly lewd and orgiastic kind, which proved to be more influential than any other nature religion in the Near East . . . The depraved nature of the Canaanite religion is indicated by the character of Anat, the sister-spouse of Baal, who was variously identified with Astarte, Asherah, and Ashtoreth in cultic worship. Cult objects such as lilies (representing sex appeal) and serpents (symbolic of fertility) were associated with the sensuous worship of Anat, and plaques recovered from Ras Shamra depicted her nakedness and fecundity"[127]

Although the Canaanite religion was crude and debased, Ivar Lissner says that it was anything but primitive, and that, "a tightly organized priesthood served regular spells of duty in the temples, which were numerous"[128] Most of these temples were dedicated to the goddess Anat whom we have seen was the sister and wife of Baal. The Ugarit tablets reveal that:

"...as was often the case in the East and in Egypt, in particular, brother and sister were married. Virginity, fertility and savagery were strangely combined in this goddess. From time immemorial, therefore, a close association existed between innocence, sacred birth, perversion and devotion to orgiastic cults. When men started to forget Baal and their religious zeal dwindled, Anat instituted a great bloodbath among the apostates"[129]

Werner Keller describes what is probably the bloodbath instituted by Anath.

> "Gruesome and ferocious are Astarte and Anath, goddesses of fertility and of war alike. The Baal-epic of Ugarit depicts the goddess Anath: 'with her might she mowed down the dwellers in the cities, she struck down the people of the sea coasts, she destroyed the men of the east. She drove the men into her temple and closed the doors so that no one could escape. She hurled chairs at the youths, tables at the warriors, footstools at the mighty men. She waded up to the knees, up to the neck in blood. Human heads lay at her feet, human hands flew over her like locusts. She tied the heads of her victims as ornaments upon her back, their hands she tied upon her belt. Her liver was swollen with laughter, her heart was full of joy, the liver of Anath was full of exultation. When she was satisfied she washed her hands in streams of human blood before turning again to other things'"[130]

We have already noted that Semiramis instituted the Mysteries when she returned from her exile in Egypt. We have also seen that Shem had successfully turned the hearts of men back to the worship of the true God during her absence. What is more likely then, that Semiramis, when she returned to Babylon, took vengeance upon those who had defected from the ranks of fire-worship, and slew them indiscriminately in a bloody reprisal designed to bring those who had remained loyal, or those who had thought of defecting, more strongly into the fold? This kind of reprisal against her apostate members would not be out of context if we recall the evil that Nimrod did against his subjects and how they adored him all the more for the suffering and death they had to endure under his rule.

Everywhere we find striking parallels in the mythology of Near Eastern nations regarding their religious beliefs and practices. The variations in names and the stories, myths, and legends used to depict the lives of their gods and goddesses are merely regional and local modifications of the same theme that originated with Nimrod and Semiramis in ancient Babylon.

So it was that Abraham left Babylon and came to Canaan only to find himself and his kin in the midst of the same religious beliefs and practices that he had rejected in Ur. Despite all that he encountered in the land of Canaan, Abraham, with the help of God, managed to keep himself pure and continue in the worship of the true God who kept His promises to him and gave him a son in his old age.

After Isaac was born, God confirmed Abraham's faith by a test in which Abraham was to take his son Isaac to the environs of Mount Moriah (some scholars say it was Mount Moreh) and sacrifice him as a burnt offering. As he was about to plunge the knife into Isaac, an angel of the Lord stopped him and said, "Do not lay your hand on the lad, or do anything to him; for now I know that you fear God, seeing you have not withheld your *son*, your only *son*, from Me" (Gen.22:12, NKJV).

Because Abraham obeyed, God once again confirmed His promise of nationhood and national birthright to his descendants. We find this in Genesis 22:15-18.

> "Then the angel of the Lord called to Abraham a second time out of heaven, and said, 'By Myself I have sworn, says the Lord, because you have done this thing, and have not withheld your *son*, your only *son*, in blessing I will bless you, and in multiplying I will multiply your descendants as the stars of heaven and as the sand which *is* on the seashore; and your descendants shall possess the gate of their enemies. In your seed all the nations of the earth shall be blessed, because you have obeyed My voice.'"

Before this event God had also told Abraham something else. After Abraham's return from the defeat of Chedorlaomer and his encounter with Melchizedek, the priest of the Most High God, he was told by the Lord God that his descendants would inherit the land of Canaan. Though Abraham did not really understand, he believed the Lord and it was accounted to him for righteousness. However, the promise of inheritance did not take effect immediately, but four hundred years after Abraham's death and burial. We find the account in Genesis 15:12-16.

> "Now when the sun was going down, a deep sleep fell upon Abram; and behold, horror *and* great darkness fell upon him. Then He said to Abram: 'Know certainly that your

descendants will be strangers in a land *that is* not theirs, and will serve them, and they will afflict them four hundred years. And also the nation whom they serve I will judge; afterward they shall come out with great possessions. Now as for you, you shall go to your fathers in peace; you shall be buried at a good old age. But in the fourth generation they shall return here, for the iniquity of the Amorites *is* not yet complete.'" (NKJV).

When Abraham died, he passed the promise of national inheritance and prosperity down to Isaac, and Isaac passed it down to his son Jacob. Jacob had twelve sons whose progeny became the chosen nation Israel. The promise of national birthright was fulfilled in Jacob's favorite son Joseph.

Chapter 8
THE EGYPTIAN LEGACY

In the 37th chapter of Genesis we read that Joseph is sold into slavery because of his brothers' jealousy and hatred of him. In chapter 41, we see that Joseph rises to power and becomes the governor of Egypt, second only to Pharaoh in power and authority. Seven years later a great famine grips the entire face of the earth. Chapter 42 tells us that Jacob sends his sons to Egypt to buy grain. Upon their arrival, Joseph immediately recognizes them but he does not reveal his identity. After questioning his brothers closely he learns that his father still lives, and that he now has a younger brother named Benjamin. Joseph is overjoyed at the news and demands that his brothers return and bring Benjamin back with them. When they return to Egypt Joseph is thrilled to see Benjamin and prepares a great feast. He finally tells his brothers who he is and requires them to return to Canaan once again and bring his father back to him.

When they relate the wonders of all that has happened to them, Jacob's spirits soar and he says: "It is enough; Joseph my son is yet alive; I will go and see him before I die" (Gen. 45:28). Jacob set out for Egypt with all his belongings and seventy-two of his kinsmen. In route he camped at Beer-sheba where he offered sacrifices to God. We read in Genesis 46:2-4 that:

> "... God spake unto Israel (Jacob) in the visions of the night (i.e. in a dream), and said, 'Jacob, Jacob', and he said, 'Here am I'. And He said, 'I Am God, the God of thy father; fear not to go down into Egypt; for I will there make of thee a great nation: I will go down with thee into Egypt; and I will also bring thee up again ...'"

Project Apostasy

    Jacob was old and growing feeble. If he had any doubts about going down into Egypt, God dispelled them immediately. What is more, he surely understood that God did not intend to bring him personally out of Egypt again. He knew that once he had entered Egypt he would never leave there alive, and that it would be his descendants, the nation Israel that God would bring out. He must also have been keenly aware of the prophecy that God had uttered to Abraham years before in which He had told him that his descendants would enter a strange land, serve the people there, and that these people would afflict them for 400 years (Gen. 15:13). Like his father before him, Jacob had faith in God's promises. He led his small band of seventy-two souls unhesitatingly into the gaping maw of certain, future captivity and slavery.

    While Egypt, Canaan, Babylon, and most of the remainder of the known world continued to worship at the altar of the idolatrous Babylonian system, Jacob entered Egypt secure in the knowledge and truth of the One True God, and that He would be with them. And God *was* with them in the beginning (this is not to say that He later abandoned them, for He never once forgot His promise to them), and they prospered and grew in the land of Goshen as long as Joseph was living and governing Egypt. When Joseph died, however, the situation took a turn for the worse. As we shall see, the Israelites were corrupted by the system that was the very antithesis of all that they believed, and of all that Abraham had taught them concerning God.

    The change in the Israelite's relationship with the Egyptians came about when there arose a Pharaoh who did not "know" Joseph, i.e. had no regard or respect for his beliefs and customs, or for those of the Israelites and their God. This unnamed Pharaoh became paranoid because the Israelites had multiplied, according to God's promise, until they "filled" the land of Egypt (Ex. 1:8-10). He was afraid the Israelites would join the enemy if war were to break out against Egypt. Consequently, he set cruel taskmasters over them, subjecting them to harsh, body and mind-breaking labor. He conscripted them for building his cities, roads, and temples, not allowing them to worship God as they had customarily done for hundreds of years. Hopelessly, they became inured to 400 long, agonizing years of cruel, relentless slavery and pagan idolatry.

    Since they were not allowed to worship God openly and undisturbed, the majority despaired, relinquishing any hope that God would ever deliver them from the horrible yoke of bondage that was destroying them body and soul. Eventually, Israel all but forgot the God of their fathers, and, for the most part, fell to worshiping the gods of the Egyptians including the Egyptian Trinity of Osiris, Isis, and Horus— the exact counterpart of the Babylonian Trinity of Nimrod, Semiramis, and Ninyas.

The Exodus

True to His promises to Abraham, Isaac, and Jacob, God raised up the prophet Moses about 430 years after Jacob's descent into Egypt. He commissioned him to go to Pharaoh and demand the release of the Israelites. Following ten severe plagues, the last of which killed all of the first-born of Egypt, Pharaoh relented and released the Israelites. God and Moses led them out with a "high hand." They left Egypt triumphantly praising God, and eager for their journey to the promised land. God produced miracle after powerful miracle as He brought the Israelites out of Egypt. They trembled in fear at the awesome spectacle of the parting of the Red Sea. And yet, even this was not enough to persuade them to abandon their inordinate desire to bow down to the inert, lifeless Egyptian idols they had become so accustomed to worshiping. Project Apostasy was going forward with all the fervor that Satan could muster.

Mount Sinai

After three months of wandering in the Wilderness of Sin, they arrived at Mount Sinai, the holy mountain of God. It was a long, arduous trip. They needed and welcomed the rest. Moses settled them on the plain that abutted the mountain, and climbed up to speak with God. When he returned to camp he related all that God had spoken. They answered, ". . . all that the Lord hath spoken we will do" (Ex. 19:8). Their oath was meaningless. It consisted of empty, shallow words uttered perhaps, to appease their own consciences and to cultivate the blessings and favor of God. They simply failed to realize that God had given His word of deliverance and national prosperity to their fathers, and that regardless of what they did or said, He would fulfill His promise without qualification. God simply cannot and will not go back on His word!

Three days later, Moses brought the people near to the base of the mountain to witness the descent of God Himself upon its lofty peak. As the people drew near, the mountain rocked and quaked as though it would split asunder. Great thunderings and lightnings accompanied the quaking. The summit was enshrouded in thick, black smoke that billowed upward into the heavens as if spewed forth from a gigantic blast furnace. Suddenly, a long trumpet-like blast split the air. As it subsided, the super-powerful voice of God reverberated from the mountain and rolled across the plain like the roaring and rumbling of a mighty herd of stampeding stallions. It thundered its way through the camp as He gave Israel His beautifully simple, all encompassing moral law.

God spoke plainly! He drove immediately and unerringly to the point. Israel had worshiped other gods for the better part of 400 years. God told them without reservation that they were no longer to put other gods before the one true God. Nor, He further stipulated, were they to make for themselves any graven images, to bow down to them or serve them. In other words, **they were to leave what they had learned in Egypt in Egypt!**

However, giving up 400 years of sating their lusts and desires with sensual, pagan rituals in the temples of Isis would make it extremely difficult for them to change their ways and honor their oath of obedience to God and Moses.

They had come out of Egypt with a "mixed multitude" (Ex.12:38). This mixed multitude probably consisted of Egyptians, Libyans, Ethiopians, and Canaanites, all of them slaves and bondmen as the Israelites had been. It was the "foreigners," as it were, who constantly stirred up the Israelites to return to Egypt and to the worship of the Egyptian gods and goddesses.

However, before God had even finished speaking to them from the mountain, the Israelites were stopping their ears and begging Moses to intercede and speak for God lest they all die. They could not tolerate the ear-splitting, fulminating sound of God's tremendously powerful voice.

Hearing, they had heard, but they had not listened. A short 40 days later, the Israelites had all but forgotten the miracles and their promises of obedience. They chose instead to listen to the satanically inspired "mixed multitude." In the ensuing period, they committed a grave error that was committed repeatedly.

The Golden Calf

Moses had returned to the mountain to receive The Law etched into two stone tablets by the finger of God. When he delayed in coming down, the Israelites grew impatient and discouraged. They and the "mixed multitude" coaxed Aaron into making a golden calf.

Why would Aaron, who had been chosen by God to be the spokesman for Moses (Ex. 4:16), and who was to be the first of the Aaronic Priesthood that would exist and function down to 70 A.D., fashion a golden calf for the Israelites to worship in the very presence of God? Well, we have already seen that the Israelites had worshiped the Egyptian gods for almost 400 years. Had Aaron been guilty of the same idolatry? Conrad seems to think so for he says:

> "... the construction of the golden bull by Aaron at the foot of Mount Sinai was not the act of a heretic, but the legitimate function of the high priest of the bull-god. In thus making the bull idol Aaron was simply following a long tradition of Israelite bull worship and had the full approval of his people."[131]

Whether Aaron was a high priest of the Egyptian bull cult, the Bible does not say. However, it is unlikely. Indications in the 32nd chapter of Exodus are that Aaron was *forced* to make the golden calf because he feared that the people would harm him if he didn't. Verse one says that the people gathered together *unto* him and requested that he make them gods to go before them. The word "unto" is the Hebrew *guwach* (goo'-akh) and means—to rush forth:—to strive. Probably egged on by the mixed multitude, the Israelites, strove with Aaron, i.e. they compelled him to do what they wished under threat of bodily harm and perhaps even death.

The JFB Commentary says that the people came against Aaron:

> "... in a tumultuous manner, to compel him to do what they wished. The incidents related in this chapter disclose a state of popular sentiment and feeling among the Israelites that stands in singular contrast to the tone of profound and humble reverence they displayed at the giving of the law. Within a space of little more than thirty days, their impressions were

dissipated. Although they were still encamped upon ground which they had every reason to regard as holy; although the cloud of glory that capped the summit of Sinai was still before their eyes, affording a visible demonstration of their being in close contact, or rather in the immediate presence, of God, they acted as if they had entirely forgotten the impressive scenes of which they had been so recently the witnesses . . . the circumstance, therefore, seems to point out 'the mixed rabble', who were chiefly *foreign* slaves, as the ringleaders in this insurrection"[132]

Regardless of whether Aaron was a high priest of the Egyptian bull cult, he acquiesced, for whatever reason, to the people's demands and made the golden calf. When it was finished, Aaron proclaimed a feast to the Lord on the following day. The Israelites rose up early in the morning and began to worship it, saying, "These *be* thy gods, O Israel, which brought thee up out of the land of Egypt" (Ex. 32:4,8).

It was a peculiar statement for them to make concerning (a) golden calf. Why would the Israelites speak of a single golden calf as "thy gods"? Were they mistaken or is the statement in Exodus 32 a translators error? Surprisingly, it is neither. The word *gods* is the Hebrew *elohim*, and is plural.

The golden calf was an imitation of the bull-god Apis whom they had learned to worship in Egypt. He seems to have originated in Egypt with Narmer-Menes whose symbol was the bull. When he forcefully united upper and lower Egypt, he spread the bull-cult throughout the land. But the bull-cult that he spread was that of the god Hap. The Greeks later called it Apis.

It interesting to note here that the first part of the name of the mighty king Narmer-Menes, bears a striking similarity to the name Nimr or Nimrod. Menes, of course, was Cush. The association of the two names would seem to indicate that the two ruled in Egypt concurrently. Nimrod conquered Egypt in very early times. The fact that the name Menes is listed second points to the probability that Nimrod set his father up as king of the First Dynasty in Egypt, while he in fact ruled over his father, and most of the known world, from Babylon. Conrad says that:

> "Narmer-Menes not only worshiped Apis and forcibly spread the gospel of the bull-god throughout Egypt, but either his adroitness or his naiveté led him to conceive of himself as a bull. In either case, at a very early date bull worship in Egypt became identical with king worship. And from the time of Narmer-Menes onward the supreme head of the Egyptian state as well as the Egyptian religion was the king. Since the king was a bull, the king was a god. For where there was bull-like power and strength, there was both kingship and godhood. Thus the triple association of *bull-god-king* seems to have been a basic feature of Egyptian civilization as early as the First Dynasty" (emphasis mine).[133]

The golden calf of the Israelites was also a representation of Saturn, the "Hidden One." We have already seen that Saturn and Nimrod are the same. The bull or young cow in Egypt had a golden solar disk between its horns. The cow, in particular, symbolized the goddess Isis, whose Grecian counterpart was Venus. Her counterpart in Babylon was Rhea or Semiramis, the goddess of fortifications, and mother-goddess of all gods. The Egyptian Apis and the Phoenician Baal were both pictured as bulls. The bull was a common representation of fertility and strength. The Phoenician god Baal was none other than Nimrod, the chief deity of Babylonians. *The JFB Commentary* says that the golden calf "was distinguished by a triangular white spot on its forehead and other peculiar marks"[134] What these "peculiar marks" were, is not disclosed, but there is historical evidence from other authors, particularly Budge, that sheds much light on the subject. We learn from Budge that:

> "Above the fore and hind legs are cut in outline, figures of vultures with out-stretched wings, and on the back, also cut in outline, is a representation of a rectangular cloth with an ornamental diamond pattern", and further, "Pliny relates (viii. 72) that the Apis bull was distinguished by a conspicuous white spot on the right side, in the form of a crescent"[135]

Conrad says that:

> ". . . the holy black bull of Apis had a white triangular blaze on his forehead, the diminutive form of an eagle on his back, the shape of a beetle on his tongue, double hairs in his tail, the figure of a crescent moon on his right side, and some twenty-four other distinct marks through which he was identified by the priests"[136]

All of these symbols had distinct cultic meanings to the priests of Apis. It is certain that the crescent-shaped white spot on the right side of the calf symbolized Isis, and that the rectangular cloth with its ornamental diamond pattern (a double equilateral triangle, if you will), was doubly symbolic of both the Babylonian and Egyptian Trinities (Nimrod-Semiramis-Ninyas; and Osiris-Isis-Horus).

We have already noted that the equilateral triangle was used to represent the Babylonian Holy Trinity. That this was true of the white triangular spot on the forehead of the Apis bull is borne out by both Hislop and Budge.

> "The ordinary way in which the favourite Egyptian divinity Osiris (Nimrod) was *mystically* represented was under the form of a young bull or calf —the calf Apis—from which the golden calf of the Israelites was borrowed". The term 'calf' can include either a bull or a cow, and, Hislop continues, "The cow of Athor (the Egyptian Isis), however, is well known as a 'spotted cow'. . . when we find Osiris, the grand god of Egypt, under different forms, was arrayed in a leopard skin or spotted dress . . . we may be sure that there was a deep meaning in such a costume. And what could that meaning be, but just to identify Osiris with the Babylonian god, who was celebrated as the 'leopard tamer'; and who was worshiped even as he was, as Ninus, the child in his mother's arms"[137]

In addition we find that:

> ". . . as the power of the triangle is expressive of the nature of Pluto, Bacchus, and Mars (all representative of Nimrod), the

properties of the square (or double triangle-shaped diamond) of Rhea, Venus, Vesta, and Juno" (all representative of Semiramis) (parentheses mine).[138]

The golden calf of the Israelites was actually an amalgam of the three elements of the Babylonian-Egyptian Holy Trinity—Apis (Nimrod-Osiris); the cow of (H)Athor (Semiramis-Isis), the female counterpart of Apis; and the leopard spotted dress (representing Osiris-Maut-Horus, or Nimrod-Ninyas), the son who was worshiped in his mother's arms. Is it any wonder that the scriptures have it correctly that the people said of the calf —"these *be* thy gods"?!

It is plain that the Israelites were worshipping the Babylonian-Egyptian Holy Trinity in a sensuous, pagan orgy accompanied by lewd dancing and perverted acts of fornication. Every one of these was an integral part of the pagan Babylonian fertility cult that was included in the Mysteries.

God considered their wanton idolatry such an abomination that He was ready to destroy them all and start over with Moses (Ex. 32:10). But Moses persuaded God to change His mind lest the Egyptians ridicule Him because He had brought the Israelites out of Egypt with great power and miracles only to destroy them in the wilderness (Ex. 32:12). And besides, Moses reminded God, "Remember Abraham, Isaac, and Israel, Your servants, to whom You swore by Your own self, and said to them, 'I will multiply your descendants as the stars of heaven; and all this land that I have spoken of I give to your descendants, and they shall inherit it forever'" (Ex. 32:13, NKJV).

Although God repented of His intent to destroy the Israelites, He did send a plague among them to punish them. The sons of Levi killed about three thousand of them with the sword. But they still did not learn the lesson. They were hell-bent-for-leather, determined to follow their lusts and desires, the consequences be damned! This is, of course, the very attitude that Lucifer displayed when he rebelled. That Satan's hand was in Israel's idolatrous leanings there is no doubt. Time after time we see him stirring up the people's hearts against God and luring them back into his perverted sense of worship.

In Leviticus 18:2-3 we find that God once again speaks to Moses to warn the people about worshipping false gods.

> "Speak to the children of Israel, and say to them, 'I *Am* the Lord your God. After the doings of the land of Egypt, wherein ye dwelt, **shall ye not do**: and after the doings of the land of Canaan, whither I will bring you, **shall ye not do**: neither shall ye walk in their ordinances'" (*their* appointed feasts, customs, and manners).

God not only commanded the Israelites to refrain from the religious rites and ceremonies of the Egyptians, He forbade them to learn the ways of the Canaanites, who, like the Egyptians, followed the Babylonish system of idolatry, and worshiped the same pagan Trinity. In Leviticus 20:1-6 God gets down to specifics and declares:

> "...again, thou shalt say to the children of Israel, 'Whosoever *he be* of the children of Israel, or of the strangers that sojourn in Israel, that giveth *any* of his seed unto Molech; he shall surely be put to death: the people of the land shall stone him with stones. And I will set My face against that man, and will cut him off from among his people; because he hath given of his seed unto Molech, to defile my sanctuary, and to profane My holy name. And if the people of the land do anyways hide their eyes from the man, when he giveth of his seed unto Molech, and kill him not: then I will set My face against that man, and against his family, and I will cut him off, and all that go a whoring after him, to commit whoredom with Molech, from among their people. And the soul that turneth after such as have familiar spirits, and after wizards, to go a whoring after them, I will set My face against that soul, and will cut him off from among his people'" (cp. I Sam. 28:7-20).

God made it very plain that He would not put up with the flagrant disregard of His laws against idolatry! He especially hated the worship of Molech with its horrible rituals of child sacrifice. He considered it the pinnacle of the idolatries to which the Israelites aspired. Children are very precious in God's sight (cp. Mat. 19:14; Mk. 10:24; Lk.18:16).

Can anyone say that by warning the Israelites to refrain from learning the ways of the heathen (Jer. 10:2), God would overlook or wink at the worship of the idolatrous, pagan, triune god of the Babylonian system?

The Bible is replete with examples of the Israelite's stiff-necked, stubborn refusal to obey God in these matters, and of their inordinate love and desires for the orgiastic rites and ceremonies of Baal-worship. In fact, there are over 80 such references throughout the Old and New Testaments.

Baal-Peor

There is a curious statement by the author of Psalm 106 that has, escaped attention, perhaps, or has been little understood by theologians, even down to our day. It is a reference to Numbers 25:2-3, which reads:

> "And they (the daughters of Moab) called the people unto the sacrifices of their gods: and the people did eat, and bowed down to their gods. And Israel joined himself unto Baal-peor: and the anger of the Lord was kindled against Israel."

The Psalmist speaks of the nation Israel during their wanderings in the wilderness, and of their idolatrous whoredoms with the nation Moab. He declares, "They have joined themselves also unto Baal-peor, and ate the sacrifices of the dead."

Kitto says that:

> "What they did was to participate in the licentious acts by which his votaries professed to honor him. 'They joined themselves to Baal-Peor' — rather, 'bound themselves with his badge;' for it was the custom in ancient times, as it is now in all pagan countries, for every idol to have some specific badge, or ensign, by which his votaries were known."[139]

But who or what is Baal-peor? And what are the "sacrifices of the dead"?

The answer to the first question is simple. The word Baal is the Chaldean for "sun" or "lord." Regarding the use of the word lord, it is used in the sense of "possessor" rather than "ruler." This is taken to mean that Baal as Lord was possessor of all things. Baal was Nimrod, and Nimrod was the direct representative of Satan. In this connection, the reference to Baal the "possessor" was an allusion to the fact that Satan is the "Great Possessor," the one who can enter and control a man mentally and bodily for his own evil purposes!

This Baal, as we have seen, was the supreme deity of the Chaldeans, and symbolized Nimrod the great sun/fire god. As the name is spelled, Baal is simply an alternate form of the Babylonian "Bel" or "Belus." This "Bel" or "Belus" was none other than Cush, the father of Nimrod, and the alleged ringleader of the apostasy after the flood. At his death his title, and all that it signified, was hereditarily passed on to Nimrod who perpetuated the legacy and the system under the evil inspiration and guidance of the "Daring One," Satan the Devil. The adjunct "peor" is the name of a mountain in Moab upon whose summit the Moabites erected a pagan shrine or high holy place in honor of the Babylonian Baal, and from which the name Baal-peor is derived.

By joining themselves to Baal-peor the Israelites immersed their minds and bodies in every despicable aspect of Nimrod-worship and the Mysteries of Semiramis. Not only did they bow the knee to Nimrod, they subscribed to every practice, ritual, custom, and tradition included in the system. Why? Because they had habitually worshiped the same god under a different name (Osiris) for almost 400 years in Egypt. Old habits die hard!

But what about "the sacrifices of the dead"? Who are the "dead" spoken of here? According to the *JFB Commentary* they are, ". . . the lifeless idols, contrasted with the 'living God'"[140] This is a plausible explanation, and modern translations have it as "sacrifices made to lifeless idols." The problem, however, lies in what the "sacrifices" were. They very likely were animals, but we must ever keep in mind that included in the sacrifices to Baal-Molech-Moloch-Chemosh, were human beings, children as well as adults. I have already noted that the priests of Baal were required to practice cannibalism. If they, then why not the laity as well. For we have seen that ". . . new features were added to that idolatry that made it still more blasphemous than before."[141]

If the Israelites were guilty of human sacrifice, (and they most likely were if they followed Baal), it was only a short step for their already depraved, pagan-oriented minds to cross the threshold into the abominable practice of cannibalism.

Because they bowed down and worshiped Baal, God was so angry with them that He sent a plague among them that would have completely destroyed them had not Phinehas the priest intervened on their behalf (Num. 25:6-8). As it was, none of that generation ever reached the promised land.

> "Your eyes have seen what the Eternal did because of Baal-peor: or for all the men that followed Baal-peor: The Eternal thy God hath destroyed them from among you" (Deut.4:3).

Chapter 9
THE DECLINE AND FALL OF ISRAEL

Following the conquest of Canaan and the death of Joshua, Israel's history consists of one political, economic, and religious tragedy after another. They failed to drive the Canaanites from the land as God had commanded (Josh. 17:13; Jdgs. 1:32, etc.), and they fell prey to the curse of failure. Israel assimilated much of the Canaanite culture and religion not heeding God's admonition to refrain from learning the way of the heathen. Leon Wood states:

> "The main area in which Israel displeased God ... was that of religion (q.v. idolatry). Many Israelites came to adopt Canaanite religious practices ... Prescribed worship ... involved religious prostitution (both physically and spiritually), and the mythology includes stories of extreme brutality and immorality. Child sacrifice and snake worship were also observed. The religion was decadent, and Israel sinned greatly in being enamored by it."[142]

During the period of the Judges, the Israelites found themselves repeatedly oppressed by the peoples who occupied the surrounding territories. Each time the oppression became unbearable they cried out to God to save them. Merciful and forgiving as ever, He heard their cries of woe and compassionately delivered them from the hands of their enemies. Incredibly, they hardened their hearts, stuck out their jaws, stiffened their necks, and returned to Baal-worship.

On six separate occasions, God severely punished the Israelites for their disobedience and crimes of idolatry. (1) The Mesopotamian Oppression (Judges 4-5); (2) The Moabite Oppression (Judges 3:12); (3)

The Canaanite Oppression (Judges 4-5); (4) The Midianite Oppression (Judges 6:1-10; 5; Ruth 1-4); (5) The Ammonite Oppression (Judges 10:6-12; 15), and (6) The Philistine Oppression (Judges 13-16). Of the first four oppressions Wood states:

> "The four punishing oppressions of Israel thus far considered did not cause the people to change their ways. In fact, their sin seemingly increased as they came to serve, not only the false gods of Canaan, but also of Syria, Sidon, Moab, Ammon, and the Philistines"(Judges 10:6).[143]

The last of these oppressions (that of the Philistines), lasted 40 years, down to the times of Samuel, Saul, and David.

Samuel

Samuel was the last of the Judges of Israel. As a young boy, God used him mightily to rebuke Eli the high priest. Eli's sons Hophni and Phinehas perverted the tabernacle worship so badly that the devout followers of God hesitated to go there. According to Wood:

> "Conditions at the tabernacle were not good at the time and they were getting worse (I Sam. 2:12-17). Eli, descended from Aaron . . . was the high priest. His two sons Hophni and Phinehas were priests. Eli, himself an earnest follower of Yahweh, was old, and his two sons were in charge of ceremonies. They were wicked men, sorely perverting the ritual and profaning the sanctuary, in a debauchery similar to that of Canaanite temples"[144]

Not only did Hophni and Phinehas take of the portions of the sacrifices allotted to them as priests of Israel, they took more than their share, even those portions designated as burnt offerings to the Lord, and ate them raw! The crowning abuse, however, was the religious prostitution they instituted in the temple of God in plain sight of the nation of Israel.

> "Now Eli was very old, and heard all that his sons did unto all Israel; and how they lay with the women that assembled at the door of the tabernacle of the congregation (I Sam.

2:22). Religious prostitution was one of the main features of the apostate Canaanite religion, and tantamount to idolatry! Josephus declares, "Eli, the high priest, had two sons, Hophni and Phineas. These sons of Eli were guilty of injustice towards men, and of impiety towards God, and abstained from no sort of wickedness. Some of their gifts they carried off, as belonging to the honorable employment they had; others of them they took away by violence. They also were guilty of impurity with the women that came to worship God [at the tabernacle], obliging some to submit to their lust by force, and enticing others by bribes; nay the whole course of their lives was no better than tyranny."[145]

Jamieson, Fausset, and Brown (p. 206) say that these women were of a strict ascetic order that were devoted to the Lord, and cite Luke 2:37 as proof. If these women were strict devotees to the service of the Lord, and if Hophni and Phinehas indeed forced them to engage in religious prostitution, bringing pagan practices and religion into the very tabernacle of God, it is understandable that He determined to kill them. They committed of the worst sort of blasphemy!

Because of the wickedness of Eli's sons, God prophesied that both of them would die in one day. "And this shall be a sign unto thee, that shall come upon thy two sons, on Hophni and Phinehas; in one day they shall die both of them" (I Sam. 2:34). Eli would live to see the oppression of Israel by an enemy once again despite all the good that God would do for them.

About 15 years later, the Philistines came against Israel. Hophni and Phinehas took the Ark of the Covenant into the field thinking that its presence would guarantee victory. They surmised that no one could stand against them because the ark was the dwelling place of God in Israel (I Sam. 4:4). How wrong they were! God allowed the Philistines to defeat them, kill Hophni and Phinehas, and capture the Ark. When news reached Eli's ears, he fell backward off his seat, broke his neck, and died. He had ruled over Israel 40 years.

After the defeat of Israel, the Philistines took the Ark to their capitol city Ashdod, and placed it in the temple of their fish god Dagon. God punished them with plagues of "tumors" (hemorrhoids) and mice. The plagues became so severe that the Philistines eagerly wished themselves rid of the Ark after only seven months. They placed it on an ox cart and sent it on its way back to Israel. It came to rest at Kirjath-Jearim in the house of Abinadab. God appointed his son Eleazar to care for the Ark. It remained in Abinadab's house for twenty years.

After the death of Eli and his sons, Samuel assumed leadership of Israel. He gained recognition as God's prophet from Dan to Beersheba, and preached and taught God's word throughout the land. During the twenty years that the Ark rested in Kirjath-Jearim, the Philistines continued to oppress the Israelites until they cried mightily to the Lord for deliverance. He heard their prayers and sent Samuel to tell them, "If you return to the Lord with all your hearts, then put away the foreign gods and the Ashteroth from among you, and prepare your hearts for the Lord, and serve Him only; and He will deliver you from the hand of the Philistines. So the children of Israel put away the Baals and the Ashteroth and served the Lord only" (I Sam. 7:3-4).

Shortly thereafter, the Israelites defeated the Philistines at Mizpah, and had all of their land restored to them. Samuel Judged Israel for the rest of his life and traveled from year to year on a circuit that included Bethel, Gilgal, and Mizpah, always returning to his home in Ramah. However, when he grew old, he transferred rulership of Israel to his sons Joel and Abijah. They turned to profiteering, bribery, and perversion of justice. The elders of Israel went to Samuel and demanded that he appoint them a king to rule over them. Very upset about this, Samuel prayed to God to deny their request. Nevertheless, God told him to do what they asked, because, He said, "they are not rejecting you but Me." God chose Saul, a Benjamite to be king over Israel.

Saul

Saul was the son of Kish. He was a head taller than anyone in Israel and according to I Sam. 9:2, there was "not a more handsome person than him among the children of Israel." Prior to his anointing he was a humble person, but his humility did not to last. After Samuel anointed him, and the people accepted him, he established his throne in Gibeah, his hometown. In the beginning, he ruled with wisdom and foresight, implementing little basic change in the people's way of life. Later however, God rejected him after he made two very serious mistakes. The first occurred during a battle against the Philistines at Micmash, only two years after Samuel anointed him king over Israel. His son Jonathan attacked and defeated a Philistine garrison at Geba, and the Philistines came against Israel with 30,000 chariots, 6,000 horsemen, and a host of infantry. The host of Israel bivouacked with Saul in Gilgal. They waited there seven days for Samuel to come and sacrifice before the Lord in order to obtain a blessing. When Samuel failed to show up, Saul became impatient and assumed the priestly role of the Levites, sacrificing before the Lord himself. Samuel arrived immediately thereafter and demanded an explanation. When Saul gave him his reasons for his brash behavior, Samuel said,

> "You have done foolishly. You have not kept the commandment of the Lord your God, which He commanded you. For now the Lord would have established your kingdom over Israel forever. But now your kingdom shall not continue. The Lord has sought for Himself a man after His own heart, and the Lord has commanded him to be commander over His people, because you have not kept what the Lord commanded you" (I Sam.13:13-14).

The second grave mistake that Saul made occurred some 20 years later during a battle with the Amalekites. God commanded him to destroy the Amalekites, to kill every man, woman, and child, and slaughter all of their livestock. However, he chose not to kill their king Agag and some of the choicest of the sheep and oxen. Saul failed in God's eyes because he would not obey divine command.

The first rejection was more or less a warning. However, he did not repent of his rebellion, and this final act sealed his fate regarding his continuing rule over God's people. Because Saul disobeyed, Samuel pronounced God's irreversible decision.

> "Has the Lord *as great* delight in burnt offerings and sacrifices, as in obeying the voice of the Lord? Behold, to obey is better than sacrifice, and to heed than the fat of rams. For rebellion *is as* witchcraft, and stubbornness *is as* iniquity and idolatry. Because you have rejected the word of the Lord, He also has rejected you from being king" (I Sam. 15:22-23).

God removed His Holy Spirit from Saul and that is when his troubles really began. Although Saul did not lead Israel into idolatry, and did not engage in idolatrous practices himself, the result of his rebellion amounted to the same thing. God removed him from being king as though he was guilty of those very acts.

Samuel anointed David, the son of Jesse, king over Israel, and the Spirit of the Lord came upon him. God blessed David in everything that he did. Although David made many mistakes, he never rebelled against God in the manner that Saul did. His kingdom prospered and grew until he became the greatest king that Israel has ever known. David ruled over Israel for forty years. He died at the age of seventy having worshiped God diligently and obediently, his heart perfect before the Lord. When David died, Solomon inherited a kingdom that stretched from Egypt to the Euphrates and worshiped the true God. Under Solomon Israel began to drift back into idolatry because his heart did not remain perfect before the Lord. Project Apostasy was alive and well, and Satan still lurked in the background.

Solomon

Solomon was the wisest man that ever lived. God blessed him mightily from the beginning of his reign. However, even with all his wisdom, power, and riches, in his later years he forgot who his God was. He allowed the apostate system to reestablish itself among God's people Israel. We find that

> ". . . he had seven hundred wives, princesses, and three hundred concubines: and his wives turned away his heart. For it came to pass, when Solomon was old, that his wives turned away his heart after other gods: and his heart was not perfect with the Lord God, as was the heart of David his father. For Solomon went after Ashtoreth the goddess of the Zidonians, and after Milcom (margin-Molech) the abomination of the Ammonites . . . Then did Solomon build an high place for Chemosh, the abomination of Moab, in the hill that is before Jerusalem, and for Molech, the abomination of the children of Ammon. And likewise did he for all his strange wives, which burnt incense and sacrificed unto their gods" (I Kings 11:3-5; 7-8).

The hill where Solomon built the high place for Molech was most likely Ophel, situated on the east side of Jerusalem and south of the Temple site. It is the same as Zion where David first erected the tent in which he placed the Ark of the Covenant, and which became known as the City of David. That Solomon should do this is not at all surprising. God warned Israel centuries before not to intermarry with the heathen because He knew it would lead to the very thing to which Solomon acquiesced. Once again, one must keep in mind that the worship of Molech (Nimrod) and Ashtoreth (Semiramis), of necessity included Ninus their son, and that all three made up the idolatrous Babylonian Holy Trinity!

The irony of the situation in which Solomon later found himself is that he was so wise and yet so vulnerable in his old age that he was unequivocally taken in by the deceit of the Mysteries! He clearly describes how this great apostate religion works in proffering its wares to those who are foolish enough to fall into the subtle trap set for them. Would that he had heeded his own wise counsel!

> "Say unto wisdom, thou art my sister; and call understanding thy kinswoman: that they may keep thee from the strange woman (q.v. the apostate church or religion), from the stranger which flattereth with her words. For at the window of my house I looked through my casement, and beheld among the simple (seducible or foolish) ones, I discerned among the youths, a young man void of understanding (of the word of God), passing through the street near her corner; and he went the way to her house, in the twilight, in the evening, in the black and dark night: and, behold, there met him a woman with the attire of a harlot (cf. Rev. 17:1-5), and subtil (crafty) of heart. (She is loud and stubborn; her feet abide not in her house: now is she without, now in the streets, and lieth in wait at every corner). So she caught him, and kissed him and with an impudent face said to him, I have peace offerings with me; this day have I paid my vows. Therefore came I forth to meet thee, diligently to seek thy face, and I have found thee. I have decked my bed with coverings of tapestry, with carved works, with fine linen of Egypt. I have perfumed my bed with myrrh, aloes, and cinnamon.

Come, let us take our fill of love until the morning: let us solace ourselves with loves... with her much fair speech she caused him to yield, with the flattery of her lips she forced him. He goeth after her straightway as an ox goeth to the slaughter, or as a fool to the correction of the stocks; till a dart strike through his liver; as a bird hasteth to the snare, and knoweth not that it is for his life. Hearken unto me now therefore, O ye children, and attend to the words of my mouth. Let not thine heart decline to her ways, go not astray in her paths. For she hath cast down many wounded: yea, many strong men have been slain by her. Her house is the way to hell, going down to the chambers of death" (Pro. 7:4-27, parentheses mine).

We have no way of knowing when Solomon wrote this. It is almost as if it were a self-fulfilling prophecy except that he probably wrote it after the fact. One can almost see each one of his "strange" wives whispering in his ear, entreating, cajoling, and plying him with flatteries until at last he fell into the very trap from which he later warned others away. Solomon's indiscretions in his old age allowed *Project Apostasy* to gain a foothold once more among the Israelites, a state of affairs that David worked so diligently to avoid. Consequently, God determined to terminate Solomon's rule, not in his day, but in the days of the reign of his son Rehoboam.

Jeroboam

During the reign of Rehoboam, God gave the ten northern tribes to Jeroboam, one of Solomon's generals.

> "And it came to pass at that time when Jeroboam went out of Jerusalem, that the prophet Ahijah the Shilonite found him in the way; and he had clad himself with a new garment; and they two were alone in the field. And Ahijah caught the new garment that was on him, and rent it in twelve pieces: and he said to Jeroboam, Take thee ten pieces: for thus saith the Lord, the God of Israel, Behold, I will rend the kingdom out of the hand of Solomon, and will give ten tribes to thee: (but he shall have one tribe for my servant David's sake, and

for Jerusalem's sake, the city which I have chosen out of all the tribes of Israel:) because they have forsaken Me, and have worshiped Ashtoreth the goddess of the Zidonians, Chemosh the god of the Moabites, and Milcom the god of the children of Ammon, and have not walked in My ways, to do *that which is* right in mine eyes, and *to keep* My statutes and My judgments, as *did* his father. Howbeit I will not take the whole kingdom out of his hand: but I will make him prince all the days of his life for David My servant's sake, whom I chose, because he kept My commandments and My statutes. But I will take the kingdom out of his son's hand, and will give it unto thee, *even* ten tribes. And unto his son will I give one tribe, that David My servant may have a light always before Me in Jerusalem, the city which I have chosen Me to put My name there. And I will take thee, and thou shalt reign according to all that thy soul desireth, and shalt be king over Israel. And it shall be, if thou wilt hearken unto all that I command thee, and wilt walk in My ways, and do *that* (which) is right in My sight, to keep My statutes and My commandments, as David My servant did: that I will be with thee, and build thee a sure house, as I built for David, and will give Israel unto thee" (I Kings 11:29-38).

When Solomon discovered what transpired between Ahijah and Jeroboam, he angrily set out to destroy Jeroboam. Unwittingly, he thought that he could simply nullify the prophecy by killing him. Therefore, it was that "Solomon sought therefore to kill Jeroboam." However, God does not utter vain prophesies. Whatever He proposes to do, He can bring to pass.

> "And Jeroboam arose, and fled into Egypt, unto Shishak king of Egypt, and was in Egypt until the death of Solomon" (I Kings 11:40).

The flight of Jeroboam into Egypt resulted in the furtherance of the downward spiral of the ten-tribed northern kingdom into the depths of the very idolatry that was the height of abomination to God. Jeroboam did not take advantage of the supreme opportunity handed him. He chose instead to listen to Satan.

Rehoboam, the impetuous young son of Solomon received the reigns of government from his father and immediately alienated the feelings of his subjects. Where Solomon taxed Israel heavily in order to carry out his many lavish building projects and add to his vast treasury, Rehoboam laid a more onerous burden upon the people through even heavier taxation. The ten northern tribes rebelled and set up Jeroboam as their king. He had recently returned from Egypt upon learning of Solomon's death.

Fearing that the people would eventually return to the House of David and to Rehoboam as their king, Jeroboam contrived to prevent such an eventuality. He was keenly aware that the Temple in Jerusalem was a strong unifying force to the tribes of Israel. Furthermore, he feared that if he allowed them to attend the Feasts there each year as they always had, he would lose control over them. He decided to split the people off to keep them from going to Jerusalem year after year.

> "And Jeroboam said in his heart, Now shall the kingdom return to the house of David: If this people go up to do sacrifice in the house of the Lord at Jerusalem, then shall the heart of the people turn again unto their Lord, *even* unto Rehoboam king of Judah. Whereupon the king took counsel, and made two calves *of* gold, and said unto them, It is too much for you to go up to Jerusalem: **behold thy gods' O Israel which brought thee up out of the land of Egypt!** (I Kings 12:26-28, emphasis mine).

These are the very words that Aaron spoke to the children of Israel at the foot of Mount Sinai!

Why was Jeroboam afraid? Was it that he simply did not trust in the promises of God, or was it because he had brought back from Egypt a personal belief in all that the Egyptian religion stood for, including a belief in their Trinity of Osiris, Isis, and Horus? Was he perhaps secretly worshipping as the Egyptians worshipped? This seems to be the case for we see that he said in his heart, "then shall the heart of the people turn again unto their Lord . . ."

Kitto says that

> "During his stay (in Egypt) he noted, with a curious eye, the institutions and strange worship of the country which

had been the scene of ancient bondage to his people. It is to be feared that much which met his view, and which could only be abhorrent to a true Israelite, inspired him with no disgust, but on the contrary drew forth his admiration; that he saw much that he deemed worthy of imitation, and that he treasured up what appeared to him to be useful hints, which might be applied when his predicted destinies were fulfilled . . . The visit was ruinous to him by filling his mind with ideas wholly alien to the Hebrew constitution; and the attempt to work out these brought disaster upon his house, and dishonor upon his name" (parenthesis mine).[146]

Evidently, he planned all along to lead the people astray. He obviously persuaded the people through his boldness. They bought into his evil machinations and became enslaved to the sin that he proposed. To continue,

"And he set the one in Beth-el, and the other put he in Dan. And this thing became a sin: for the people went to worship before the one, *even* unto Dan. And he made an house of high places, and made priests of the lowest of the people which were not the sons of Levi. And Jeroboam ordained a feast in the eighth month, on the fifteenth day of the month, like unto the feast that is in Judah, and he offered upon the altar. So did he in Beth-el, sacrificing unto the calves that he had made: And he placed in Beth-el the priests of the high places which he had made. So he offered upon the altar which he had made in Beth-el the fifteenth day of the eighth month, *even* in the month which he had devised of his own heart; and ordained a feast unto the children of Israel: and he offered upon the altar, and burnt incense" (I Kg. 12:29-33).

Because of Jeroboam's sin there followed years of tumultuous upheaval, political intrigue, murders, assassinations, and wicked kings who followed his example. They plunged the northern kingdom even farther into the blasphemous idolatry of the apostate Babylonian religion and its worship of a triune god.

The one true God thundered out His dire warnings repeatedly but Israel would not listen. The stubborn, objurgatory refusal of the Israelites to turn back to the one true God eventually brought about their downfall and swept them into captivity. Thoroughly fed up with their flagrant disregard of His commandments and statutes, God brought swift and sudden retribution at the hands of Shalmaneser. This Assyrian king carried the Israelites captive to the very seat of the pagan, idolatrous system of Baal-worship to which they were so wont to cling.

Carried out in a series of campaigns, the captivity left the land practically devoid of inhabitants. Wild animals began to multiply rapidly and attack the sparse numbers that remained. These appealed to Shalmaneser for help to defend against the ravagings of the wild beasts. The king graciously complied and repopulated the land with the devout disciples of the hated Baal-worship. Samaria subsequently became the capitol of the now defunct northern kingdom. The peoples of the Southern Kingdom gave the peoples of the Assyrian Empire that settled in Samaria, the name Samaritans, an epithet that, in those days, and even in the days of Jesus, carried a vile and despicable a connotation. Devout Jews (Pharisees) of New Testament times hated and maligned these people.

After Nebuchadnezzer, carried her into captivity, a remnant of Judah returned to the land about 70 years later, and their descendents are still there today. There followed a period of about 400 years in which they were ruled over by the Persians, the Ptolemies, the Seleucids, and the Romans. Following the Maccabean revolt, and by the time of Jesus, the Roman Empire was firmly in control and Herod the Great, an Idumean by birth, administered the government in Israel.

Although there is no biblical evidence that Jesus or the Apostles ever taught a Trinitarian Doctrine, by the 4th century A.D., it began to creep into the writings of the early church fathers. In later chapters we will discuss the reasons why such a non-biblical doctrine made its way into Christian literature and how it has led millions to worship an idolatrous Trinity-in-unity.

Chapter 10
CHECK IT OUT!

Why Check It Out?

Mainstream evangelical Christian churches today teach the Trinitarian Doctrine as fact. Scores of well-known evangelists, preachers, and teachers assume that the Godhead is a trinity. Nevertheless, can anyone say with certainty that it is a fact when the Bible does not contain the word "trinity," and there is no all-encompassing statement about the trinity-in-unity that lends validity to the doctrine? No! All one can say with certainty is that it is implied. When something is implied, it is true by indirect indication, or inferred. To imply that something is true without checking the facts is speculation. To say that the Holy Spirit is a "person" because the Bible speaks of the Holy Spirit as demonstrating quasi-personal activities is exegesis of the worst sort. In fact, it is eisegesis; i.e. reading something into the text that is not there. The Roman Catholic Church, the bastion of the Trinitarian Doctrine, categorically states that mainstream evangelicals err when they speak of the Holy Spirit as a person because it "speaks," it "hinders," it "indwells," etc. Says she:

> "When a quasi-personal activity is ascribed to God's Spirit, e.g. speaking, hindering, dwelling (**Acts 8:29; 16:7; Rom. 8:9**), one is not justified in concluding immediately that in these passages God's Spirit is regarded as a person; the same expressions are used in regard to rhetorically personified things or abstract ideas (see **Rom. 6:6; 7:17**). Thus the context of the phrase 'blasphemy against the Spirit' (**Mt.**

12:31; cf. Mt. 12:28; Lk. 11:20) shows that reference is being made to the power of God"[147]

Even in light of this plain, matter-of-fact statement, the Roman Catholic Church ignores her own teaching and accepts the trinity-in-unity as fact. Mainstream evangelical Christianity follows her lead, like it or not. Therefore, a discussion of the Trinitarian doctrine is pertinent to our understanding of what follows in the succeeding chapters. We need to know if the trinity-in-unity is valid within the religious structure that we call Christianity.

Now that we have seen the ancient historical origins of the apostasy, and the Trinitarian Doctrine and its effects upon the God's chosen nation Israel, let's take a look at how can go about evaluating the doctrine itself.

A discussion of the art of evaluating a doctrine is pertinent to our understanding of what follows in the succeeding chapters, so that we may know if the Trinitarian Doctrine has any validity within the religious structure we call Christianity.

What Is A Doctrine?

What is a "doctrine?" This is a question that all of us should ask ourselves from time to time in order to make sure that the minister or teacher is teaching God's truth. Unfortunately, too many of us do not take the time to check things out. Therein lies the reason behind the multitude of religious beliefs extant within Christianity today. Because the many lethargically accept the blandishments of modern day "prophets" and self proclaimed "ministers" of God, they go astray, leaning to fables and belief systems that are diametrically opposed to God's teachings. They are "... carried about by every wind of doctrine, by the sleight of men, *and* cunning craftiness, whereby they (false ministers and prophets) lie in wait to deceive . . ." (Eph. 14:4).Too many accept a doctrine as truth when it is nothing but a mish-mash of truth and error cleverly disguised as the truth. A doctrine, however, is not necessarily a rigid, unyielding, dogmatic espousal of truth.

A doctrine, in its most basic of terms, is simply a teaching. Thus, it is "Something that is taught . . . [from the Latin doctrine, teaching, learning, etc.], (*The American Heritage Dictionary*, New College Edition, 1976). It naturally follows that where there is a doctrine there is a teacher. After exhaustive research and considerable thought, if that teacher arrives at an incorrect conclusion, his doctrine or teaching is wrong! Therefore, it is up to the reader or listener to discover the truth or error of the teacher's teaching.

The average would be Christian might walk into a local bookstore-paraphernalia-trinket house, pull a book about the Holy Spirit off the shelf, go home, plop down in an easy chair, and without the Bible and the Holy Spirit as his guides, suck up an ocean of endlessly recycled spiritual-sounding drivel about the "personhood" of the Spirit and its place in the Godhead as the third member of the Trinity. However, before he accepts what he reads in a book or hears from the pulpit, he should take copious notes, ask God for understanding, and carefully study every single point the author or preacher makes. He should then compare it to what the Bible has to say on the subject—not what he *thinks* the Bible has to say—but what it actually says. Before he accepts any doctrine, he needs to check it out! But how does he do that? If he listens to the inveiglements of some of the established Christian theologians concerning the Trinitarian Doctrine, he can't, for:

> "The true understanding of the personality of the Holy Spirit is covered by so many layers of ignorance, indifference, and prejudice, that it would take a prolonged effort to scrape them off and cast them away" [148]

Could it be that it is futile to try to understand the "mystery" of the Holy Trinity? Are the ignorance, the indifference, and the prejudice so deep, so ingrained in our minds, that no one can clear it away in a lifetime of study and effort? Is the only way to be at peace with explaining and illustrating the Holy Trinity, to just accept it on "faith," and be done with it? God forbid!

Much of evangelical Christianity feels strongly about the faith issue for it will not put forth the prolonged effort needed to put the matter to rest. It seems ever reluctant to attempt to apply the scraper and "scrape away and cast off" these onerous layers of misunderstanding. It is afraid of what it might find at the bottom! Therefore, it waxes content with remaining ignorant, indifferent, and prejudiced when it comes to unraveling the so-called mystery of the Holy Trinity.

There is a way to clear the air, to know the truth, once and forever. Follow the principles outlined below and They will lead you to the truth about the Trinitarian Doctrine, or any doctrine you care to tackle. Remember this—**healthy skepticism is no sin!** Do not be gullible! **Prove** whether the teacher, preacher, evangelist, or author is telling you the truth. The last thing you should ever want to do when it comes to your personal salvation is buy his arguments and his doctrines just because he says it is so!

Search The Scriptures!

Search the Scriptures like the Bereans did (Acts 17:11). Simply looking up isolated Scriptures may not be enough. One must look up every scripture associated with the subject under study. This is how the converted mind must study the Bible, but without the Holy Spirit, one cannot even understand it this way. This is the very reason why so many say, "I read and read, but I just can't seem to understand the Bible." It is also the reason why so many are, "Ever learning, and never able to come to the knowledge of the truth" (II Tim. 3:7).

There is one church in America that uses the example in Isaiah 28:9-13 as the biblical example of how to study the scriptures. However, close examination of these verses reveals that God did not give them as a model for studying the scriptures. Verse 7 states that the religious leaders of Israel were teaching the people lies and profaning the judgments of God because they were getting drunk. God is mocking Ephraim because they listened to the words of the pagans instead of Him. He told them how they should worship Him but they would not listen. He mocks them because through their teachings they mimicked the prophets as though they were teaching little children in a school.

The Ephraimites were deeply involved in idolatry and God says in verse 13 that their power would eventually be broken, that teachings of the pagans would eventually entrap them. The result would be that they would become the captives of foreign nations because they had listened to the babblings of the pagans instead of the truth of God.

In Matthew 13:10 and Mark 4:11-12, we see that because the Israelites were still listening to the babblings of the pagans, God did not want them to understand His word. Consequently, Christ spoke to them in parables. However, they wanted to interpret God's word their way. They would not listen to Jesus, just as the majority of people do today.

The Bible reveals much of God's truth only by searching thoroughly back and forth in it. Many do not understand this principle and so cannot come to a right knowledge of God's word. The disobedient who refute God's word and refuse to accept the truth, continue resolutely to follow the traditions of men.

The Bible was not written to be studied only chapter-by-chapter, section-by-section, or book by book. You cannot come to a full understanding of God's word by studying it only this way. You must understand the principle given here! You must look up every verse dealing with the subject under study, evaluate them within context, analyze them, and most importantly, ask for God's help in understanding them. Then, and only then will you get the true, overall picture of what God is telling you.

Extra-Biblical Sources

Should we use extra-biblical sources? We should make ample use of these, but do not use them of and by themselves to establish doctrine. However, you need a broader knowledge from extra-biblical sources such as encyclopedias, dictionaries, and concordances or you will not know the historical background. If you do not know the historical background, you cannot know the circumstances surrounding the writing of the Biblical text. The historical aspects have an important bearing on what the Scripture means. You must read the Bible consistently to gain a broader knowledge of what is going on.

Word Studies

It is essential that you do word studies on your own. Either purchase, or go to the library and use such helps as *Strong's Exhaustive Concordance*, *The Englishman's Greek Concordance*, Bible dictionaries, lexicons, etc.

Here is an example of what you might find. In Ephesians 2:15 it says, "Having abolished in His flesh the enmity, *even* the law of commandments contained in ordinances . . ." The word "abolished" used here is the Greek *kartageo*, and means—to abolish, destroy, make of no effect, to make void, etc. This same word is found in Luke 13:7 where it is translated "cumbereth." If you insert the word abolish here it does not make sense for it would read, "... why abolish it the ground?" However, upon further investigation you will find that *kartageo* can also mean—to cumber, i.e. burden the ground. This is a much more sensible rendering within the context.

What Does The Scripture Say?

Having determined the correct word usage, you must now ask yourself—"what does the Scripture say"? An example often given as "proof" of the Holy Trinity is Genesis 1:26. It reads, "Then God said, 'Let **Us** make man in **Our** image, after **Our** likeness...'"

This scripture does not say that God is plural in nature or even hint at a trinity. The words "us" and "our" do not necessarily mean that God was talking to himself or Jesus and the Holy Spirit as "persons" of a Trinity. He could have been talking to His council of Elders or his angels. The word (God) used here, is the Hebrew *Elohim*, which when applied to the One God is the plural of majesty. It does not mean that there is more than one God in the Godhead! To say that God, as presented here, is a trinity, or that it implies a definite number in the Godhead, such as three, is speculative theological nonsense! Any Jewish or Hebrew scholar will tell you that the Old Testament holds no such concept as a triune God. Isaac Asimov, voicing the same opinion, has stated:

> "To Christians, who consider God to be a trinity of three co-equal aspects— Father, Son, and Holy Spirit—the 'let us' (Gen. 1:26) might be viewed as the three aspects of the trinity communing among themselves. This is an interesting thought, which would explain the verse neatly, but **there is no sign anywhere in the Old Testament that the Jews accepted the notion of a trinity**" (emphasis mine).[149]

Therefore, the scripture does not say that God is a trinity—unless one views it subjectively, i.e. from the presupposition that the Holy Spirit is a person!

What Does The Scripture Mean?

Now that you have determined what the scripture does or does not say, you need to ask yourself —"What does the scripture mean?" As an example, let us look at Luke 1:35, another verse that Trinitarians use as evidence of the Holy Trinity.

The angel Gabriel came to Mary and said to her, "... The Holy Ghost shall come upon thee, and the power of the Highest shall overshadow thee. . ." The key to the meaning of this verse is the little word "and." The Greek word here is *kai*. Strong says that it is "apparently a primary article having *a copulative and sometimes also a cumulative force*; and, also, even, so, then, too, etc." The translators used it here in the **copulative sense**, i.e. of joining two actions. It appears, then, that two things occurred: (1) The Holy Spirit came upon Mary, and (2) The power of God overshadowed her.

The intent of the translators was to show that the Holy Spirit, as the third member of the Trinity, came upon Mary and through "His" power, impregnated her. To translate it any other way would have been treasonous. King James was a devout Trinitarian. However, should they have translated in the copulative sense?

Let us return to the reference cited earlier from Eph.2:15. Once again, it reads, "Having abolished in His flesh the enmity, *even* the law of commandments contained in ordinances ..." The Bible uses the same Greek word *kai* here, but in the **cumulative sense**, i.e. to intensify instead of to join. In this example, the meaning is quite clear. The "enmity" and "the law of commandments contained in ordinances" mean the same thing.

Now, if the Holy Spirit and the power of God were not the same, i.e. if the Holy Spirit *is* the third person of the Trinity, then God apparently sent the Holy Spirit to rest upon Mary, and then, using the Holy Spirit as an instrument of transference, caused His power to overshadow her. Thus, to use the word *kai* in the copulative sense is entirely correct.

If, however, we substitute the word "even," i.e. *kai* is used in the **cumulative sense** as in Eph. 2:15, no distinction between the **Holy Spirit** and the **Power of God** is indicated. The effect then becomes one of intensification rather than connection, and **The Holy Spirit and the Power of God are the same!**

There are two other words in the text that deserve close study— "power" and "overshadow". The word "power" is the Greek *dunamis* (from which we get our word dynamite), and means *miraculous power*. The word "overshadow" is the Greek *episkiazo* and means—to envelope or invest with **preternatural** (miraculous or superhuman) **influence**. In both cases, the text designates a **power** or **force**.

Nevertheless, what does the text say about the Holy Spirit? The Greek word *pneuma* is used, and in every case, it is neuter in gender! Putting all this together and using the cumulative sense of the word *kai*, we would have—"The Holy Spirit (pneuma) will come upon you, **even** the (miraculous) power of the Highest will overshadow (invest) you (with miraculous or superhuman influence). In light of this, the **Holy Spirit** and the **Power of God** are indistinct, inseparable, and the same! The overshadowing consisted of an influence, a **power**, not a person! The coming of the Holy Spirit upon Mary, the investing of a superhuman influence was nothing more, or nothing less than God's creative **force** or **power**, which He calls His **Holy Spirit**. God used the same **power** to create the universe, and Jesus performed miracles by it! There is no Trinity indicated here!

List And Evaluate Scriptural References In Context!

As you do this, ask yourself—is this scriptural reference essential to the argument? If it is, circle it. After you have done this, determine which translation is the best translation available for these verses. After reading several translations, determine how much variation there is among translators. If there is a significant variation, it will be because there is a certain amount of obscurity associated with the text. If you find that the translators always expresses the same thought , that part of the scripture really belongs there with few exceptions.

Is The Doctrine Oversimplified?

A good example of oversimplification pertaining to the Trinitarian Doctrine is that the Holy Spirit is a person simply because Jesus and the authors of the New Testament personify it. The idea is that since they refer to the Holy Spirit in the masculine gender, it **must** be a "person." However, we have already pointed out that in every case in the New Testament the word translated *Spirit* is the Greek word *pneuma*, and is neuter in gender!

Simply appending a personal pronoun to a word or thing that does not possess gender does not automatically invest it with a personality. We Americans say of a ship or an airplane—"She's a beauty," or of our country—"I really love her" or we call her our "Motherland." We even give hurricanes feminine or masculine names. None of these things has inherent personalities *per se*. We ascribe personalities to them when we anthropomorphize or personify them.

This is what the writers of the New Testament did by attaching the masculine pronoun to the Holy Spirit. However, they could just as well have attached the feminine pronoun. Why they did not do so? To choose the feminine pronoun would have led to the idolatrous dictums of Theosophical Doctrine. Theosophy is the doctrinal belief of such sects as Buddhism, Taoism, Hinduism, etc. These ancient religions invariably embraced and taught a Trinitarian concept, which included a feminine element in the Godhead. In light of this, the Trinity would have been two parts masculine and one part feminine. This is exactly what we have encountered in the Babylonian and Egyptian ideas of the Trinity.

Nevertheless, why is it always rendered as a masculine Spirit? Why did they personify it at all? The answer is very simple. Scripture always presents God the Father as being masculine. Now God *is* a Spirit, that is, He is composed of spirit essence, which has inherent, eternal life. God is also holy. Therefore, can we not call Him *The* Holy Spirit? Of course, we can! Logically, then, every manifestation of the Holy Spirit (He speaks, He intercedes, He testifies, He commands, He leads, He guides, He appoints, etc.) is not that of a separate person, but is **the creative, sustaining, miraculous force and power of the One True God** endowed with the very personality of God Himself. The term Holy Spirit describes, and is, the very personality, nature and character of Almighty God manifested in our lives. It gives us the **power** to become Godlike, to qualify to become the very sons of God and heirs with Jesus Christ of all that is!

G.H. Pember says of the personification of the Holy Spirit:

> "... on turning to the New Testament, we find, whereas the Greek expression for the Spirit ... is neuter, yet whenever, to emphasize his personality, the gender of a connected pronoun is changed, the pronoun becomes masculine (John 16:13-14). Again, the adjective (*parakletos*) is sometimes used substantively (independent in existence or function; not subordinate), and applied to the Holy Spirit as the Comforter: in such a case it is invariably found in the

masculine gender, although, grammatically, it might just as well have been made feminine -- John 14:16, 26; 15:26; 16:7" [150]

Trinitarians base this personification, the doctrine that the Holy Spirit is a person, on a technicality. Technicalities cannot be the bases of doctrines. One must base doctrines upon sound, well-grounded theology, and upon sound use of Scripture. They have to relate consistently to other doctrines. They must fit like a piece of precision machinery without being forced. There is no way that you can accept the idea of a Trinity without forcing it.

What Are The Presuppositions–Assumptions–Philosophies Underlying This Concept?

Does the author state his presuppositions and assumptions? If he does not, where is he coming from? Catholics and Protestants cannot find anything wrong with the Trinitarian Doctrine because of what they have always been taught and accepted without question. The assumption is automatic that their preachers and teachers are correct. When you accept this, the most reasonable, intelligent, and rational interpretation of the Scriptures is Roman Catholic (whether you are Catholic or Protestant), for it is out of Catholicism that the modern concept of the Holy Trinity is derived.

If you do not know what the presuppositions and assumptions are, or what the overall philosophy is, you will probably miss something. You will not know where the author, preacher, or teacher is going with his doctrine. It is not something that simply hangs in midair, but is a living, active thing that has direction. It will go where it goes with or without you. You must be the one who decides which direction you will go.

Is The Doctrine Rational–Does It Make Sense?

God is rational; He is not the author of confusion! You must believe that the truth will eventually make sense. Here is a good example. Has the Holy Spirit, as the third "person" of the Trinity always existed, or did God create it as He created the angels? If it was present as a "person" in the beginning, why is this not revealed in the only two accounts of the beginning in the Bible (Gen.1:1, John 1:1-3)?

It is strange, for it was by the **power** of the Holy Spirit that God the Father did the creating. These two accounts do not say that the Holy Spirit, as a separate, distinct person, did the creating. John 1:1-3 says that God did the creating. The means employed, the Holy Spirit, was none other than the **creative-force, power, and divine authority** of God the Father.

Listen To Your Heart or Gut-Feeling

We talk about intuition, but what is it? Intuition is the accumulation of all past experiences. Use this intuition in matters of doctrine. Let your conscience be your guide. If your conscience tells you something is wrong with the idea behind a doctrine, give it the benefit of the doubt. It just may be the urging of the Holy Spirit working with your spirit (I Cor. 2:11) to guide you toward the truth.

If you can accept the Holy Spirit as a **power, a force, or a supernatural, miraculous influence** rather than a "person," you will be accepting the truth, and you shouldn't get hurt by it. It hurts only those who hate the truth!

Chapter 11
THE MAGIAN LEGACY

No one can write a history of the Christian era without including the Church of Rome. However, most writers of the development of Christianity following apostolic times are unaware that when they speak of the Roman Catholic Church, they are not speaking of the true Christian Church.

The Roman Catholic Church, because of what it became about 400 years after the death of Christ, is not the Church of God! No matter how authentic its beginnings may have been the nefarious doctrines of the Babylonian Mysteries rapidly corrupted whatever truth the Catholic Church may have retained. It became a syncretistic amalgamation of orthodox Christian teachings, and near eastern dogma (Gnosticism) that has since been a curse to all that have been deluded and deceived by its spiritual darkness.

Anyone who has read a history of Roman Catholicism and especially a history of the Papacy (such as Malichi Martin's *The Decline and Fall of the Roman Church*); can readily see that this is no Christian church! She is not, and never was what God intended His church to be. From the moment that the Catholic Church established herself in Rome, she has been thoroughly Babylonian. She has ever been a church which has made men "twofold more the children of hell" instead of sanctifying them as God's Church was commissioned to do.

Despite her atrocities, and in the face of all that she has done in the name of religion to gain power over the lives of men, she still has the temerity to call herself "holy"! In God's eyes, she is a cup full of abominations! Boettner says of her that:

> "She applies to herself the term 'holy', but the fact is that through the ages and in her official capacity the Roman Church has been guilty of the most atrocious crimes, practiced in the name of religion, including murder, robbery, persecution of all kinds, bribery, fraud, deception, and practically every other crime known to man" [151]

We see the first satanic flickerings of her beginnings around 36 A.D. in the person of one Simon the Magus. However, before we learn of him, it is important that we know what a "Magus" is, and how the "Magi" have influenced religion, and Christianity in particular, through the ages.

The Magi were a caste of priests established by Nimrod. They were in power and politically active in Babylon, and particularly in Ur of the Chaldees, during the time of Abraham. These Magi gave rise to the Universal or Catholic Church, and we can trace her earliest origins back to a time prior to the Noachian Flood. The grand design upon which Satan built her was the evil conspiracy masterminded by the arch-deceiver himself. His aim was the insidious corruption of God's Church (read Acts 8).

The Rab-Mag

The first place in the Bible that mentions a part of the word Magus is Jer. 39:3.

> "And all the princes of the king of Babylon came in, and sat in the middle gate, *even* Nergal-sharezer, Samgar-nebo, Sarsechim, Rab-saris, Nergal-sharezer, Rab-mag, with all the residue of the princes of the king of Babylon."

What is the meaning of the term "Rab-mag?" The *ISBE* states:

> "The word is a compound, the two parts seemingly being in apposition and signifying tautologically the same thing. The last syllable or section of the word, *magh*, was the designation among the Medes, Persians, and Babylonians for priests and wise men. Its original significance was 'great' or 'powerful'...The first syllable, *rabh*, expresses practically the same idea, that of greatness, or abundance in size, quantity, or power.

Thus it might be interpreted the 'all-wise' or 'all-powerful' prince, the chief magician or physician. It is, therefore, a title and not a name, and is accordingly put in appositive relations to the proper name just preceding, as 'Nergal-sharezer, the Rab-mag,' translated fully, 'Nergal-sharezer the chief prince or magician.'

"In harmony with the commonly accepted view, the proper rendering of the text should be, 'All the princes of the king of Babylon came in, and sat in the middle gate, to wit, Nergal-sharezer, Samgar-nebo, Sarsechim, [the] Rab-saris, Nergal-sharezer, [the] Rab-mag . . .'" [152]

The *Companion Bible*, in a footnote to Jer. 39:3, says that:

"Nergal-sharezer, Rab-mag = Nergal-sharezer, chief of the physicians (or magi). Only four names of persons in this verse, not six" [153]

Jeremiah depicts a time of military occupation by the Chaldeans. They forced their way into Jerusalem from the north side and established a position opposite the middle gate, the gate that occupied the middle wall between the upper and lower city.

Nergal-sharezer and *Samgar-nebo* are proper names formed from the Chaldean idols Nergal and Nebo (II Kings 17:30; Isa.46:51). *Rab-saris* means, "Chief of the eunuchs." *Rab-mag* is the "chief of the magi." He accompanied the expedition in order that its leaders might know their fate beforehand through his astrological skill. The term *Mag* is Persian and means "great," or "powerful." The magi were a priestly caste among the Medes. They supported the Zoroastrian religion.

Kitto says that there were four classes of Babylonian adepts—the magicians, the astrologers, the sorcerers, and the Chaldeans. It is not certain to which of these the Magi belonged, but the opinion of most is that they were either of the magicians or the Chaldeans. Of the last of these, he writes:

"This is the only one of these orders which can be recognized in the Assyrian sculptures, from the peculiar dress of the functionary, and from the distinctive offices in which he is seen to be engaged, which show that he was certainly a priest, and therefore a magician or a diviner of one of the classes mentioned here; for it is known that in other countries, and eminently in this, the priests were also diviners" [154]

It is in this official capacity that we find Daniel after Nebuchadnezzar takes him captive to Babylon. However, referring once again to Jeremiah we read that:

"A sword *is* upon the Chaldeans, saith the Lord, and upon the inhabitants of Babylon, and upon her princes, and upon her wise *men*" (Jer. 50:35).

The word "princes" here is the Hebrew *saw* (Strong 8269) and means—a head person of any rank or class, captain (that had rule), chief (captain), etc. We see this word in the title *Rab-saw-is*. By extension, we see only two classes of people spoken of in Jer. 50:35: (1) the citizens of Babylon, and (2) the Chaldeans, princes, and wise men, all of whom are the same class. The Chaldeans were a special class of Babylonians, the Magi. They became so common that whenever the book of Daniel mentions them, it is talking about this special class of priests, not merely the citizens of Babylon.

The Magi

It is axiomatic that when one nation conquers another, the government changes form, and the society may bow to the whims of the conquerors, but the religion does not. In almost every case, the religion of the vanquished state conquers the conquerors.

When the Medo-Persian Empire came to power, Magianism became extremely popular. The great Magian teacher Zarathrusta, or Zoroaster as the Greeks knew him, concocted a religion which featured a great conflict between the forces of good and evil. According to Herodotus, he was contemporary with Hystaspis or his father, but other sources place him anywhere from 600-1000 B.C. Nevertheless, he completely reformed the Persian religion. The Magi are said to owe to Zoroaster their monopoly of priestly functions because they were his own "tribe." The principle deity worshiped by the Zoroastrians was Ahura-Mazda. Thus, Mazdeism became an alternate name for Zoroastrianism. By any name, it was an active, proselytizing, missionary religion, which was always ready to form a syncretism with any other system. Easton, in his article on Zoroastrianism in the *ISBE*, says:

> "As a matter of fact, after Israel's contact with Persia the following elements, all known to Mazdeism, appear, and apparently for the first time: (1) a formal angelology, with six or (seven) archangels at the head of the developed hierarchy; (2) these angels are not mere companions of God, but His intermediaries, established (often) over special domains; (3) in the philosophical religion a corresponding doctrine of hypostases; (4) as a result, a remoter conception of God; (5) a developed demonology; (6) the conception of a supreme head (Satan) over the powers of evil; (7) the doctrine of immortality; (8) rewards or punishment for the soul immediately after death; (9) a schematic eschatology, esp. as regards chronological systems; (10) a super-human Messiah; (11) bodily resurrection; (12) a rationalized, legalistic conception of God's moral demands." [155]

In many of the so-called Christian denominations extant today we see much of what was called Mazdeism, q.v. 1, 2, 5, 6, 7, 8, 10, and 11. Of course, there has always been among the Israelites a belief concerning angels, demons, bodily resurrection, and a rationalized, legalistic conception of God's moral demands.

Moreover, what is the teaching of Protestantism today? Why, just what Zoroastrianism espoused —The Great Conflict! According to most of Christianity so-called there is a great battle going on between God and Satan for the possession of men's souls. In addition, the soul, regardless of where it goes after death, lives on eternally either basking in the sublime presence of God, or suffering in hell fire forever, crackling, spitting, boiling, bubbling, and writhing in excruciating agony, but never burning up. Thus the soul is pictured as being immortal, a doctrine that the Bible never espouses (see Ezek. 18:4, 20). Burning in hell fire forever, while never being consumed is not death, but eternal life albeit agonizing. Death is the complete cessation of life both physically and spiritually. Moreover, who do the Protestants follow in these doctrines? Why, the Roman Catholic Church of course—like it or not! The concept of the immortality of the soul did not come from the Bible, but, as we have readily seen, from ancient Babylon! Satan was no less intelligent back then than he is today. He designed Roman Catholicism so that even today it bears an incredible resemblance to Zoroastrianism, or Magianism.

The Magian system originally rebelled violently against Zoroastrianism after the fall of Babylon, but later incorporated its doctrines and began to revere Zoroaster as a great teacher. While Satan is the great mastermind behind the whole system, Zoroaster became the driving force behind Magianism, and ultimately Simon the Magus and the Roman Catholic Church. Tradition says that Simon was a student of Zoroaster and a member of the priesthood of a mystery religion. He was not only a magician and a sorcerer, but also, perhaps, an astrologer. He was the pawn, as was Nimrod, in a great global conspiracy by Satan and his demons to overthrow, destroy, thwart, and prevent the plan of God from working out on time. As the 8th chapter of Acts introduces Simon the Magus, we are witnessing the first shadowy beginnings of the Roman Catholic Church.

The Mysteries took control of God's church from within. History traces the big, organized church, which became the church of Satan the Devil, back to a time prior to the Noachian Flood. The grand design upon which Satan built her was the evil conspiracy (Project Apostasy) master-minded by the arch-deceiver himself. His aim was the insidious corruption of God's Church (read Acts 8).

Simon the Magus

Perhaps the most renowned of the Samaritans during apostolic times was a devoutly religious man named Simon. We know little of his life except that he was born at Gitton, a small village in Samaria and educated in Egypt. Schooled at Alexandria, he learned the scientific and religious lore of the Egyptians, becoming adept in the black magic of the Mysteries. The Samaritans knew him as a sorcerer with a great following. So adept was he at his trade that he was thought of as being "the great power of God" (Acts 8:10). All of the people of Samaria listened to his teachings because he had bewitched them for so long a time.

Then Philip, an evangelist and a man of God appeared on the scene (probably the city of Shechem or Sychar, as Kitto maintains. It was the chief seat of the Samaritans, not the city of Samaria), preaching the Kingdom of God and persuading many of the truth of Christ. So great were his powers of persuasion against the Babylonian system that the Samaritans believed and were baptized. Kitto says that:

> "Among these converts was a man who had before been held in high reverence by the people of the place. His name was Simon; and he is described as one of those men, partly philosopher and partly charlatan, of whom there were many in that age, who pretended to have, and perhaps deluded themselves into the belief that they actually had, a special intercourse with the hidden spiritual world; and who, either by aid of the powers of darkness, were enabled to work real wonders in support of their pretensions, or by their acquaintance with the secrets of natural science now familiar to us, but then known only to adepts, were enabled to produce effects which astonished the uninstructed..."[156]

Philip so impressed Simon by his abilities that Simon fell in with him, and for some time, continued with him. He learned all that he could about his newly found religion. It was patently obvious to Simon that the validity of Philip's preaching and miracle-working powers were far above his own. Consequently, he abandoned his sorceries for the time being in favor of the higher and nobler teachings of Philip concerning Christ.

Simon possessed considerable powers of his own, but he could not heal the sick and the dying or restore strength and health to the lame and helpless. Philip could do these things and Simon immediately developed a desire to possess such powers. He seems to have thought that he could strengthen his influence upon the people by adhering to the new cause rather than being hostile to it.

He introduced himself to Philip, professed a belief in Christ, and Philip baptized him. We can never be sure whether his belief was sincere or feigned. It is apparent that he was not spiritually converted. However, there is evidence that his historical belief in what Philip taught was very strong. Regardless, he expected to be able to gain possession of the same powers that Philip displayed by attaching himself to the unsuspecting evangelist.

The Birth of Simony

Simon was a master deceiver, and it seemed to Philip and his retinue that God had truly converted him. However, as Kitto maintains, and as the biblical account illustrates, this simply was not the case. When Peter arrived in Samaria to lay hands on the people that Philip had previously baptized, that they might receive the Holy Spirit, he immediately discerned in Simon an ungodly spirit. Peter refused to lay hands on Simon, but he could not so easily dismiss the magician. Simon offered Peter money and asked him to grant him the power of the laying on of hands. Peter refused his money and pronounced a curse upon him.

Take Your Money. . .

Many have misunderstood and concluded that Peter's anger and refusal stemmed simply from the offer of the money for the gift of the Holy Spirit, the **Power of God** to bring men to salvation. Such was not the case. The offering of the money was not the vital issue. Such a thing was common practice among the Samaritans of Simon's day, and later, among the Roman Catholics. Later Christian scholars named it "Simony" after the Biblical example.

The real issue was the "gall of bitterness" and the "bond of iniquity" which Peter perceived in Simon. Peter knew immediately that Simon had neither truly repented nor been truly converted. He recognized that Simon desired the **power** for his own self-centered, egotistical, illegal, and unethical monetary gain. Simon was already charging his followers for his sorceries, and receiving a lucrative income. His "gall of bitterness" resulted because of the works of Philip and Peter caused him to lose his business. His "bond of iniquity" was simply that he had not given up his beliefs in the works of the Mysteries.

When he tried to purchase the **power and authority of God** demonstrated through Peter by the laying on of hands, Peter simply told him to take his money and go to hell with it for thinking he could buy the gift of the Holy Spirit (J.B. Phillips translation). From that day forward, Simon became Peter's bitter enemy. Christianity became the means by which he would continue to spread his corrupt and degrading brand of idolatrous religion (q.v. the Babylonian Mysteries and its blasphemous Trinitarian Doctrine). The simple-minded truthfulness of the Galilean fisherman broke his proud spirit.

The Birth of the Roman Catholic Church

Following his unsuccessful encounter with Peter, Simon reverted quickly to his former beliefs and practices. Apparently, he founded his own brand of "Christianity," and his own church, which consisted of a blasphemous mixture of what Christian doctrine he had learned from Philip, and the doctrines of Baal worship he had learned in Egypt. He led the people into idolatry in much the same way that Semiramis did after Shem had turned their hearts back to God following the death of Nimrod. He came to be considered the "Patriarch of Heretics." Eusebius says that:

> "Simon . . . we have understood to have taken the lead in all heresy; from whom also, down to the present time, those that followed his heresy, still affected the modest philosophy of the Christians, so celebrated for purity of life among all. From this, however, they appeared again to depart, and again embrace the superstitions of idols, falling down before the pictures and statues of this selfsame Simon . . ." [157]

Where did Simon establish his church? Did he remain in Samaria, or did circumstances force him to go elsewhere? Indications are that it was the latter. With the apostles teaching and working throughout the land of Samaria, Simon's syncretistic religion may not have been able to maintain a foothold. However, there was certainly one place where it would have been most welcome—Rome. Again, we read in Eusebius that:

> ". . . the enemy of salvation devising some sort of scheme of seizing upon the imperial city for himself, brought thither Simon . . . Coming to the aid of his insidious artifices, he attached many of the inhabitants of Rome to himself, in order to deceive them . . . Justin writes (to Antonine), 'and after the ascension of our Lord into heaven, certain men were suborned by demons as their agents, who said they were gods . . . Simon, a certain Samaritan . . . was one of the number, who, in the reign of Claudius Cesar, performed many magic rites by the operation of demons, was considered a god, in your imperial city of Rome, and was honored by you with

a statue as a god, in the river Tiber, (on an island) between the two bridges, having the inscription in Latin, *Simoni Deo Sancto*, which is, To Simon the Holy God; and nearly all the Samaritans . . . worship him, confessing him as the Supreme God'" [158]

By what name did the people of the city of Rome know Simon? Was it by the title "Simon the Magus"? This is not likely! Satan continued to run true to course. Even as he presents himself as angel of light, so did Simon. He took the name "Peter." Was there a better way to attach himself to the Christian community there than to appropriate the very name of one of the chiefest of the apostles? After all, the Christians at Rome had never seen Peter, and Simon, for all they knew, was the real thing. Hislop says that:

". . . it can be shown to be by no means doubtful that before the Christian era, and downwards, there *was* a 'Peter' at Rome, who occupied the highest place in the *Pagan* priesthood. The priest who explained the Mysteries to the initiated was sometimes called by the Greek term, the Hierophant; his title was 'Peter'—i.e. 'the interpreter' [159]

As the first "Peter" of what was to become the Roman Catholic Church, Simon was also the first "Pope." These words in the Chaldean mean, "opener of secrets," an epithet equally applied to Nimrod. Elaine Pagels, quoting Irenaeus, an early church father, concerning the two sources of tradition about the apostolic succession, says:

". . . one of these derives from God . . . The other comes from Satan—and goes back to the Gnostic teacher Simon Magus (literally, magician), Peter's archenemy."[160]

Besides setting himself up as the first Pope, Simon evidently declared himself to be God incarnate and Messiah to his followers. Had he not learned of the death and resurrection of Jesus from Philip, he most likely would not have had the temerity to attempt to duplicate them. Hippolytus says that he had himself buried alive at his own request, confident that he would rise on the third day. This ill-fated venture ended in failure. According to Kitto:

"It appears ... that ... when he had digested his views into something of a system, he claimed to be nothing less than the incarnate God, and as such became an object of worship to his followers. His deity consisted of certain Aeons, or persons, all of which, collectively and severally, he declared to be manifested in himself. Hence he professed to appear as the Father in respect to the Samaritans, as the Son in respect to the Jews, and as the Holy Ghost in respect to all other religions; but that it was indifferent to him by which of these names he was called. According to Jerome, he declared of himself: 'I am the Word of God; I am the perfection of God; I am the Comforter; I am the Almighty; I am the whole essence of God.' He ... did not require purity of life; but taught that actions were in themselves indifferent, and that the distinction of actions as good or evil was a delusion taught by the angels to bring men into subjection.[161]

We see in these pronouncements the basic elements of the Trinity; the Father, Son, and the Holy Spirit as being incarnated in one "person," of the same essence and homogeneous. As we have already seen, this is an espousal of the doctrine, which originated in the Babylonian Mystery Religion. A part of Satan's grand design, it is not a part of God's design for mankind in the scheme of things. It is a prevarication meant only to delude and mislead men down the pathway to destruction. But the Trinitarian Doctrine has persisted through the vehicle of the Holy Roman Catholic Church until today it is embraced not only by her but also by her daughters, the myriad denominations that came out of her in protest, but who still adhere to so many of her errant doctrines. However, the world will know the truth, and God will be triumphant over the powers of darkness that hold men in their sway. Satan's time grows ever shorter and God will expose his deceptive plan for what it is.

Chapter 12
THE ROMAN LEGACY

The Holy Trinity, as understood by the Universal Church, and taught by them as an infallible doctrine, is supposed to have been around since the days of the apostles. Cornelius J. Hagerty says that:

> "The same discipline which today requires missionaries to teach the Trinity has been in force from the days of the apostles. Without faith in the Trinity no one can be regarded as a Christian"[162]

Mr. Hagerty is correct! The Trinitarian Doctrine *has* been in force since the days of the apostles. It has also been in force since the days of Nimrod and Semiramis and the establishment of the Babylonian Mysteries! However, neither of these facts explicitly implies, nor are they proof that Jesus or the original apostles ever taught the Trinitarian doctrine. Mr. Hagerty is misleading by innuendo. In fact, he contradicts himself when he states that:

> "The use of the term God to apply indifferently to any one of the three persons, or to all of them, or to the three as if the one nature subsisted absolutely, **did not develop during the life of the apostles**, or early (Catholic) fathers, but after the Council of Nicea [325 A.D.] (Parenthesis, and emphasis mine).[163]

Despite this, Mr. Hagerty asserts dogmatically that, "without faith in the Trinity no one can be regarded as a Christian." What else can we expect him to say? To claim otherwise would brand him an infidel in the eyes of the Church and the great religious system, which he serves. He further asserts that to be a Catholic, and a Catholic theologian (as he himself is), and not to be devoted to a belief in the Trinity, is heretical. He declares:

> ". . . whether they realize it or not, devotion to the Trinity is the center of **Catholic** life" (emphasis mine).[164]

If what Mr. Hagerty implies is true, where is the proof? If the apostles preached a Trinitarian Doctrine, they must have received it from Jesus. If they received it from Jesus, he must have taught it not only to the original apostles, but to His disciples and the masses as well! How could He not have done so concerning so important a doctrine? However, we find that Jesus never spoke to the masses except in parables. Why did he speak to them only in parables? In his own words, he did it in order to hide the meaning of what He was saying (Mat. 13:10-11). If the Godhead is a Trinity, Jesus must have revealed it, if not to the masses, at least to his disciples during his ministry on earth.

However, Jesus was a Jew and grew up in a Jewish household. From his youth up, he learned about Jewish monotheism, the belief in a single God. He never strayed from or compromised that belief his entire life. Jesus taught the Jewish monotheism that he learned from his youth up and passed that monotheistic belief on to his disciples. He says in John 17:3, "This is eternal life, that they may know You, the **only** true God, and Jesus Christ whom You have sent." In john 5:44, he asks, "How can you believe, when you receive glory from one another and you do not seek the glory that is from the *one and only* God?" In these verses the word "only" is the Greek *monos* and means "alone, only, only one." It designates a single person, not more than one. There is no Trinitarian Doctrine in this unless we have lost touch with the English language or have changed the meaning of "one" to mean "more than one."

Mark 12: 28 present us with another clear-cut example of Jesus' monotheistic teaching. When a young lawyer approached Jesus with the question, "What commandment is foremost of all," Jesus answered him by quoting Deuteronomy 6:4, "Hear O Israel, the Lord our God the Lord is One!" When the Scribe agreed with him and said, "Right, Teacher; You have truly stated that he is one, and **there is no one else besides him,**" Jesus commended him and told him, "You are not far from the kingdom of God." Here was a great chance to teach a Trinitarian

Doctrine, but Jesus, true to his Jewish upbringing, presented God the Father as the One and only true God. The word "one" that Jesus used is the Greek *heis*. The New American Standard Exhaustive Concordance and Strong's Exhaustive Concordance have it the same when they say that it is a primary number and means "one" or "only." According to Barnes, when Jesus said,

> "Hear O Israel," "This was said to call the attention of the Jews to the great importance of the truth about to be proclaimed." *The Lord our God* ... Literally, "Yahweh, our God, is one Yahweh." The other nations worshipped many gods, but **the God of the Jews was one, and one only. Jehovah was undivided**; and this great truth it was the design of the separation of the Jewish people from other nations to keep in mind. This was the "peculiar" truth which was communicated to the Jews, and this they were required to keep and remember forever" (Emphasis mine).[165]

In addition, the *JFB* Commentary declares of Jesus' statement "Hear O Israel, the Lord our God is One God,"

> "This every devout Jew recited twice every day, and the Jews do it to this day; thus keeping up the great ancient national protest against the polytheisms and pantheisms of the heathen world: it is the great utterance of the national faith in One Living and Personal God—'One Jehovah!'"[166]

K. H. Bartels, under the word "one" in the *New International Dictionary of New Testament Theology*, says, "The unity of God is particularly stressed in Deut. 6:4."[167] In stressing the unity of the God of Israel, one must, by default, excluded all other gods. However, that is not to say that one cannot speak of other gods so-called. Bartels goes on to say that although the Shema excluded all other gods but the One God of Israel, early Israel still spoke of the existence of other gods."[168]

Nevertheless, Israel never acquiesced to polytheism. Quite to the contrary,

> "Explicit monotheism became increasingly dominate from the 7th cent. B.C. (e.g. 1 ki. 8:60; Jer. 2:11; and especially in

Isa. 41:29; 43:10; 44:8). But the unique reality of God was firmly anchored in the faith of Israel from the first. This forms the basis of the call to unity among the people (Mal. 2:10). The words of Deut. 6:4f. form the š^{e}ma‛, i.e. the daily confessions by Jews of the unity of God, the basic creed of Jud., by which it separates itself from all paganism and idolatry. . ."[169]

Jesus and his disciples knew nothing about a Trinity much less teach it because it would have gone against the first principle of Old Testament teaching about God."[170] Indeed, where in the pages of the Bible does Jesus ever refer to himself as God? He does not. Neither does he ever refer to himself as part of a triune deity. Trinitarians merely assume that he does! Further, where does the Bible ever use the explicit term "Trinity?" No such instance exists!

> "The term 'Trinity' is not a Biblical term, and we are not using Biblical language when we define what is expressed by it as doctrine."[171]

No Trinitarian Teaching

Jesus does state that He and the Father are one. However, nowhere does he say that he, the Father, *and* the Holy Spirit are one in the respect that they form a triune Godhead. In what respect, then, are Jesus and the Father "one?" Trinitarians automatically assume that he and the Father are co-equal and co-eternal. Consequently, they do not understand that the "oneness" Jesus speaks of is a functional oneness, i.e. they are one in purpose and will, not in substance, equality, or eternal existence.

However, If you insist that Jesus taught a Trinitarian Doctrine to the original apostles, what about Paul? He was not one of the original twelve, but he was an Apostle nonetheless. Did Paul preach a triune God? If so, did he receive it from the original twelve? If not from them, did he receive it from Jesus? No! For had he received it from the original twelve he would have been preaching a gospel received from men. He declares in the book of Galatians:

> "But I certify to you, brethren, that the gospel which was preached of me is not after man. For neither received it I of

man, **neither was I taught it but by the revelation of Jesus Christ**" (Gal. 1:12).

From whom did he receive it? Verse 12 says that he received it directly from Jesus Christ! After his conversion, Paul presumably spent time in the deserts of Arabia where he received the gospel directly from Jesus Christ through revelatory means, and then returned to Damascus where he remained for three years before he had contact with any of the other Apostles! He received none of the gospel from them, and he did not receive a Trinitarian Doctrine from Jesus! Had he not received a monotheistic doctrine from Jesus, why would he have made such a clear cut statement in 1 Corinthians 8:6 claiming that for those in the Faith, there is but one God? "Yet for us there is *but* **one God, the Father**, from whom are all things and we *exist* for Him; and **one Lord, Jesus Christ**, by (through or for) whom are all things, and we *exist* through Him"(see also Rom. 3:30; 15:6; 1 Cor. 8:4; Eph 4:6; 1 Tim 2:5; Jas 2:19). Paul distinguishes between God the Father and His Son Jesus, the Messiah. Jesus is Lord, but he is not God in the sense that God the Father is God (with a capital G).

Paul was the apostle to the heathen, Gentile nations. God sent him to the lost sheep of the House of Israel to call them out of the paganism that they had practiced for so many years. They already believed in a triune God because they were part of the Babylonian Mystery Religion! In Revelation 18 God says of this great apostate system:

> ". . . come out of her, my people, that ye be not partakers of her sins, and that ye receive not of her plagues" (Rev. 18:4).

Undoubtedly, one of these sins was the false, abominable Trinitarian Doctrine! God did not say, "Come out of her but retain the Trinitarian Doctrine." He said, "come out" in the sense that they were to forsake that system in its totality—including any belief in a triune God!

Paul speaks of the "mystery of iniquity" already working in the church at Thessalonica at a time when all of the apostles were still alive, and the gospel rapidly spread throughout the Gentile world. This mystery of iniquity was none other than the workings of the Babylonian Mystery Religion of which Simon Magus was a devout disciple.

Excommunication

The Mysteries quickly infiltrated the churches established by Paul in Asia Minor. Paul's writings demonstrate that the new converts were reluctant to give up their former beliefs and practices. The reason was simple.

> "For there are certain men crept in unawares, who were before of old ordained to this condemnation, ungodly men, turning the grace of our God into lasciviousness, and denying the only Lord God, and our Lord Jesus Christ" (Jude 4).

One of the ways they denied Jesus was by teaching a Holy Trinity! These men were totally libertine in their outlook. They taught that the grace of God was license to do anything one wanted to do, or teach anything one wanted to teach, as long as one did it or taught it in the name of Jesus Christ! Consequently, those who disagreed with their viewpoint (q.v. true Christians), were summarily excommunicated because the dissenters stood in the way of the express purpose of the establishment of a hierarchical authority. This, largely, has always been a standard to which the devotees of the Babylonian Mystery Religion, the Roman Catholic Church, and Protestantism have always flocked. There was never a pyramidal structure of government in God's Church, (except where men have sought to pervert God's government), and there was never meant to be (see Matt. 20: 25-26) One such case of excommunication is found in III John.

> "I wrote unto the church: but Diotrephes (a name which means—nourished by Zeus—the Greek name for Nimrod), who loves to have preeminence among them, receiveth us not. Wherefore, if I come, I will remember his deeds which he doeth, prating against us with malicious words: and not content therewith, neither doth he himself receive the brethren, and forbiddeth them that would, **and casteth them out of the church**" (III John 9-10, parenthesis mine).

We cannot establish with certainty that Diotrephes was a disciple of the Mysteries or a follower of Simon Magus, but why else would he be so quick to ostracize and ex-communicate God's people? Was his sole reason for casting them out one of a desire for absolute authority?

If so, it was still not a godly spirit, which prompted him to act in this manner. Regardless of his reasons, he made himself an enemy of true Christianity by his actions. If we can count him among those libertines, it is highly likely that among the beliefs he tried to force upon the true believers was of a doctrine of a Holy Trinity as taught by the Mysteries. This doctrine is a flagrant denial of the true nature of Almighty God, and of Jesus Christ! Declares James Hastings:

> "The Christian doctrine of God (q.v.) as existing in three persons and one substance is not demonstrable by logic or scriptural proofs . . ."[172]

No Trinitarian Definition

Before 325 A.D., there was no satisfactory terminology concerning the Holy Trinity that defined the Holy Spirit. Hagerty says that:

> "Although the dogma (concerning the Holy Trinity) was sufficiently comprehended from the first to enable bishops to recognize heretics like Theodotus who taught that Jesus Christ was not God and Sebellius who taught that Father and Holy Ghost were the same person, it was not until the Council of Nicea (325 A.D.) and the great theological discussion which followed that a satisfactory terminology was worked out" (comments mine).[173]

By whom was it "sufficiently comprehended?" Present day theologians do not comprehend it well enough to explain how it works! Those who did not accept the Trinitarian Doctrine were heretics only in the eyes of the Roman Catholic Church, not in the eyes of God. The controversies that raged among the theologians at the Council of Nicea did not revolve around the matter of whether or not the Holy Trinity existed, but rather "How do we define it"?

The Arian Heresy

The Council of Nicea was convened primarily because Arius, a priest at Alexandria, Egypt proclaimed that there was only one God, that this God created Jesus Christ (Christ was therefore not divine), and that the Holy Spirit was in turn created by Jesus Christ (likewise, the Holy Spirit was not divine).

Alexander, the bishop of Alexandria, Egypt, bitterly disputed Arius' claims. He maintained that God the Father was unbegotten; that there was no time when the Father and the Son did not exist (therefore, the Father *and* the Son are consubstantial, and Arian "Adoptionism" was a flagrant error). However, he remained silent about the divinity or consubstantiality of the Holy Spirit. The controversy raged on until it involved not only Egypt, but also Libya, Upper Thebes, and eventually the entire Greek-speaking world, as well as the Roman Empire. What was the result of all this haggling over the divinity of God and Christ?

Men who desired to elevate the creature to the level of the Creator resoundingly condemned the Arian heresy. Their aim was to set the Virgin Mary side by side with her son. The Council of Nicea, persuaded by the representatives of the Christianity, so-called, of Egypt, declared that there were three persons in the Trinity—the Father, the Virgin Mary, and the Messiah, their son.

Constantine the Great, Emperor of Rome, and recently "converted" from Mithraism to Christianity, became gravely concerned about the unity of his empire. Fearing that the Arian controversy might precipitate an unwanted religious and political schism among his subjects, he dispatched Hosius, bishop of Cordova, Spain to Alexandria to attempt reconciliation between Arius and Alexander. Hosius failed and Constantine convened the Council of Nicea. Three hundred and eighteen bishops and presbyters from all over the empire converged upon Nicea to settle the matter for the last time. Arius was condemned for his heresies, and the bishops formulated the Nicene Creed. The Creed, thus stated, says this:

> "We believe in the one and only God, the Father, maker of all things, visible and invisible; and in only one Lord, Jesus Christ, the Son of God, the sole-begotten of the father, that is to say, of the Father's substance, God of God, Light of Light, true God of true God; begotten not made, con-substantial (homoousious) with the Father, by whom all things were made; who for us and for our salvation came down, became incarnate, became man, suffered, was raised again on the

third day, ascended into heaven and will come again to judge the living and the dead; and in the Holy Spirit . . ."[174]

Notice carefully that the formulators of the creed fully agreed that Christ was indeed divine, not created, not made from nothing, and that there was indeed no "Adoptionism" as Arius maintained. However, what of the divinity of the Holy Spirit and its consubstantiality with God and Christ? Although the Nicene Creed postulated a belief in the Holy Spirit, it said nothing about its divinity or consubstantiality. Nevertheless, the early church fathers had long assumed the idea of the consubstantiality of the Holy Spirit with the Father and the Son.. Hagerty observes that:

> "In all churches, according to the testimony of Justin, Tertullian, Cyprian, and other early Fathers, catechumens were baptized in the name of the Father and the Son and of the Holy Ghost. Adults were not admitted to baptism without instruction and interrogation concerning the Trinity."[175]

Of course, this was the Catholic Church's way of keeping the true believers out for fear that they would expose her!

Athanasius

There was one man at the Council whose tenacity and perseverance in establishing his doctrines and beliefs is a monument to the abilities and power of a single person to change the course of religious history. His name was Athanasius. He became the bishop of Alexandria in 328 A.D. after the death of Alexander. He was a mere deacon in 325 when the Council convened. Largely, he was responsible for defending the consubstantiality of Jesus with the Father. It was there also that he began his work of defending the consubstantiality of the Holy Spirit with both of them.

> "Rufinis relates that this (Athanasius) when quite a boy played with others of his own age at a sacred game: this was an imitation of the priesthood and the order of consecrated persons. In this game therefore Athanasius was allotted the Episcopal chair, and each of the other lads personated either a presbyter or a deacon. The children engaged in this sport

> on the day in which the memory of the martyr and bishop Peter was celebrated. Now at that time Alexander bishop of Alexandria happening to pass by, observed the play in which they were engaged, and having sent for the children, enquired from them the part each had been assigned in the game, conceiving that something might be portended by that which had been done. He then gave directions that the children should be taken to the church, and instructed in learning, but especially Athanasius; and having afterwards ordained him deacon on his becoming of adult age, he brought him to Nicea to assist him in the disputations there when the synod was convened."[176]

What Alexander perhaps saw in Athanasius was not just intellect but ambition and natural leadership abilities as well. These, he must have surmised, coupled with political astuteness and acumen would make Athanasius a likely successor to his (Alexander's) See, and a formidable enemy to the dissenters from the Catholic faith. Alexander was not to be disappointed.

At the Council of Nicea Athanasius defended the consubstantiality of the Father with the Son with such dispatch that Eusebius, bishop of Nicomedia, and Theognis, bishop of Nicea, both of whom sided with Arius, became embittered against Athanasius "because he had so vigorously withstood them in the synod while the articles of faith were under discussion."[177] Eusebius thereafter worked diligently to have Athanasius removed from the bishopric of Alexander and to set up Arius in his stead. Eusebius' goal was to expunge completely the doctrine of consubstantiality. He wrote to Athanasius asking him to reinstate Arius, but Athanasius adamantly refused. Eusebius and Theognis then brought seditious charges against Athanasius. Constantine commanded an audience with him but found him innocent of all charges. Having failed to unseat Athanasius; Eusebius, Theognis, and their cohorts fled into exile. Nevertheless, even in exile they continued to work for the reinstatement of the Arian doctrine. Athanasius, formidable foe that he was, became even more recalcitrant. Eventually, he was victorious.

Eusebius returned from exile, went immediately to Alexandria to meet with Athanasius, and convoked a synod, all to no avail. All of the bishops who attended this synod sided with Athanasius. They agreed to the divinity of the Holy Spirit and included it as consubstantial to the Trinity. They finally put the Arian heresy to rest and "Christianity" officially adopted another of the pagan doctrines of the Babylonian Mysteries. Never would there again be a controversy over the divinity of Jesus or the Holy Spirit. The Trinitarian Doctrine would be forever entrenched in the Roman Catholic faith and credo. Declares Hagerty:

> "A clear summary of Christian Faith in the Trinity is contained in the Athanasian Creed. The date of this composition is probably the end of the fifth century, after the great Trinitarian and Christological controversies were over. At Nicea in 325 A.D., the divinity of Christ was upheld; in 381 A.D., the first Council of Constantinople declared the Holy Ghost to be of the same substance as Father and Son. In 431 at Ephesus, the unity of Christ's person was asserted when Mary was held to be the Mother of God. In 451 at Chalcedon the hypostatic union of two unconfused natures in one divine person was defined. After that preachers and catechists needed a creed in which the faith as defined by the great councils was manifestly and unequivocally stated."[178]

The Athanasian Creed

> "The Catholic faith is this, that we worship one God in Trinity and Trinity in unity, neither confounding the persons, nor dividing the substance. For there is one person of the Father, another of the Son and another of the Holy Ghost. But the Godhead of the Father, of the Son and of the Holy Ghost is all one, the glory equal, the majesty co-eternal. Such as the Father is, such is the Son, and such is the Holy Ghost. The Father uncreated, the Son uncreated, and the Holy Ghost uncreated. The Father eternal, the Son eternal, and the Holy Ghost eternal and yet they are not Three Eternals, but One Eternal. And as there are not Three Uncreated, nor Three Incomprehensibles, but One Uncreated, and One Incomprehensible; so likewise the Father is Almighty, the Son Almighty, and the Holy Ghost Almighty; yet they are

not Three Almighties, but One Almighty . . . The Holy Ghost is of the Father and of the Son; neither made, nor created, nor begotten, but proceeding (from them both).

"So there is one Father, not three Fathers, one Son, not three sons; one Holy Ghost, not three Holy Ghosts. And in this Trinity there is nothing before or after, nothing greater or less; but the three Persons are co-eternal, and co-equal. So that in all things, as before said, the Unity in Trinity, and the Trinity in Unity is to be worshipped. **He therefore that will be saved, must think thus of the trinity.**

"Furthermore, it is necessary to everlasting salvation, that he also believe rightly the incarnation of our Lord Jesus Christ. For the right Faith is, that we believe and confess, that our Lord Jesus Christ, the Son of God, is God and man. God, of the substance of the Father, begotten before the world; and man, of the substance of his mother, born into the world. Perfect god and perfect man, of a rational soul and human flesh subsisting. Equal to the Father as touching his Godhead, and inferior to the Father as touching his manhood. Who, although he be God and man, yet he is not two, but One Christ. One, not by conversion of the Godhead into flesh, but by taking of the manhood into God. One altogether, not by confusion of substance, but by unity of person. For as the rational soul and flesh is one man, so God and man is one Christ, who suffered for our salvation, descended into Hell, rose again the third day from the dead. He ascended into Heaven, he sitteth on the right hand of the Father, God Almighty, from whence he shall come to judge the quick and the dead. At whose coming all men shall rise again with their bodies, and shall give account of their own works. And they that have done good shall go into life everlasting and they that have done evil into everlasting fire. This is the Catholic Faith, which except a man believe **faithfully and firmly, he cannot be saved.**"[179]

Thus, with the councils of Nicea, Constantinople, Ephesus, and Chalcedon, the Roman Church overwhelmingly declared the Unity in Trinity and the Trinity in Unity a doctrine of faith. She impressed it into the minds of Catholic theologians and catechists alike. What Satan had inspired, what Nimrod and Semiramis had spread throughout the known world, and what Simon Magus had injected into Christianity, was now an undeniable requisite for salvation. Instead of Nimrod, the name of God the Father had been substituted; instead of Ninus, the name of Jesus Christ the Son; instead of Semiramis, the name of the Holy Spirit, divinized, personified, and changed from the female gender of the original Babylonian Trinity into the male gender of the "Christianized" Trinity of the fifth century A.D.

Early Roman Catholic theologians from the very beginnings of New Testament times borrowed the idea of a Holy Trinity, not from Scripture, but from ancient paganism, and subsequently "Christianized it." The concept of a triune God in the Catholic Church, three persons in one, inseparable, equal, and of one substance, was not based upon a clear revelation of God-breathed scripture, but upon the writings of ancient pagan philosophers such as Plato, Socrates, and Aristotle.

Plato's Influence

Plato mostly influenced the Christian (Catholic) idea of God, and Augustine, who lived and wrote after the Council of Nicea advanced and "Christianized" Plato's world of "ideas," identifying them with the mind of God. Plato, however, received most of his ideas from his expansive world travels, and especially from the Egyptians, among whom he lived for some time in order to learn their manners and customs (q.v. religious beliefs).

Augustine learned of Plato's philosophy from Plotinus who was a pantheist. Where Plato believed that the idea of "the Good" was God, and that the material world was nothing more than an imitation of the world of ideas (in other words, it's all in your mind, nothing is real), Plotinus, the father of Neo-Platonism, believed that God was so exalted that He was inaccessible to man's knowledge (the same incomprehensibility expressed by the Athanasian Creed). Augustine rejected Plotinus' ideas as being "too dangerous," but introduced Plato's philosophy into Catholic religious thought and labeled it "Christian." He employed it extensively to strengthen and magnify the Trinitarian Doctrine.

Chapter 13
The Great Mystery

What Is the Holy Trinity?

According to Evangelical Christianity, the Holy Trinity is a mysterious amalgam of God the Father, God the Son, and God the Holy Spirit three distinct persons—and yet they are one, inseparable, and of the same essence. How this is possible is not quite clear to millions of believing, professing Christians.

Perhaps a simple example will serve to illustrate this lack of clarity and understanding. Billy Graham says of Dr. David McKenna that he:

> "... once told me that he was asked by his small son, Doug, 'Is God the Father God?' He answered, 'Yes.' 'Is Jesus Christ God?' 'Yes.' 'Is the Holy Spirit God?' 'Yes.' 'Then how can Jesus be His own Father?'" [180]

How indeed can Jesus be His own Father? The answer is that he cannot! If the Holy Spirit is a distinct person of the Godhead, we have a gigantic dilemma on our hands that is unexplainable in terms of the Trinitarian Doctrine. Jesus Christ came into being through the power of the Holy Spirit, who, if he were the third "person" of the Trinity, would make Him the Father of Jesus! However, is the Holy Spirit, as a distinct person, the father of Jesus Christ? No! God the Father is! Then if the Holy Spirit is the father of Jesus Christ, and if God the Father is the father of Jesus Christ—Oh well, you see what I mean!

The question that little Doug asked his father was very profound for his young years. It deserved a satisfactory answer. However, Dr. McKenna did not give him one.

"David thought quickly (too quickly perhaps). They were sitting in their old 1958 Chevrolet at the time. 'Listen, son,' he replied, 'under the hood is one battery. Yet I can use it to turn on the lights, blow the horn, and start the car.' He said, 'How this happens is a mystery—but it happens!'" (Parenthesis mine).[181]

Dr. McKenna very neatly dodged the issue with a nonsensical answer that does not even come close to illustrating what he, and millions of others view as the Holy Trinity. The fact that the one battery's power operates the lights, blows the horn, and starts the car is no mystery! It is as simple as knowing that all three were connected to the same **power source**. Anyone with a basic knowledge of electricity could have understood to what Dr. McKenna referred. If he had said that the battery itself was analogous to God the Father, and that the **power** that proceeded from the battery to operate the lights, the horn, and start the car, was analogous to the Holy Spirit, (God's creative power in action) he would have been correct! Doug was probably more confused after his father's inept explanation than before he asked. At least Doug was doing something the Trinitarians seem loathe to do—he was thinking about the incongruities of what he had probably been taught from early childhood.

However, undaunted by the lack of any clear and concrete evidence in the Scriptures for a triune God, the Trinitarians continue to teach their doctrine as an unadulterated fact with as much fervor and dedication as modern science teaches the theory of evolution.

If the Holy Trinity is such a mystery to millions of Evangelical Christians, why is it that the Trinitarian Doctrine is one of the most accepted and least understood doctrines extant in the Christian world so-called today? Why all the difficulty surrounding it? Jesus Christ said that one of the reasons the Holy Spirit would be sent into the world was to guide us into all truth (Jn. 16:13), and God's word cannot be broken (Jn. 10:35)! Why do Evangelical Christians not believe this? The answer is that they continue to follow Catholic doctrine despite themselves! What are the difficulties surrounding the Trinitarian Doctrine? Dr. Graham sums it up for us succinctly:

"The Bible teaches us that the Holy Spirit is a living being. He is one of the three persons of the Holy Trinity. **To explain and illustrate the trinity is one of the most difficult assignments to a Christian**" (emphasis mine).[182]

Mr. Graham need not be embarrassed over his dilemma for he is not alone. There have been many learned minds, would be "Christian" theologians that have struggled to "explain" and "illustrate" the Holy Trinity since the Council of Nicea in 325 A.D., without much success. Despite oft-repeated attempts throughout the centuries to define the Trinity in clear and precise terms, their failures have been obvious. The reason is simple. Each of these theologians, these would be purveyors of the truth, begins with the preconceived notion that the Holy Spirit is a "person" and therefore a member of the Holy Trinity.

Is The Holy Spirit A Person?

Dr. Billy Graham is a world-renowned evangelist of high moral character and one of the most respected theologians living today. It is safe to say that when he speaks from the pulpit, he speaks for the majority of mainstream Christianity. Is he, however, correct in his assumptions about the Holy Spirit and the Holy Trinity, or is he, like hundreds of other theologians, merely parroting a belief instituted thousands of years ago and disseminated by the founders of the Babylonian Mysteries? Has he, have they, given their minds over to a doctrine which constitutes idolatry in the eyes of God? Are we not, if we give our minds over to a doctrine, which depends exclusively upon rank theological speculation rather than sound scriptural exegesis, guilty of idolatry? According to A.W. Tozer:

"The essence of idolatry is the entertainment of thoughts about God that are unworthy of Him."[183]

By this definition, most books about the Holy Spirit are idolatrous!

If the Holy Spirit is not a person, millions of people throughout the world are deceived. If what most of the books on the Holy Spirit and the Holy Trinity say is not true, and if by Tozer's definition they are idolatrous, these millions of deceived are worshipping God in vain because they follow the traditions of men instead of the common-sense teachings of God and Jesus (Mt. 15:9; Mk. 7:7).

Books, Books, and More Books

There are literally hundreds of books on the market about the Holy Spirit and the Holy Trinity! King Solomon wrote of the writing of many books about three thousand years ago. Says he:

> ". . . of making of many books *there* is no end; and much study (margin) *is* a weariness of the flesh" (Eccl. 12:12).

This prophetic statement was never truer than it is today! Walk into any bookstore and browse for a while. You will find the shelves filled with a dizzying array of endless titles publicizing every subject imaginable. It seems that no area of the print media is left untouched or is immune to the avalanche of materials pouring forth from the typewriters of hundreds of authors, including those involved in the writing of Christian literature so-called.

Most often the subjects of these books consist of the same insipid, reconstituted pabulum, dished up in pedantic portions which are viewed as spiritual, good for the soul (another mystery), and relevant in all respects to one's personal salvation. The idea seems to be that by ingesting this steady, bland diet of spiritual mush, one can build one's spiritual muscles as it were, and thereby obtain the strength to ward off the evil machinations of the Devil while somehow working one's way into heaven. What it all really amounts to in many cases is a mish-mash of nonsensical exegetical procedure. It is a frenetic attempt to proselytize the masses and convert them into pseudo "born-again believers," "Christians so-called" who "give their hearts to the Lord," and their money to the evangelist! Franky Schaeffer makes an interesting though disdainful observation about these books. Says he:

> "The publishing houses churn out (measured by the ton) a landslide of material which can scarcely be called books, often composed of the same themes which are viewed as spiritual, rehashed endlessly by writers who would be better employed in another trade."[184]

Mr. Schaeffer refers to the deluge of materials in the areas of Christian arts and culture that the publishers are passing off as Christian when, in fact, they have nothing or very little to do with true Christianity or the Bible. His statement, however, fits just as well those books that deal with profound doctrinal issues, and *especially* the Holy Spirit and the Holy Trinity. In a footnote to the above statement, Schaeffer writes:

> "In looking at the diversity of the Scripture itself as well as its content and form, one can hardly imagine that the Bible has anything to do with the present narrow sloganeering aspects of evangelical Christianity. It seems to me that if it had been written along the lines of what much of evangelical Christianity represents today . . . it would be a three page pamphlet printed probably in words of one syllable, preferably on pink paper (because pink sells), possibly with a scratch and sniff section on the back to simulate some spiritual experience while reading it. In contrast, the real Bible, the word of God, is solid, human, verifiable, divine indeed."[185]

The Bible, the word of God, is indeed solid and verifiable in all of its aspects whether in the areas of art, culture, history, or doctrine. Being thusly verifiable, and taken in its true sense under the guidance of the Holy Spirit, it categorically rejects the Trinitarian Doctrine as wholly pagan and idolatrous.

Too many are addicted to spiritual mediocrity because they are too willing to accept the Trinitarian Doctrine as fact without proving or disproving it for himself or herself. Modern Christianity, in Franky Schaeffer's words, exhibits one outstanding feature, its addiction to mediocrity!

Is The Word "Trinity" In The Bible?

Where in the Bible do you ever find the word "Trinity"? Where does it state explicitly and unequivocally that the Father, Son, *and* the Holy Spirit are of equal essence? Karl Barth says that:

"The Bible lacks the express declaration that the Father, Son, and the Holy Spirit are of equal essence and therefore in an equal sense God Himself. And the other express declaration is also lacking that God is God thus and only thus, i.e. as the Father, the Son, and the Holy Spirit. These two express declarations which go beyond the witness of the Bible are the twofold content of the church doctrine of the Trinity." [186]

Barth is correct! Nowhere does the Bible (regardless of what Trinitarian theologians may wish to read into it) express such a relationship as (the Catholic and Protestant) church doctrines espouse!

Where Do We Get The Word Trinity?

If the word Trinity is not a Biblical term, where did it originate? According to James Hastings:

"The term **TRIAS** was first used by Theophilus of Antioch (c. A.D. 180), and although not found in Scripture was thereafter used as a brief designation for the doctrine..."[187]

The Encyclopedia of Ethics and Religion reinforces this historical but non-biblical aspect of the Trinitarian Doctrine.

"The term 'Trinity' (from the Latin *trinitas*) appears to have been first used by Tertullian, while the corresponding Greek term 'Triad' . . . appears to have been first used by Theophilus the Christian Apologist . . ."[188]

Actually, the use of the term Trinity by Theophilus and Tertullian was the first time for eastern Christian philosophy so-called. We have already seen that pagan religions used the Trinitarian concept and the term Trinity extensively for thousands of years prior to the advent of Christianity. According to the *ISBE*:

"The term 'Trinity' is not a Biblical term, and we are not using biblical language when we define what is expressed by it as a doctrine."[189]

Christian Vocabulary

When we use the term "Trinity" we are employing "Christian vocabulary," not biblical language. There is a vast difference between Christian vocabulary and biblical language. Christian vocabulary has adopted such words and phrases as "Rapture," "Secret Rapture," the "Immortal Soul," "When I get to heaven," "Pre-millenialism," "Post-millenialism," the "Holy Trinity," etc.

These words and phrases are neither biblical terms nor even sound biblical principles. They are, in the light of cold, hard, analysis, merely the verbal meanderings of deceived minds clutching at spiritual straws in the winds of spiritual darkness. They are the buzzwords of confused men who are "Easter-egging," looking, searching, running to and fro, tossed by every wind of doctrine, and trying desperately to find answers to concepts that have no basis in true Christianity, let alone in the real world.

Although he does not mention these words and phrases, Franky Schaeffer talks about the Christian vocabulary in rather uncomplimentary terms. The principle, however, is applicable to all of the Christian vocabulary *per se*. In referring to the meaning of such words and phrases that consistently crop up in the Christian vocabulary he says that:

> "Odd phrases have crept into the Christian vocabulary, A little private Christian language in itself . . . words such as 'full-time Christian service' have crept in. What is full-time Christian service? Are the rest of the Christians part time Christians? What do all these slogans mean . . . what do all these phrases mean . . .?" The answer? In a vacuum they are merely what they sound like and so often are—spiritual babblings of those addicted not to biblical Christianity, but mediocrity."[190]

And The Beat Goes On–And On–And On–And On

Despite substantial evidence to the contrary, evangelical Christianity continues to embrace a doctrine that has no basis in Scripture. Its adherents obviously refuse to look thoroughly into its historical background, for if they did, they could not deny its origins. Historical literature thoroughly documents the Trinitarian Doctrine's pagan origins so that even nonprofessionals can easily understand if they care to expend the time and effort to ferret out the truth. It is incredible in the least that one can still advocate a belief in the Holy Trinity when the overwhelming evidence dictates otherwise. Nevertheless, advocate it they do—even though they admit that they cannot prove the doctrine scripturally!

> "The Christian doctrine of God (q.v.) as existing in three persons and one substance is not demonstrable by logic or Scriptural proofs, but is . . . a necessary hypothesis."[191]

If it is not demonstrable by logic or Scriptural proofs, then why bother with it? If it is not demonstrable by logic and Scriptural proofs, then why is it a "necessary hypothesis"? It is "necessary" because evangelical Christianity refuses to admit the truth, and because it refuses to admit that there is no such thing as a Holy Trinity as it conceives of it, or otherwise. Thus, it must have a hypothesis to support its views (much the same as evolutionists), and to attempt to discredit (for its own subtle motives), the fact that the Trinitarian Doctrine is categorically pagan!

Consequently, Christianity so-called continues to teach the Trinity as an undeniable fact irrevocably and unalterably evident in the pages of the Bible when it is at best a doctrine that is inexplicable, tenuous, and untenable. All this notwithstanding, Christianity so-called continues to believe in a fanciful, obscure doctrine concocted by men, for men, to circumvent a blind, misdirected effort to understand the true nature and character of the Godhead.

Chapter 14
THE HOLY SPIRIT IN THE OLD TESTAMENT

The "Plurality" of the Godhead

If you ask a Trinitarian to prove the existence of the Holy Trinity in the Bible, he might well take you to the very first verse of Genesis. Having turned there and read it to you, he might well say to you, in the words of Eric S. Fife:

> "It is of more than usual significance to note that the plurality of the Godhead is mentioned as early as the first two verses of the Bible."[192]

Mr. Fife, because he is a Trinitarian, would have you believe that the use of the plural to describe the Godhead in Genesis 1:1-2 refers to a Trinity. Yet, on page 24, he states:

> "The Holy Spirit was not created or begotten but **proceeds** from the Father."[193]

We will speak of this later, but first, let us look more closely at the Trinitarian concept of the plurality of the Godhead. In order to understand the Godhead in the Old Testament, one must look at it from the viewpoint of the Old Testament writers, and here there is no evidence to support the concept of the Trinity. The ISBE states:

> ". . . there is no indication of a belief that the Spirit of God was a material particle or emanation from God. The point of view of Biblical writers is nearly always practical rather

than speculative. They did not philosophize about the Divine Nature."[194]

Again:

> "In a great number of passages... God and the Spirit are not thought of as identical... of course this does not mean that God and the Spirit were two distinct beings in the thought of the OT writers, but only that the Spirit had functions of His own in distinction from God. The Spirit *was* **God in action**, particularly when the action was specific, with a view to accomplishing some particular end or purpose of God" [such as creating] (brackets mine).[195]

Unlike the Old Testament writers, today's evangelicals spend a great deal of time philosophizing about the relationship of the Holy Spirit to the Godhead. The arguments are endless. It is amazing in the least that the Trinitarians cannot get a handle on the truth of the make-up of the Godhead when there is more than ample evidence, and there exists such practical statements concerning the Holy Spirit. Nevertheless, practicality be damned, they continue to defend their pet doctrine with all the fervency they can muster. Example? Most works about the Holy Spirit are replete with statements such as the following by Billy Graham:

> "God unfolds His revelation of Himself in the Bible progressively. But there are indications from the very beginning of the book of Genesis that God subsists in three persons—the Father, the Son, and the Holy Spirit—and that these three persons constitute the One God. Christianity is Trinitarian, not Unitarian. There is only one God, not three, so it is clear that the Christian faith is not polytheistic. The Bible begins with the majestic statement: 'In the beginning God created the heavens and the earth'" [Genesis 1:1] (emphasis mine).[196]

Has Mr. Graham been reading Mr. Fife's book, or has Mr. Fife been reading Mr. Graham's? The point is that evangelicalism in the main agrees *in toto* about the Trinity. To believe that there are "indications" that God subsists in three persons from the passage just quoted is to give credence to the Roman Catholic teaching about the Holy Trinity, and by extension, to condone the Trinitarian error of the Babylonian Mysteries! Mr. Graham's bases his reasoning on personal communications from Hebrew scholars and the concepts singular, dual, and plural (as it applies to more than two). It is the plural use of the word God (*Elohim*) that Mr. Graham (and thousands of others) claims is indicative of a Holy Trinity, three persons in one, inseparable, and of one essence. However, if we are to believe the Bible for what it actually says, and from what has gone before, this cannot possibly be true. The word "God" in Genesis 1:1, as we have already witnessed, is "Elohim," and is, as Mr. Graham states, plural. According to William F. Dankenbring, it is more than just plural; it is also uni-plural.

> "The Bible reveals that the Creator of all things is the true God. In Genesis 1:1 we read, 'In the beginning God created the heaven and the earth.' The Hebrew word for God here is "Elohim" and is a uni-plural word. It literally means 'The Mighty Ones.' It denotes more than one individual person— even as our English words 'family', 'church', 'congregation' denote more than one individual."[197]

Mr. Dankenbring writes, not as a Trinitarian, but as a Binitarian, i.e., he believes there are two Gods in the Godhead and that the Holy Spirit is a power or force that emanates from God the Father.

Does the Elohim of Genesis 1, as Mr. Graham and Mr. Fife claim, indicate a Holy Trinity, or does the Godhead now consist of a lesser number and subsist in the dual sense as Mr. Dankenbring insists? Scriptures, after all, clearly reveal the Godhead in such a manner that there should be no speculation involved as to its make-up. Daniel 7:9-10 describes the One God of the Godhead is as the *"Ancient of Days."* The account never graphically describes Holy Spirit. The only evidence that we ever see of it appearing in material form is found in the New Testament when it descends upon Jesus in the form of a dove immediately after His baptism (John 1:32). Although the Holy Spirit was active in the creation process, the Bible does not speak of it as the third "person" of the Godhead. According to Mr. Graham's Hebraic scholars, the plural sense of the word "Elohim" indicates more than two.

Thus, he concludes automatically that there are three. However, the Old Testament never speaks of the Godhead in terms of three.

> *"The term (Holy Spirit) in its latter sense (as a person)* **does not occur in the O.T.** . . . In Ps. 51:11 and Isa. 63:10f, we find the expression 'Thy Holy Spirit' and 'His Holy Spirit,' but the meaning is not that of later Christian thought (of the Holy Spirit as a person). *All that is meant is that God deals with men by His Spirit, and that this Spirit is holy because it is the Spirit of God who is Himself holy.* This, indeed, is the characteristic thought of the O.T.; the distinction is made between God as a Spirit and the spirit of His Divine Spirit. **the Spirit of the divine Spirit is his very life principle,** whereby He can carry on all His diverse activities. . ." (Parentheses and emphasis mine).[198]

Then what about Genesis 1:26; 3:22; 11:16, and Isa. 6:8? Again, Evangelical Christianity applies the same interpretation—that there are elements of a Trinity here. Consequently, they use these verses as "proof" texts. Let us see what Mr. Graham says of them. On page 29 of *The Holy Spirit*, he states:

> "As we have seen concerning creation, even from the beginning God gives us glimpses of the truth that the Godhead consists of more than one person."[199]

We cannot overly emphasize that the Godhead consists of only one person. There are over 6000 references in the Old Testament with which the writers use singular pronouns to describe the One God. Evangelicalism bases its belief that the Godhead consists of exactly three persons upon the biased assumption that the Holy Spirit is a person, not upon the clear revelation of God-breathed Scripture. Mr. Graham continues:

> "I have italicized some of the key words. In Genesis 1:26, God said, 'Let *us* make man in *our* image, according to *our* likeness; and let them have rule over the fish of the sea, and over the birds of the sky, and over the cattle, and over all the earth, and over every creeping thing that creeps on the

earth.' Further, in Genesis 3:22 the Lord God said, 'Behold, the man has become like one of *us*, knowing good and evil.' And in Genesis 11:6, 7, the Lord said, 'Behold, they are one people, and they all have the same language. And this is what they begin to do, and now nothing which they purpose to do will be impossible for them. Come, let *us* go down and there confuse their language, that they may not understand one another's speech!' When Isaiah heard the voice of the Lord saying, 'Whom shall I send, and who will go for *us*?' he answered, 'Here am I. Send me.'"[200]

Again, because of a preconceived notion taught by Catholics and Protestants alike, the words "our" and "us" are construed as including three persons. However, we have already seen that this was not the concept held by the Hebrews or the Israelites, and it is not the concept held by the Jews today. (See Isaac Asimov, "*In The Beginning*", p. 59).

What holds true for Genesis 1:26 holds true for every other Old Testament Scripture, and for every New Testament Scripture concerning the Holy Spirit. In God, there is no variance. He is the same yesterday, today, and forever (Heb. 13:8).

For all this, the history behind the concept of Trinity, the Hebraic and Jewish denial of a triune God, and ample evidence, secular and Biblical, which speaks loudly and clearly, against the Trinitarian Doctrine, Evangelical Christianity persists in believing a fable.

Let us go back to the second verse of Genesis 1 for a moment. It talks about the Spirit of God "moving" upon the face of the waters.

> "And the earth was (became) without form and void; and darkness was upon the face of the deep. And the Spirit of God moved upon the face of the waters."

Here is yet another "proof" text used to illustrate that the Holy Spirit is a person based upon its activity. This is what Mr. Graham says about it.

> "The Hebrew word for 'moving' means 'brooding' or 'hovering'. Just as a hen broods over her eggs for the purpose of hatching them and bringing forth new life, so the Holy Spirit brooded over the original creation of God for the

purpose of filling its void with life in various forms. The creation recorded in the rest of Genesis 1, together with Genesis 2, resulted. Thus, from the beginning the Holy Spirit was active in creation along with the Father and the Son"[201]

There is no doubt that the Holy Spirit was active in the creation process, but the Bible does not say that It was active as a person! Mr. Graham implies personhood through activity in Genesis 1:2. However, mere activity does not assign personhood to that which is active. The word "Spirit" is the Hebrew *Ruwach* (roo-akh) and means—wind, or by resemblance, breath, i.e. a sensible (or even violent) exhalation. *Hastings' Bible Dictionary* declares:

> "The LXX rendering, *epephereto*, suggests the movement of wind over the face of the waters, but the Hebrew verb (moved) denotes rather the **vitalizing energy of the divine spirit**, giving life to creation that is about to be called into being by God's word . . . It will be clear from what has been said that in the development of the O.T. the Spirit is the **living energy** of a personal God. **It is not an independent hypostasis.** (Emphasis mine).[202]

As to the anthropomorphosis connected with the Holy Spirit in the Old Testament and the New Testament as well, *The New Catholic Encyclopedia* states:

> "Very rarely do the O.T. writers attribute to God's Spirit emotions or intellectual activity (Isa. 63:10; Wis. 1: 3-7). When such expressions are used, they are **mere figures of speech** that are explained by the fact that the *Ruah* was regarded also as the seat of intellectual acts and feeling (Gen. 41:8). Neither is there found in the O.T. or in Rabbinical literature the notion that God's Holy Spirit is an intermediary being between God and the world. This activity is proper to the angels, although to them is ascribed some of the activity that elsewhere is ascribed to the Holy Spirit of God" (emphasis mine).[203]

Repeatedly we see that the very religion whose heart and soul revolve around the Trinitarian Doctrine, and who has bequeathed this doctrine to the Protestants, teaches that the **Holy Spirit is not a person in the O.T.** Yet, Protestants continue to believe otherwise without researching the facts. They invariably use the same method employed by the evolutionists to establish the ages of fossils and fossil strata (i.e. they date the fossils according to the strata in which they find them, and they date the strata according to the index fossils they find in them). In the case of the Trinitarians it is not so much circular reasoning as it is reliance upon the exegetical meanderings of late nineteenth and early twentieth century revivalists whose utterances concerning the Holy Trinity were based upon the traditions of the early Catholic fathers. In fact, Billy Graham says that:

> "Matthew Henry says it (*Elohim*) signifies the plurality of persons in the Godhead, Father, Son, and Holy Ghost. This plural name of God . . . (confirms) our faith in the doctrine of the Trinity . . ."[204]

To the contrary, no less an authority than the *Encyclopedia of Ethics and Religion* states:

> "The Old Testament could hardly be expected to furnish the doctrine of the Trinity . . . It is exegesis of a mischievous, if pious, sort that would discover the (Trinitarian) doctrine in the plural form, 'Elohim', of the Deity's name" (parenthesis mine).[205]

It is significant that, according to Peloubet:

> "Elohim denotes the **idea of power of effect or strength** concerning God as Creator, Governor, and upholder of the universe."[206]

He also states:

> "The plural form of Elohim has given rise to much discussion. **The fanciful idea that it referred to the Trinity of persons in the Godhead only finds supporters among scholars.** It is either what grammarians call *the plural of majesty*, or it

denotes the *fullness* of divine strength, the *sum of the powers* displayed by God" (emphasis mine).[207]

The Power of the Holy Spirit

The Semitic writers were prolific in their use of anthropomorphisms to describe God in a manner that made Him "live," as it were. Although they thought of Him as being infinite, the anthropomorphic view brought Him down to a personal level in the lives of His children. Turning once again to Peloubet, we see that:

> "The anthropomorphisms in which the Old Testament abounds are used in order that man may realize that God is not merely a force . . . but is a real person with mind, will, heart, feelings like His children, but in an infinite degree . . . We use the same expressions today. 'When the Bible speaks,' says Sanday, 'of the hand, arm, mouth, lips, and eyes of God,' when He makes 'bare His mighty arm, and musters His hosts with a shout,—all this is but a vivid conception of His being, His intelligence, His activity, and **universal power**; and testifies to the warmth and intensity of the religious feelings of the writers.'" (Emphasis mine).[208]

"That's all well and good," you might say, "but doesn't that apply to the Holy Spirit?" Well, yes, it does, in a way, but the Holy Spirit was never thought of as being a "personal" entity.

> "Just as the ancient Israelites spoke anthropomorphically of God's hand, and face, so they spoke of His breath, i.e. His vital **power** or **spirit**, which was active and as efficacious as God Himself."[209]

This is the very idea presented in Genesis 1:2 when the *Ruach* moved over the face of the waters. It is the same idea presented as the Lord God bends over the lifeless clay form of Adam and breathes into his nostrils the breath (*ruach*— **vital force or power**) of life. Even Hagerty, who is a staunch Roman Catholic Trinitarian, admits that the Holy Spirit as it is presented in the Old Testament is not a person but a **force** or **power**, which emanates from God.

> "The Spirit of God is mentioned frequently in the Old Testament. It means at least an **action, force,** or **energy** from God that enlivens, forms, strengthens creatures on whom it acts." (emphasis mine).[210]

Again, with reference to the Old Testament Jews, Hagerty says:

> "References to the Spirit of God in the Old Testament signified for the great majority of the Jews no more than the **force, activity,** or **energy** of God." (Emphasis mine).[211]

Time after time, the very church that has palmed the Holy Spirit off as a distinct "person," and the third member of the Holy Trinity, contradicts itself when it states the unadulterated truth. If the Spirit of God was not a person in the Old Testament, it is not a person in the New Testament, and therefore not a member of a so-called Holy Trinity! God does not change to suit the whims and fanciful imaginations of men be they pagan or Christian. There is neither variableness nor shadow of turning with the great Creator God of this universe. However, if there were, and if God, at some point decided that He should become a Trinity on a lark in order to satiate pagan man's inordinate desire to worship Him as such, where is the proof? Such a God would not be deserving of worship. Where indeed can we find in the pages of the Bible during the period between the close of the prophetic age of the Old Testament and the opening of the Messianic age of the New, a clear and precise message calling for a change in the number of the members of the Godhead? We cannot, for there is none.

As a parting thought before we turn to a discussion of the Holy Spirit in the New Testament, let us take one more look at what the Roman Catholic Church has to say about the Holy Spirit in the Old Testament.

> "The OT (Old Testament) clearly **does not envisage god's spirit as a person**, neither in the strictly philosophical sense, nor in the Semitic sense. **God's Spirit is simply God's power.** If it is sometimes represented as being distinct from God, it is because the breath (ruach) of Yahweh acts exteriorly. Isa. 48:16; 63:11; 32:15." (Emphasis mine).

What are we to conclude about the Holy Trinity when the bastion of Christianity, and the defender of the faith concerning the Trinitarian Doctrine, makes such dogmatic claims? Her teaching on the Holy Trinity as an official doctrine bearing upon personal salvation beginning in 325 A.D. was a calculated ploy to gain and hold pagan "converts" to Christianity who flocked to her standard by the thousands. Why? Because they were not required to renounce their former beliefs and practices in order to be a part of all that was the Church of Rome with her ritual, ceremony, pomp, and circumstance, the majority of which she derived from the Babylonian Mysteries, and to which the "converts" had been accustomed for so many hundreds of years. If the Spirit of God was not a "person" in the Old Testament, it is not a "person" in the New Testament, and therefore not a member of a so-called Holy Trinity! God does not change to suit the whims and fanciful imaginations of men be they pagan *or* Christian.

Chapter 15
THE HOLY SPIRIT IN THE NEW TESTAMENT

Regardless of one's viewpoint concerning the Holy Trinity in the Twentieth Century, all roads, from the 4th Century onward, ultimately lead to the philosophical and "Christian" schools of Alexandria, Egypt. The conception of a triune God is older than Egypt itself.

Generally, every city and town had its triad, which consisted of a local deity, and two other gods associated with him. The latter shared his authority and power, but were much less honored and revered by the inhabitants. Of the three, two were usually gods, one old, one young. The third was a goddess. She was usually the wife of the older god, and the mother of the younger. The younger god, the son, possessed all the authority, power, and abilities of the older. Thus, we see in this formula the exact duplication of the Nimrod-Semiramis-Ninyas triad of the Babylonian Mystery Religion.

Both systems were theosophical in nature, and both had their roots in the same Satanic deception that originated with Cain on the Plain of Shinar. Theosophical Doctrine, which teaches the existence of a feminine element in the Godhead, was the common denominator of all pagan religions. The Bible categorically denies any such idea.

Nevertheless, present-day Trinitarians persist in the notion that the Trinity is fully revealed in the pages of the New Testament as the Father, Son, and Holy Spirit. From a purely theosophical standpoint, the only person of the Trinity who could represent the female essence is the Holy Spirit.

The Roman Catholic Church, ever true to her pagan origins was quick to recognize this apparent opening and seized the opportunity to elevate the Virgin Mary to the Godhead. Thus, it is she who really is the Holy Spirit in Roman Catholic dogma. However, she is not the original. She is a substitute of the role model established by Semiramis in Babylon and adopted by the Egyptians in the goddess Isis.

In the south of Egypt, the worship of Isis persisted until the opening of the 5th Century. It was about this time that in other parts of Egypt, the Virgin Mary took the place of Isis, and Christ took the place of Horus, her son. Isis, the "Mother of God," was no longer Isis, but Mary, the "Mother of God." This most blatant of heresies virtually steamrolled its way into Christianity. How was this possible?

> ". . . the probability that many of the heresies of the early Christian Church in Egypt were caused by the survival of ideas and beliefs connected with the old native gods which the converts to Christianity wished to adapt to their own creed . . . the rapid growth and progress of Christianity in Egypt were due mainly to the fact that the new religion . . . so closely resembled that which was the outcome of the worship of Osiris, Isis, and Horus."[212]

Therefore, it was that thousands entered Roman Catholic "Christianity." However, the gospel did not come to the masses of Egypt with the power and authority required to suppress Roman Catholicism's pagan teachings. Had it done so the Isis-Mary heresy would never have attained a foothold, the Arian heresy may never have materialized, and the Council of Nicea might never have been convened. However, because of thousands of years of superstition, the new converts who had given their worship and devotion to Semiramis, Isis, Diana, Athena, Artemis, and Aphrodite found it an incredibly simple matter to transfer their adoration to Mary and continue unrestrained to pay homage to their blessed Trinity.

But we are talking about the beginning of the 5th Century, 400 years after the birth of Christ. The term "Trinity" was not used until late in the 2nd Century by Theophilus a Christian apologist (c. 180). Since then the Trinitarian Doctrine has become firmly entrenched in western religious thought. There are, however, beginnings of a movement among Biblical scholars to refute any qualified Trinitarianism in the New Testament. R.L. Richardson declares:

"There is the recognition on the part of exegetes and Biblical theologians, including a constantly growing number of Roman Catholics, that one should not speak of Trinitarianism in the New Testament without serious qualification. There is also the clearly parallel recognition on the part of Historians of dogma and systematic theologians that when one does speak of an unqualified Trinitarianism, one has moved from the period of Christian origins to, say, the last quadrant of the 4th Century. It was only then that what might be called the definitive Trinitarian dogma "one God in three persons" became thoroughly assimilated into Christian life and thought"[213]

The Philosophers

The single factor that allowed this definitive Trinitarian dogma to become "thoroughly assimilated into Christian life and thought" was the output of the already mentioned philosophical schools of Alexandria. Therefore, one cannot speak of the history of the Trinitarian Doctrine in the New Testament era without mentioning the role of the philosophers.

We have already seen that Plato influenced Christian thought with his purely abstract theories concerning the make-up of the Godhead. Subsequent philosophers merely followed Plato's lead, and their influence spilled over into the Christian Church through the writings of early Roman Catholic Fathers such as Clement, Origen, Eusebius, Cyprian, Tertullian, and later, Augustine, who is said to have written no less than thirteen treatises on the Holy Spirit.

That the "Christian" idea of God has been influenced by Plato is common knowledge among theologians, exegetes, and historians, but few of the laity are aware of this fact. What is more, fewer are familiar with the method he used. His was the allegorical method (a literary style which uses symbolic representations to illustrate concepts difficult to explain), and he used it to explain just about everything that was otherwise unexplainable, including the Holy Trinity.

The Alexandrian catechetical school followed Plato's reasoning. It held Clement and Origen in high esteem and considered them to be the greatest of the Greek Church theologians. As the leaders of the church, they used Plato's allegorical method to explain and illustrate Scripture. Hubert Jedin says of this school:

> "Its thought was influenced by Plato: its strong point was theological speculation. Athanasius . . . had been included among its members . . ."[214]

We have already seen that Athanasius, more than any other, was responsible for establishing the divinity of the Holy Spirit at the Council of Nicea in 325 A.D. His efforts eventually led to the acceptance of the Trinity as a prime Roman Catholic doctrine. Nevertheless, the concept of the Holy Trinity, and the Trinitarian Doctrine as a whole, as it was presented in the Roman Church, was derived directly from Plato's teachings. Hagerty says that:

> "Christian philosophers and theologians have always followed Socrates, Plato, and Aristotle in distinguishing between substance and accidents, reality and appearance, nature and phenomena."[215]

Nevertheless, Plato, Aristotle, Socrates, and later Greek and Roman theologians were never able to explain fully the Trinity through the allegorical method. Gibbon testifies of Plato that:

> "The vain hope of extricating himself from these difficulties, which must ever oppress the feeble powers of the human mind, might induce Plato to consider the divine nature under the threefold modification—of the first cause, the reason, or *Logos*, and the soul or spirit of the universe. His poetical imaginations sometimes fixed and animated these metaphysical abstractions; the three *archical* or original principles were represented in the platonic system as three Gods, united with each other by a mysterious and ineffable generation . . ."[216]

Despite a lack of Scriptural evidence for this "mysterious and ineffable generation," the Platonists and Neo-Platonists among the early church Fathers used the respectability of this pagan philosopher's name as the fulcrum upon which to support the "truth" of the nature, the generation, the distinction, and the equality of the three divine persons of the mysterious Triad.

Athanasius and the Council of Nicea

The emperor Constantine demonstrated considerable favor to the Christians of his empire after his "conversion" from Mithraism. There was a rapidly growing body of Christians but the vigor and unity of the church and the empire was being threatened by the Arian Heresy. Arius admitted to the divinity of the Father, but categorically denied the divinity of the Son. He had nothing whatever to say about the Holy Spirit.

It is understandable that it was to the best interest of Constantine and the empire that the unity of the Church be maintained. Hosius, Bishop of Cordova, suggested to him that if he would convoke a synod of the whole Church, both east and west, the matter could be resolved. Constantine himself could not have cared less about the Arian dispute. His motivation for bringing the matter to a close was purely political.

From Alexandria came the sharp-minded young bishop Athanasius, who was the protégé of former bishop Alexander. Gibbon says of him:

> "We have seldom an opportunity of observing either in active or speculative life, what effect may be produced, or what obstacles may be surmounted, by the force of a single mind, when it is inflexibly applied to the pursuit of a single object. The immortal name of Athanasius will never be separated from the Catholic doctrine of the Trinity, to whose defence he consecrated every moment and every faculty of his being."[217]

The Arian controversy was not the only one that threatened the stability of the Church and the empire by 325 A.D. The Macedonians freely admitted the consubstantiality of the Son with the Father but denied the existence of three gods. It was to the Arian and Macedonian disputes that Athanasius mostly applied himself.

The disputes chiefly revolved around the consubstantiality of the Father and Son but the opinions expressed about the Son were extended and applied to the Holy Spirit. The relationship of Christ to God was held only by a small group of Arians, and perhaps even a smaller group of delegates sided with Athanasius. The majority of the delegates stood between the two extremes. They rejected Arius' view and refused to accept Athanasius'. However, the young bishop won out. Arius was humiliated and exiled for his beliefs.

Athanasius established not only the consubstantiality of the Son with the Father but also that of the Holy Spirit with the Father and the Son. Moreover, he introduced into Roman Catholicism for the first time, a consistent definition of the Holy Trinity. By this, the victorious Athanasius cleared up the ambiguous language of some of the respectable "doctors," confirmed the faith of the Catholics, and condemned the Macedonians. The deity of the Holy Spirit was ratified and the mysterious Trinitarian Doctrine was received and accepted by every nation and every church in the Christian world so-called.

Unfortunately, the truth of the matter had been overlooked in the confusion generated by multitude of differing opinions. The synod was blinded by Athanasius' intellectual prowess and his brilliant defense of the Trinitarian concept. Had these learned scholars bothered to check the facts as they presented themselves, and followed the example of the Bereans, they would not have been taken in by so obvious a Satanic ploy. They would have seen through Athanasius' definition of the Holy Trinity for what it was, an echo of past generations of ignorance and superstition so loved and embraced by the pagans. James Bonwick says that:

> "Though it is usual to speak of the Semitic tribes as monotheistic; yet it is an undoubted fact that more or less all over the world the deities were triads. This rule applies to eastern and western hemispheres, to north and south. Further, it is observed that, in some mystical way, the triad of three persons is one . . . The definition of Athanasius . . . applied to the trinities of all heathen religions."[218]

What conclusion can we draw from this? Namely, Trinitarianism is not unique to Christianity. Christianity adopted paganism's Trinitarianism as conceptually true. However, the Hebraic concept, or if you prefer, the Jewish concept of the Godhead patently denies such a probability. "**Christianity added the Trinitarian terms to the Jewish description of God.**"[219]

It follows that if the Trinitarian terms were not present in the original, i.e. the Old Testament, they are not present in the New, except where they are insinuated by the mistaken notions of men who would rather cling to a lie. These, largely, do so in order to solicit the affections of the people rather than obey the word of God.

Modern Trinitarianism seems determined to ignore the facts regardless of how many times they confront them. The entire basis of present day Trinitarian Doctrine rests with the early Church Fathers. However, even they are ignored by the Trinity-in-Unity advocates when they speak against the Holy Spirit as a person. Hagerty declares:

> "St. Augustine was the first to teach explicitly that communicating the divine nature to the Son the Father communicates His will fecund with power to spirate so that the Son cooperates with the Father in spirating the Holy Ghost. Hence, the Holy Ghost **proceeds from the father and son as a common product of their will-act.** St. Augustine says the Son is active principle, together with the Father, of the Holy Ghost; both spirate because both have the same nature, energy, and will." (emphasis mine).[220]

What could be clearer! To spirate is to breathe in the sense of the Old Testament *ruach* which was considered to be **God's active life principle.** If, as Augustine says, this spiration is the active principle of the Father and Son of the Holy Spirit, then **the Holy Spirit is the nature, energy, power, force, and will of the father and son**, not a person! Moreover, if the Holy Spirit is not a person, there can be no Holy Trinity in the Christian Godhead!

The "Plurality" In the New Testament

The account of the beginning found in John 1:1-3 supposedly reveals, if not a Trinity, the beginnings of a Trinitarian "understanding" of God. In Genesis 1:2, the Holy Spirit is spoken of a brooding like a dove over the face of the waters, but no personality is indicated. It is merely assumed by the Trinitarians. In John 1:1-3 the Holy Spirit is not even mentioned, and yet, we know that it was present. The Trinitarians working from a preconceived notion, again begin to clutch at straws and draw mistaken conclusions. Because the Father and Son are supposedly mentioned, the inference is that automatically there must be an element of Trinitarianism. However, according to Dr. W. N. Clark:

> "There is no Trinity in this; but there is a distinction in the Godhead, a **duality** in God. This **duality** is used as a basis for the idea of an only-begotten Son, and as a key to the possibility of an incarnation." (Emphasis mine).[221]

If there is no Trinity in this the very beginning of all things, how can there be a Trinity subsequent to these events unless God, as we have already alluded to, decided on a lark to change His nature to appease the pagan elements of society and therefore allow them to dictate the manner in which they should worship Him. There is no evidence for such a change. Regardless, man stubbornly refuses to accept such a notion, and even Dr. Clark, who denies the Trinitarian concept above, almost acquiesces a page later when he says:

> "The New Testament begins the work [of illustrating a concept of a Holy Trinity], but does not finish it; for it contains no similar teaching (like John 1:1-18 concerning the divinity of Christ) with regard to the Holy Spirit. The unique nature and mission of Christ are traced to a ground in the being of God; but similar ground for the divineness of the Spirit is nowhere shown. Thought in the New Testament is never directed to that end. Thus the Scriptures take the first step toward a doctrine of essential Trinity, or threeness in the being of one God, **but they do not take that second step by which alone the doctrine could be completed.**"(Emphasis mine).[222]

Why would God, through His holy and incorruptible word, take that first step toward a doctrine of "essential" Trinity and not take the second step which would complete it, leaving no doubt in the mind of mankind as to His true character and make-up? He would not do that! Nevertheless, man, who likes to make up his own God, cannot resist the notion that his make-believe God likes to play guessing games. Consequently, we are led to believe, Trinitarianism though merely "hinted at" in the New Testament and not really revealed as an immutable truth, is fully developed throughout its pages. Nothing could be farther from the truth! God does not play guessing games! The gospel of John, as well as the remainder of the New Testament, does not contain a sharply delineated doctrine of the Trinity, not even in the baptismal formula of Matthew 28:19. The text should read "into" the name of the Father, and of the Son, and of the Holy Spirit. There is no indication that the Father, Son, and the Holy Spirit are three distinct persons here for the baptism is to be accomplished in the "name," singular, not "names", plural, of the Godhead. The singular word "name" merely denotes the object and purpose of the baptismal rite and is the final definition of the "Name" of the one true God, i.e. God the Father, or *Yahweh Elohim*. God the Father is "*The* Holy Spirit," and this name denotes the character and make-up of the true Godhead. The true Godhead is holy and is spirit. This holiness and spiritness is manifested as **the active life principle, the energy, force, and power** by which God imparts His will upon the universe. However, the Trinitarians are still not convinced.

The "Personhood" In the New Testament

The personhood of the Holy Spirit in the New Testament is viewed strictly from the presupposition that God is a Trinity. Regardless of facts, to the contrary this error seemingly cannot be dislodged from the minds of present day Evangelicals, or, for that matter, from the teachings of the Catholic Church. We have already seen that she categorically denies the existence of the Trinitarian Doctrine prior to the 4th Century A.D. However, despite her denial she espouses the "gradual revelation" of the personhood of the Holy Spirit in the pages of the New Testament. She declares:

> "Although the NT (New Testament) concepts of the Spirit of God are largely a continuation of those of the OT, in the NT there is a gradual revelation that the Spirit of God is a person."[223]

If the New Testament concept is merely a continuation of the Old Testament concept of the Spirit of God, how can It be a person? It cannot for it was not a person in the Old. Nevertheless, the Evangelicals persist in following the Roman Catholic Trinitarian Doctrine with the attitude "Let's teach it, all the way, to the hilt, the truth be damned, amen." Billy Graham is a leader in the dissemination of this attitude. Says he:

> "The Bible teaches that the Holy Spirit is a *person*. Jesus never referred to 'it' when He was talking about the Holy Spirit . . . He spoke of the Holy Spirit as 'He' because He is not a force or thing but a person. **Whoever speaks of the Holy Spirit as 'it' is uninstructed, or perhaps even undiscerning**" (emphasis mine).[224]

According to Dr. Graham, then, such people as Abraham, Isaac, Jacob, Moses, David, the prophets, and even modern day Jewry were and are, either uninstructed or undiscerning about the true makeup of the Godhead. Regardless of the fact that the Jews are biblical monotheists, and reject Jesus Christ as the true Messiah, they have been the keepers of Gods oracles through the ages and have kept much of His truth intact (Rom. 3:1-2). Moreover, they are monotheistic!

It is illogical in the face of mountains of material written by scholars and historians in the past, that modern day evangelicalism should continue to cling to the Trinitarian Myth. When one looks closely at what eminent biblical scholars have to say about the make-up of the Godhead, one cannot but believe that Mr. Graham et. al., are the ones who are uninstructed and undiscerning. They either have not read, or choose to ignore their predecessors in biblical scholarship, who have looked at what the ancients have had to say with an unbiased eye. Consider the following:

> "In thinking of the personality of the Holy Spirit the most obvious and important 'truth' to stress is that 'He' is a person", or "Because the Holy Spirit is a person, we can **and indeed must treat him as a person**," or "When Jesus promised that the Holy Spirit would descend upon man, He seemed to particularly stress the fact of His personality by use of the personal pronoun."[225]

It is not enough that we **must** treat the Holy Spirit as a person just because Jesus stressed the fact of His personality by the use of the of the personal pronoun, we must also believe that those who fail to accept the personhood of the Holy Spirit are in a sorry state indeed. Mr. Graham candidly states:

"Anyone who fails to recognize this (that the Holy Spirit is a person) is robbed of his joy and power. Of course a defective view of any member of the Trinity will bring about this result because God is all important."[226]

Many people today who do not hold to the Trinitarian view are not robbed of the joy and power of the Holy Spirit. Obviously, Mr. Graham has not considered that perhaps his view of the Godhead is defective! It is precisely because God is all-important that the non-Trinitarians do not believe Him to be a triune God. We need only be reminded that the personal pronoun upon which the Evangelicals lay so much stress could just as well have been rendered "she," and would have been grammatically correct.[227]

However, the Evangelicals are still not convinced. They preach from their lofty pulpits that 1 John 5:7-8 is proof beyond reasonable doubt that God is indeed a Trinity. Their "proof" hinges of the formula presented in the last part of the verse 7 and the first part of verse 8.

> "For there are three who bear witness in heaven: the Father, the Word, and the Holy Spirit: and these three are one. And there are three that bear witness on earth: the Spirit, the water, and the blood; and these three agree as one."

These verses indeed seem to imply that God is composed of three "persons." However, upon further investigation it will be seen that the last part of verse 7 and the first part of verse 8 are glosses, which were not a part of the original manuscripts. In fact, the rendering in the margin (NKJV), states that, "NU (the modern eclectic or 'critical' text), M (Majority text) omit the rest of v. 7 and through *on earth* of v. 8, a passage found in Greek in only four or five very late mss. The verses should read, "For there are three who bear witness in heaven: the Spirit, the water, and the blood; and these three agree as one."

Notice that it says: **these three agree as one, not that they are one!** From the *JFB Commentary on the Whole Bible*, we read:

> "The only Greek mss. *in any form* which support the words 'in heaven, the Father, the Word, and the Holy Ghost, and these three are one; and there are three that bear witness in earth,' are the *Montfortianus* of Dublin, copied evidently

from the *modern* Latin Vulgate; the *Ravianus*, copied from the *Complutensian Polyglot*; a ms. at Naples, with the words added in the margin by a recent hand; Ottobonianus, 298, of the fifteenth century, the *Greek* of which is a mere translation of the accompanying Latin. **All the old versions omit the words.** The oldest mss. of the *Vulgate* omit them: the earliest *Vulgate* ms. which had them being Wizan Burgensis, 99, of the eighth century. A scolium quoted in *Matthaei*, shows that the words did not arise from fraud, for in the words in all *Greek* mss. 'there are *three* that bear record'. As the Scholiast notices, the word 'three' is *masculine*, because the three things (the Spirit, the water, and the blood) are symbols of **the Trinity**. To this Cyprian, 196, also refers, 'of the *Father, Son, and Holy Spirit*, it is written, '*and these three are one*' (a unity).' There must be some mystical truth implied in using 'three' (Greek) in the masculine, though the antecedents, 'spirit, water, and blood,' are neuter."[228]

Charles F. Pfeifer and Everett F. Harrison state that:

"The text of this verse should read, Because there are three that bear record. The remainder of the verse is spurious. Not a single manuscript contains the Trinitarian addition before the fourteenth century, and the verse is never quoted in controversies over the Trinity in the first 200 years of the church era." (emphasis mine).[229]

Peak's Commentary on the Bible states:

"The famous interpolation after 'three witnesses' is not printed even in the **RSV**, and rightly. It cites the heavenly testimony of the Father, the Logos, and the Holy Spirit, but it is never used in the early Trinitarian controversies. No respectable Greek ms. contains it. Appearing first in the late 14th century Latin text, it entered the Vulgate and finally the NT [New Testament] of Erasmus."[230]

From the *Plain Truth Magazine*, a publication of the Worldwide Church of God at Pasadena, California, comes these quotes from the Emphatic Diaglot:

> "... it is likely this verse is not genuine. It is wanting in every ms. of this epistle written before the invention of printing, one excepted, the Codex Montfortii, in Trinity College, Dublin ... It is wanting in both the Syriac, all the Arabic, Ethiopic, Coptic, Sahidic, Armenian, Slavonian, etc., in a word, in all the ancient versions but the Vulgate; and even of this version many of the most ancient and correct mss. have it not. It is wanting also in all the ancient Greek fathers; and in most even of the Latin."

And further:

> "I John 5:7 ... is not contained in any Greek manuscript which was written earlier than the fifth century. It is not cited by any of the early Greek ecclesiastical writers; nor by any of the early Latin fathers, even when the subjects upon which they treated would naturally have led them to appeal to its authority. It is therefore evidently spurious; and was first cited (though not as it now reads) by Virgilius Tapensis, a Latin writer of no credit, in the latter end of the fifth century; but by whom forged, is of no great moment, as its design must be obvious to all."[231]

Regardless of quote after quote denying the authenticity of these verses and the obvious design for which they were intended, present day evangelicalism blatantly ignores the implications and continues to heap error upon error regarding the true make up of the Godhead.

It is ironic that in espousing the Trinitarian Doctrine the Evangelicals cannot avoid the use of the word "power" in describing the personhood of Holy Spirit. However, this does nothing to diminish their use of it while they seemingly ignore its import.

Chapter 16
A Faith That Fails

Eric Fife in his book The Holy Spirit, Common Sense and the Bible, states:

> "The Bible teaches the Trinity in unity. We **must accept this on faith** and remember that if we had complete proof there would be no room for faith" (emphasis mine).²³²

Why must we accept such an untenable doctrine on faith without complete proof? There is no reason! Evangelical Christianity accepts Trinitarianism on faith without proof because it cannot explain the inexplicable, allegorically or otherwise. Hence, the inexplicable must be accepted on faith. If one cannot accept the inexplicable on faith, and if there is no room for faith *and* complete proof, what is the alternative? There is but one – to deny the existence of the Trinity! However, as we shall see later, the Evangelicals will not even allow this!

Evangelical Christianity, largely, does not resort to reliable exegesis to arrive at the truth concerning the proof of the Trinity, but to theological speculation of the highest order. This sort of exegesis is contrary to Biblical teaching. In his letter to the Thessalonians, Paul admonishes them: "Test (prove) all things, hold fast to what is good" (1 Thess. 5:21, NKJV). This admonition resulted because the Jews of Thessalonica refused to hear the word of God as preached by Paul and Silas. They were not persuaded by Paul's teachings, as were the Greeks. They became jealous of Paul's following among the Greeks. Because Paul preached Jesus a king, the Jews rioted and accused Paul and Silas of treason against Caesar. They were subsequently hidden in the house of Jason, a Greek convert. For fear of their lives, the brethren sent them to Berea to preach the word there.

> "Then the brethren immediately sent Paul and Silas away by night to Berea. When they arrived, they went into the synagogue of the Jews. These were more fair-minded than those (Jews) at Thessalonica, in that they received the word with all readiness, and searched the scriptures daily *to find out* whether these things were so. Therefore many of them believed, and also not a few of the Greeks, prominent women as well as men. But when the Jews from Thessalonica learned that the word of God was preached by Paul at Berea, they came there also and stirred up the crowds" (Acts 17:10-13, NKJV).

They would not give up! They refused to hear God's word in Thessalonica, and when they learned that Paul preached it in Berea, they went there and caused more trouble! However, notice that the Bereans accepted the word. Why? Because they searched the scriptures daily and **proved** that what Paul and Silas said was true! Contrary to what Mr. Fife says, their proof was complete as far as they were able to prove God's word with the aid of the Holy Spirit and the resources at their command. They based their "faith" upon proof, not upon the premise that faith is the alternative to a lack of complete proof. They believed! Faith is not just another word for belief; it is belief in action! Belief combined with action amounts to obedience, and obedience is accorded by God as righteousness (Jas. 2:23). Acts 17:11, then, seems to indicate that, contrary to what Mr. Fife says, "complete" proof does not negate faith, but enhances and strengthens it!

There are many examples of faith in Hebrews 11. Let us look at the example of Abraham, the **Father of the Faithful.**

> "By faith (i.e. as a result of action through belief), Abraham obeyed when he was called to go out to the place which he would *afterward* receive as an inheritance. And he went out, not knowing where he was going" (Heb. 11:8, parenthesis mine).

We have already seen that Abraham obeyed because he had proved, through scientific investigation, that there was but one true God. It follows naturally that he did not obey out of an empty faith as an alternative last resort. He obeyed because his proofs were conclusive! His proofs did not negate his faith but rather strengthened it to the point that he was willing to forego his present lifestyle, and the prestigious position he enjoyed as a leading scientist among his peers, in order to obey the will of God. His faith continued to remain strong even when God chose to test him (Gen. 22:1-2).

However, Mr. Fife and others of his ilk remain unmoved from their position about the Holy Spirit and the Trinity. He steadfastly maintains that: "The Bible states the Trinity as fact but does not explain it."[233] Obviously, Mr. Fife has never considered that the reason the Bible does not "explain" the Holy Trinity is that there is no Holy Trinity to explain. He further states:

> "To comprehend the nature of God is impossible to fallen man. Although we seek to understand Him . . . we must begin by realizing that it is not possible to understand Him perfectly."[234]

The key to understanding Mr. Fife says is the phrase "fallen man." Mr. Fife is quite correct in his assumption that fallen man cannot understand the nature of God, and the Bible quite clearly points this out (Rom. 8:7). To have a carnal mind is to resist God, God's laws, and God's truth. The carnally-minded man cannot understand the things of God because he dwells on the things of the flesh (Rom. 8:5).

However, what can we say about redeemed man? Can he understand the nature of God? Can the man who has truly repented, who comes to God with a childlike attitude of awe and respect, who has been baptized, and through the laying on of hands has received the gift of the Holy Spirit, understand the nature of God? Certainly, he can!

The man who has the Holy Spirit dwelling in him is no longer fallen but redeemed, a son of God, and co-heir with Jesus Christ, of all that is. Whenever the Holy Spirit joins with the spirit of man (I Cor. 2:10-12), the man's mind is opened to the truth. God lifts the veil of darkness from that persons mind making it possible for him to begin to comprehend the nature of God, and the truth begins to penetrate that mind like an unstoppable flood rolling over the land. It is as though there were scales over the eyes that drop off and the man sees the glorious light of the gospel of Jesus Christ for the first time. Like the Bereans, he accepts the truth with all readiness of mind no longer deceived by spurious doctrines nor turned to fables.

If Mr. Fife et. al. would just pursue the matter of the Holy Trinity to its logical conclusion, they would not, with all deference to their sincerity, be able to say as he does: "The subject is just too exalted for man to understand."[235]

If the subject is "too exalted for man to understand," how can he be so certain that the Bible teaches the Trinity as fact? The point is that he cannot. Neither can anyone else who resorts to faith without proof. Faith without proof like faith without works is dead!

After unequivocally stating that man cannot understand the Trinity, Mr. Fife has the temerity to tell us that: "The supreme purpose of the Bible is to reveal God."[236]

If this is true, and if the Bible reveals God as a Trinity, why do Mr. Fife and Evangelical Christianity in general not understand the concept? Why is the subject too exalted to understand? Why, if God gave the Bible to us for the express purpose of revealing our Creator, does it not clarify the "mystery" of the Holy Trinity? Because there is no concrete evidence in the Bible that God is a Trinity!

The faith espoused by those who would have you believe that God is a Trinity is an empty faith. It is a faith born of man and depends upon man for its dissemination. It is a faith that is destined ultimately to fail. It is a faith whose roots are anchored in the unproductive soil of pagan beliefs and superstitions! It is no faith at all but an advocacy for the acceptance of a doctrine whose tenets rely on theological speculation and misinterpretation of the word of God!

Welcome Aboard the Insanity Express

Someone has said that the human mind is not capable of fully understanding the mystery of the Trinity, and that he who would try to understand the mystery fully will lose his mind. Moreover, he who would deny the Trinity will lose his soul.

This does not leave us much of a choice. The only choice left, if you accept such an absurd statement, is "just accept the Trinity on faith." If you try to solve the mystery, you will find that you have just bought a one way ticket on the "Insanity Express" bound for the land of "Mental Oblivion." If you deny the Trinity, you will lose that illusive, unexplainable, ethereal substance called the soul. Who could ever hope to extricate himself from the horns of such a dilemma?

Let us recognize this for what it really is—religious intimidation pure and simple! Such irresponsible theological nonsense has been the earmark of Christianity so-called for hundreds of years! God does not use such intimidating tactics and neither should those who would be His ministers! Those who preach such things are resorting to fear tactics and emotional experiences designed to whip the masses into lemming-like obedience in order to lead them over the precipice of spiritual darkness into the all consuming fires of pagan idolatry!

Present day leaders of Evangelical Christianity are doing precisely the same thing that the religious leaders of Jesus' day were doing.

> "Woe to you, Scribes and Pharisees, hypocrites! for you travel land and sea to win one proselyte, and when he is won, you make him twice as much a child of hell as yourselves" (Mt. 23:15).

What a stinging indictment against the established hierarchy! Evangelical Christianity sells its goods and services much more efficiently than did any of the Scribes and Pharisees, but they do it in much the same manner.

Anyone who is familiar with sales knows that one of the most effective tactics used to close a sale is the "take-away." Intimate to someone that he may not qualify for your product or service, make him think that you are going to take it away from him, and usually, he will buy it out of fear of losing it when in fact he does not have it in the first place. How does this work in the religious world?

Largely the "sellers" threaten the laity with such statements using the same take-away tactics used by salesmen. The "salesmen" in this case are would be prophets and ministers of God. They hawk their religious wares like carnival barkers at a sideshow, except they do it via television, radio, and books all across America and the world. They design their pitches to appeal, not to the intellect, but to the emotions. They prey on the fears of those who are looking for a religious "experience."

Day in and day out, Evangelical Christianity spews forth such wry inducements as,

> "Anyone who fails to recognize this (that the Holy Spirit is the third "person" of the Trinity), is robbed of his power and joy." (Parenthesis mine).[237]

What self-professing Christian in his right mind would want to be deprived of the power and joy of the indwelling of the Holy Spirit?

The main thrust of the Trinitarian Doctrine is the belief that the Holy Spirit is a "person." The would-be "salesmen" skillfully weave this false premise into the fabric of the Christian vocabulary as a means of duping the masses. It is religious fear mongering at its worst. To quote Billy Graham again:

> "Whoever speaks of the Holy Spirit as 'it' is uninstructed, or perhaps even undiscerning."[238]

To be uninstructed is to be uneducated and ignorant of the facts. No self-respecting Christian wants to wear this label, nor does he want to have this kind of albatross hanged around his neck for all the world to see. To avoid the shame of ignorance he swallows the concept of the Trinity hook, line, and sinker! He listens to the words and traditions of men instead of the solid, verifiable word of God. Anyone who tells you that you are uninstructed and ignorant is telling you that your opinion is worthless. He is telling you in less than subtle terms that you do not have your religious and spiritual act together if you dare question his views. Do not be intimidated by this form of reasoning. There is nothing wrong with questioning anybody's views! God says that we are:

> "Not (to) believe every spirit, but (to) test the spirits, whether they are of God." Why? "Because many false prophets have gone out into the world" (I John 4:1).

If, as A.W Tozer has said, entertaining thoughts of God that are not worthy of Him is idolatry, we must conclude from the foregoing that the Trinitarian concept is pure idolatry! It is not a doctrine of the true God but of the god of this world, Satan, who continues to spread his false doctrines through his grand scheme for the destruction of mankind—Project Apostasy!

Endnotes

[1] Anthony F. Buzzard and Charles F. Hunting, *The Doctrine of the Trinity, Christianity's Self Inflected Wound*, p. 1.
[2] Ibid., p. 3.
[3] Ibid., p. 3.
[4] Ibid., p. 4.
[5] A. W. Tozer, *Knowledge of the Holy*, p. ix.
[6] Ibid., p. 3.
[7] Ibid., p. 3.
[8] Ibid., p. 4.
[9] Ibid., p.4.
[10] Ibid., p. 6.
[11] Ibid., p. 7.
[12] Ibid., p. 6
[13] Robert Jastrow, God and the Astronomers, p. 14.
[14] Ibid., p.14.
[15] Ibid., p. 11.
[16] Henry M. Morris, *Scientific Creationism*, p. 5.
[17] Robert Jastrow, *God and the Astronomers*, p. 11.
[18] William F. Dankenbring, *Beyond Star Wars*, p. 249f.
[19] Ibid., p. 251.
[20] Ibid., p. 294f.
[21] F. N. Peloubet, *Peloubet's Bible Dictionary*, pp. 222-224.
[22] James Hastings, *Hastings' Dictionary of the Bible*, Art. Eholim, p.299.
[23] E. W. Bullinger, *The Companion Bible*, Appendix 41, p. 35.

[24] William F. Dankenbring, *Beyond Star Wars*, p.250.
[25] Joseph Bryant Rotherham, *Rotherham's Emphasized Bible*, p.33.
[26] E. W. Bullinger, *The Companion Bible*, appendix 19, pp. 24, 25.
[27] E. A. Wallace Budge, *The Gods of the Egyptians*, vol. I, p. 62
[28] Garner Ted Armstrong, "Angels," a taped sermon delivered at Tyler, Texas, 1984.
[29] E. A. Wallace Budge, *the Gods of the Egyptians*, Vol. I, p. 85.
[30] Ibid., Vol. II, p. 61.
[31] Garner Ted Armstrong, "Angels," a taped sermon delivered at Tyler, Texas, 1984.
[32] Jack Randolph Conrad, *The Horn and the Sword*, p. 112.
[33] C. F. Keil and F. Delitzsch, *Commentary on the Book of Genesis*, pp. 68-69.
[34] Adam Clarke, *Clarke's Commentary, The Old Testament*, vol. 1, Ages Digital Library, Albany, OR., 1997, p. 77.
[35] C. F. Keil and F. Delitzsch, *Commentary on the Book of Genesis*, p. 68.
[36] Adam Clarke, *Clarke's Commentary, The Old Testament*, vol. 1, Ages Digital Library, Albany, OR., 1997, p. 78.
[37] Ibid., p. 78.
[38] William Whiston, *The Works of Josephus: The Antiquities of the Jews*, Bk. I, Chap. II, sec. 2, p. 31,
[39] Ibid., Bk. I, Chap, II, sec. 2, p. 31ff.
[40] Ibid., Bk. I, Chap. II, sec. 3, p. 32.
[41] E. A. Wallace Budge, *The Gods of the Egyptians*, vol. I, p. 414.
[42] Albert M. Rehwinkle, *The Flood*, pp. 28-30.
[43] C. F. Keil and F. Delitzsch, *Commentary on the Old Testament: Genesis*, p. 81
[44] Ibid., p. 81
[45] Ibid., p. 83.
[46] Colin Brown, Editor, *New International Dictionary of New Testament Theology*, Vol. 3, pp. 277, 278.
[47] Crichton, *International Standard Bible Encyclopedia*, Vol. V., Art. Sons of God, 2 (2), p. 2835.
[48] William Whiston, *The Works of Josephus, The Antiquities of the Jews*, Bk. I, Ch. 3 (73), p. 32.
[49] R. H. Charles, *The Book of Enoch or I Enoch*, pp. 13-15.

50 Ibid., p. 18.
51 Anthony F. Buzzard, *Our Fathers Who Aren't in Heaven*, p. 19
52 Ibid., Footnote, Ps. 29:1; 89:6; Dan. 3:5; Job 38:7, p.147.
53 Ibid., pp. 147, 148.
54 John Pilkey, *Origin of the Nations*, p.147.
55 Ibid., p. 147.
56 Ibid., p. 21.
57 Alexander Hislop, *The Two Babylons*, p. 134
58 T. G. Pinches, *International Standard Bible Encyclopedia*, Art. "Ham", p. 1324.
59 William Whiston, *The Works of Josephus: The Antiquities of the Jews*, Bk. I, Ch. V, (1), p. 35.
60 Alexander Hislop, *The Two Babylons*, p. 27f.
61 John Pilkey, *Origin of the Nations*, p. 163.
62 Alexander Hislop, *The Two Babylons*, p. 28).
63 John Pilkey, *Origins of the Nations*, p. 164.
64 Alexander Hislop, *The Two Babylons*, p. 51f.
65 Charles Rollin, *Rollin's Ancient History*, Vol. I, p. 442.
66 Alexander Hislop, *The Two Babylons*. p. 217.
67 Ibid., p. 50.
68 Charles Rollin, *Rollin's Ancient History*, Vol. I, p. 444.
69 E. A. Wallace Budge, *The Gods of the Egyptians*, Vol. I, p. 33f.
70 William SteuartMcBirne, *The Search for the Twelve Apostles*, p. 176.
71 Ibid., p. 177.
72 E. A. Wallace Budge, *The Gods of the Egyptians*, Vol. I, p. 484.
73 Ibid., Vol. I, p.476.
74 Ibid., Vol. I, p. 485.
75 Alexander Hislop, *The Two Babylons*, p. 287.
76 Ibid., p. 226.
77 Ibid., p. 227, cp. Gen. 3:5-7.
78 Ibid., p. 230.
79 Ibid., p. 34.
80 Charles Rollin, *Rollin's Ancient History*, Vol. I, p. 240).
81 Ibid., Vol. I, p. 204f..
82 Ibid., Vol. I, p. 242.
83 James G. Frazer, *The Golden Bough*, Bk. I, p. 236.
84 William L. Shirer, *The Rise and Fall of the Third Reich*, Vol. I, p. 6.

[85] Charles Rollin, *Rollin's Ancient History*, Vol. I, p. 234.
[86] Marilyn Ferguson, *The Aquarian Conspiracy*, p. 193f.
[87] James G. Frazer, *The Golden Bough*, Bk. I, p. 41.
[88] Alexander Hislop, *The Two Babylons*, p. 32
[89] E. A. Wallace Budge, *The Gods of the Egyptians*, Vol. I, p. 34f.,
[90] Ibid., Vol. I, p. 36.
[91] Herman Hoeh, *The Plain Truth Magazine*, Feb. 1966, pp. 18, 47.
[92] E. A. Wallace Budge, *The Gods of the Egyptians*, Vol., p. 246.
[93] Alexander Hislop, *The Two Babylons*, p. 62, 66f.
[94] Alexander Hislop, *The Two Babylons*, p. 141.
[95] Ibid., p.74f.
[96] George Rawlinson, *The History of Herodotus*, p. 75).
[97] E. A. Wallace Budge, *The Gods of the Egyptians*, p. 280.
[98] Charles Rollin, *Rollin's Ancient History*, Vol. I, p. 51.
[99] Ibid., Vol. I, p. 58).
[100] Alexander Hislop, *The Two Babylons*, p. 67.
[101] James G. Frazer, *The Golden Bough*, Bk. I, p. 33.
[102] Ibid., Bk. I, p. 34).
[103] Ibid., Bk. I, p. 35,
[104] Charles Rollin, *Rollin's Ancient History*, Vol. I, p. 62.
[105] Loraine Boettner, *Roman Catholicism*, p. 141-42.
[106] Ibid., p. 134
[107] Alexander Hislop, *The Two Babylons*, p. 69.
[108] E. A. Wallace Budge, *The Gods of the Egyptians*, Vol. I, p. 462.
[109] Alexander Hislop, *The Two Babylons*, p. 307.
[110] Ibid., p. 65).
[111] Ibid., p. 32f.
[112] Ibid., p. 36
[113] Ibid., p. 19.
[114] Clay, *The International Standard Bible Encyclopedia*, Art. Ur of the Chaldees, p. 3039.
[115] T. G. Pinches, *The International Standard Bible Encyclopedia*, Art. Chaldea, Vol. I, p. 589).
[116] F. N. Peloubet, *Peloubet's Bible Dictionary*, Art. Chaldeans, p. 113.
[117] William Whiston, *The Works of Josephus: Antiquities*, Bk. I, Chap. VII, (2), p. 38).
[118] Ibid., Bk, I, Chap. VII, (1), p. 38.

[119] Robert Jamieson, A. R. Fausset and David Brown, *Commentary on the Whole Bible*, p. 25.
[120] Leon Wood, *A Survey of Israel's History*, p. 47.
[121] Werner Keller, *The Bible As History*, p. 78.
[122] Ibid., p. 80.
[123] Leon Wood, *A Survey of Israel's History*, p. 47.
[124] Ibid., p. 47.
[125] Werner Keller, *The Bible As History*, p. 264.
[126] Leon Wood, *A Survey of Israel's History*, p. 207-208.
[127] R. K. Harrison, *Old Testament Times*, p. 168f.
[128] Ivar Lissner, *The Silent Past*, p. 39).
[129] Ibid., p. 40).
[130] Werner Keller, *The Bible As History*, p. 266.
[131] Jack Randolph Conrad, *The Horn and the Sword*, p. 107.
[132] Robert Jamieson, A. R. Fausset and David Brown, *Commentary on the Whole Bible*, p. 78f.
[133] Jack Randolph Conrad, *The Horn and the Sword*, p. 72,
[134] Robert Jamieson, A. R. Fausset and David Brown, *Commentary on the Whole Bible*, p. 79.
[135] E. A. Wallace Budge, *The Gods of the Egyptians*, Vol. II, p. 350.
[136] Jack Randolph Conrad, *The Horn and the Sword*, p. 75.
[137] Alexander Hislop, *The Two Babylons*, p. 46.
[138] E. A. Wallace Budge, *The Gods of the Egyptians*, Vol. II, p. 252f.
[139] John Kitto, *Daily Bible Illustrations*, Vol. I, p. 466.
[140] Robert Jamieson, A. R. Fausset and David Brown, *Commentary on the Whole Bible*, p. 446.
[141] Alexander Hislop, *The Two Babylons*, p. 62.
[142] Leon Wood, *A Survey of Israel's History*, p. 207f.
[143] Ibid., p. 222.
[144] Ibid., p. 230.
[145] William Whiston, *Antiquities of the Jews*, Bk. V, Chap. X, sec. 1, p. 338, Baker.
[146] John Kitto, *Daily Bible Illustrations*, Vol. I, p. 856.
[147] *The New Catholic Encyclopedia*, Vol. 13, p. 575.
[148] Eric S. Fife, *The Holy Spirit, Common Sense and the Bible*, p. 17.
[149] Isaac Asimov, *In The Beginning*, p. 59.
[150] G.H. Pember, *Earth's Earliest Ages*, p. 261.

151 Loraine Boettner, *Roman Catholicism*, p. 27.
152 Walter G. Clippinger, *The International Standard Bible Encyclopedia*, p. 2522.
153 E. W. Bullinger, *The Companion Bible*, p. 1073.
154 John Kitto, Daily Bible Illustrations, p. 383f.
155 Burton Scott Easton, *The International Standard Bible Encyclopedia*, p. 3157.
156 John Kitto, *Daily Bible Illustrations*, Vol. II, p. 681.
157 Eusebius Scholasticus, *Ecclesiastical History*, Bk. II, Ch. 13, p. 63.
158 Ibid., Bk. II, chap. 13, p. 62).
159 Alexander Hislop, *The Two Babylons*, p. 208.
160 Elaine Pagels, *The Gnostic Gospels*, p. 45.
161 John Kitto, *Daily Bible Illustrations*, Vol. II, p. 684, 685.
162 Cornelius J. Hagerty, *The Holy Trinity*, p. 154.
163 Ibid., p. 120.
164 Ibid., p. 40
165 Albert Barnes, *Barnes' Notes on the Bible*, Vol. 12, pp. 656-657.
166 Robert Jamieson, A. R. Fausset, and David Brown, *Commentary on the Whole Bible*, p. 975.
167 K. H. Bartels, *New International Dictionary of New Testament Theology*, Art. "heis," Vol. 2, p. 720.
168 Ibid., p. 720.
169 Ibid., p. 720.
170 Anthony F. Buzzard, *Who is Jesus?*, p. 1.
171 Benjamin B. Warfield, *International Standard Bible Encyclopedia*, Art. Trinity, p. 3012.
172 James Hastings, *Hastings Dictionary of the Bible*, [revised], Art. Trinity, p. 1015.
173 Cornelius J. Hagerty, *The Holy Trinity*, p. 156.
174 Ibid., p. 95, quoted from Hughes, *A History of the Church*, Vol. I, p. 19.
175 Ibid., p. 153.
176 Socrates Scholasticus, *The Ecclesiastical History*, Bk. I, chap. XV, p. 20.
177 Ibid., Bk. I, chap. XXII, p. 26).
178 Cornelius J. Hagerty, *The Holy Trinity*, p. 176.
179 Ibid., pp. 176-178.
180 Billy Graham, *The Holy Spirit*, p. 28.

[181] Ibid., p. 28
[182] Ibid., p. 28,
[183] A. W. Tozer, *The Knowledge of the Holy*, p. 6.
[184] Franky Schaeffer, *Addicted To Mediocrity*, p. 23.
[185] Ibid., p. 20).
[186] Karl Barth, *Doctrine of the Word of God*, p. 473.
[187] James Hastings, *Hastings' Dictionary of the Bible*, Art. Trinity, p. 1015.
[188] James Hastings, *The Encyclopedia of Ethics and Religion*, Vol. 12, Art. Trinity, p. 458).
[189] Benjamin B. Warfield, *The International Standard Bible Encyclopedia*, Art. Trinity, p. 3021.
[190] Franky Schaeffer, *Addicted To Mediocrity*, p. 41.
[191] James Hastings, *Hastings' Dictionary of the Bible*, Art. Trinity, p. 1015.
[192] Eric S. Fife, *The Holy Spirit, Common Sense and the Bible*, p. 25).
[193] Ibid., p. 24.
[194] E. Y. Mullins, *The International Standard Bible Encyclopedia*, Art., The Holy Spirit, p. 1406.
[195] Ibid., p. 1407.
[196] Billy Graham, *The Holy Spirit*, p. 28.
[197] William F. Dankenbring, *Beyond Star Wars*, p. 247.
[198] *Harper's Bible Dictionary*, Art. Holy Spirit, p. 265.
[199] Billy Graham, *The Holy Spirit*, p. 29.
[200] Ibid., *The Holy Spirit*, p. 29.
[201] Ibid., p. 35.
[202] James Hastings, *Hastings' Bible Dictionary*, Art. Holy Spirit, p. 390.
[203] *The New Catholic Encyclopedia*, Vol. XIII, p. 574.
[204] Billy Graham, *The Holy Spirit*, p. 29.
[205] *Encyclopedia of Ethics and Religion*, p. 458.
[206] F. N. Peloubet, *Peloubet's Bible Dictionary*, p. 224.
[207] Ibid., p. 224.
[208] Ibid., p. 224.
[209] *New Catholic Encyclopedia*, Art. Spirit of God, Vol. 13, p. 574.
[210] Cornelius J. Hagerty, *The Holy Trinity*, p. 131.
[211] Ibid., p. 132.
[212] E. A. Wallace Budge, *The Gods of the Egyptians*, vol. II, p. 220.

[213] R. L. Richardson, *The New Catholic Encyclopedia*, vol. 14, Art. Holy Trinity, p. 295.
[214] Hubert Jedin, *Ecumenical Councils of the Catholic Church*, p. 29.
[215] Cornelius J. Hagerty, *The Holy Trinity*, p. 179.
[216] Edward Gibbon, *The Decline and Fall of the Roman Empire*, Vol. I, p. 676.
[217] Ibid., Vol. I, p. 698).
[218] James Bonwick, *Belief and Modern Thought*, p. 396.
[219] Elaine Pagels, *The Gnostic Gospels*, p. 49.
[220] Cornelius J. Hagerty, *The Holy Trinity*, p. 171.
[221] W. N. Clark, *An Outline of Christian Theology*, p. 167.
[222] Ibid., p. 168.
[223] *The New Catholic Encyclopedia*, Vol. 13, p. 575.
[224] Billy Graham, *The Holy Spirit*, p. 22
[225] Eric S. Fife, *The Holy Spirit, Common Sense and the Bible*, pp. 18-19.
[226] Billy Graham, *The Holy Spirit*, p. 32.
[227] G. H. Pember, *Earth's Earliest Ages*, p. 261.
[228] Robert Jamieson, A. R. Fausset and David Brown, *Commentary on the Whole Bible*, p. 1510.
[229] Charles F. Pfeifer and Everett F. Harrison, *Wycliffe Bible Commentary*, p. 1477
[230] *Peak's Commentary on the Bible*, p. 1038.
[231] Plain Truth Magazine, pp. 30, 31).
[232] Eric S. Fife, *The Holy Spirit, Common Sense and the Bible*, p. 22.
[233] Ibid., p. 22.
[234] Ibid., p. 18.
[235] Ibid., p. 23.
[236] Ibid., p. 33.
[237] Billy Graham, *The Holy Spirit*, p. 32.
[238] Op. Cit., p. 22-23.

About the Author

Jesse Acuff is pastor of Covenant-House One, a non-denominational house church which focuses on and teaches the Gospel of the Kingdom of God. He lives with his wife Bernice and his mother Helen Lewey in Aurora Colorado. He is a former school teacher who holds a Bachelor of Sience degree in Education with a concentration in Biology and Earth Science from Minot State College, Minot North Dakota, and a Master of Arts in Religion with a concentration in the Bible from Bethany Bible College and Seminary in Dothan, Alabama. He is presently working on a Doctorate of Biblical Studies at Colorado Theological Seminary. He has been a student of the Bible for over thirty years and has done extensive research on the Trinitarian Doctrine and its impact on Evangelical Christianity.

Mr. Acuff has self-published several articles on the internet (covenanthouse1.org) and has one article (*The Pre-trib Rapture: Fact or Fiction, Truth or Hoax?*) in the Journal for Radical Reformation, published by Restoration Fellowship, Morrow, Georga.

Made in United States
Orlando, FL
25 August 2023